Praise for
From Ace to Zummo

"I have enjoyed Ellin Dodge's books for over twenty-five years. I find her website to be very informative and I wanted to say thank you for her contributions to numerology over the years. Her books been a joy to read and refer to other students to use for reference."
—Rhavda Cooper Emison, numerologist

"This book is a must for all critter lovers. I cannot live without it."
—Marsha Mason, actress

"After rescuing a beat-up, furless terrier of uncertain age who I wanted to name Harry, I called Ellin for information on the name and was assured that his name and mine would bond into a healthy, entertaining, supportive relationship. After seven years together, I still don't know how old Harry is—he's a Hollywood dog and won't reveal his age—but to his vet's surprise, he's grown a full furry coat, he laughs at my jokes, he's intelligent, and we're extremely compatible and considerate of each other's idiosyncrasies. Ellin knew that Harry was the perfect companion name for me!"
—Valorie Armstrong, TV-film actor

"Ellin Dodge has done it again. . . . Helping me understand me and my favorite pet pooch through the magic of numbers."
—Heidi Foglesong, TV personality and radio talk show host

"Ellin Dodge's insight, wit, and wisdom have made naming a pet an exercise in enlightenment! You'll find no rehashing of human names and values in this delightful book. Her analyses of these pet names and their numerological basis have the uncanny ability to speak to us from both the animals' and the owners' perspectives—telling us in many ways what to expect and how to . please our beloved companions. Enjoy!"
—Lynne Alvarez, playwright

A Fireside Book

Published by Simon & Schuster
New York London Toronto Sydney Singapore

FROM ACE to ZUMMO

A Dictionary of
Numerologically Based Names
for Your Pet

Ellin Dodge

FIRESIDE
Rockefeller Center
1230 Avenue of the Americas
New York, NY 10020

For information regarding special discounts for bulk purchases,
please contact Simon & Schuster Special Sales:
1-800-456-6798 or business@simonandschuster.com

Designed by Diane Hobbing of SNAP-HAUS GRAPHICS

Manufactured in the United States of America
10   9   8   7   6   5   4   3   2   1
Library of Congress Cataloging-in-Publication Data

Dodge, Ellin.
From Ace to Zummo : a dictionary of numerologically based names for your pet / Ellin Dodge.
p. cm.
Includes bibliographical references (p.   ).
1. Pets—Names. 2. Numerology. I. Title.

SF411.3 .D64 2002
929.9'7—dc21   2002026788
ISBN 0-7432-1585-0 (trade pbk.)

For Vicki George and her brood: Sam the Doberman;
Tyler, Joey, Marylou, and Molly, all Wheaten Terriers

Acknowledgments

For help and encouragement: World traveler, Susan Williams Stockard; Laura Greenberg, of Del Mar, California; Heidi Foglesong; Shelly Segal; Don Talbot and Beth Meyer-Lohse, of Phoenix, Arizona; Rona Barrett, of Santa Ynez, California; Marcela Landres and Trish Todd at Simon & Schuster in New York; literary agent Jim Schiavone, of West Palm Beach, Florida; and Sammy the Yorkie, whose magical appearance reinforced my belief in angels.

Contents

FROM ACE to ZUMMO

Ages ago a heartfelt prayer
   Arose from a man in deep despair.
The Father heard. "His need is great—
   For such poor mortals I'll create
A loyal friend, who'll stay close by
   To love, to share, to live and die.
His willing slave, who'll ask no more
   Than just to worship and adore,
Who cannot speak or lift a hand
   To help—but will understand."
And so it came to pass at morn
   An answered prayer—*a dog was born.*

                     —*Author Unknown*

Compassion for the person who never has known
   An aloof and charming cat;
Who never has watched her artful ways
   While baiting a fake fur rat.
Comfort the person who never receives,
   In hours of sadness and woe,
The lingering touch of an intuitive cat
   In a way only she seems to know.
Pity the man who does not know
   A feline aristocrat.
He'll never understand the bond that exists
   Between man and the mystical cat.

                     —*Ellin Dodge*

Introduction

A visit from angels? Maybe! . . . When a downcast Yorkshire Terrier pup showed up at my doorstep just as I was picking up my Sunday newspaper, I thought, "Fred slipped out." But when I saw the friendly pixie staring up at me, I realized his face was too small to be my Yorkie Fred, and I knew I had a visitor. After scooping him up and calming his shivers, I set off in search of his home, eventually finding a notice taped to a cluster of mailboxes: "Little Boy Missing Yorkie." Soon after, I met the boy's mom, who explained that she was going to take the little Yorkie to the pound because he could not be housebroken. She had convinced her son it was best for the pet since her unaccommodating, live-in boyfriend regularly shooed the boy's feisty little Yorkie out the door. I looked down at the vivacious puppy, now begging to be held, and thought, "Here's a dog with real attitude." Within minutes, his AKC papers, food, bed, travel box, and the mother's gratitude arrived at my door—now a two-Yorkie household . . . but that's just part of the story.

Littlest Yorkie was named Sam, and after a few days it was time for a physical, so both Yorkies went to see the vet. Sammy, a year and a half old according to his AKC papers, was pronounced healthy, but ten-year-old frisky Fred was drinking too much water and the vet diagnosed him with late-in-life diabetes. Within two weeks of Sammy's arrival, Fred passed on, but he wasn't forgotten. Sammy, once a dog who couldn't be housebroken and who was accustomed to running away, had learned valuable life lessons from Fred in their brief time together. Soon, Sammy was using the doggy-door exit to the backyard and staying inside the house when the front door was opened: He had taken on new social graces.

And Sammy's first family? The mysterious neighbors were never seen after Sammy came here to live, though his unique arrival makes one wonder if they were predestinating angels, intending to replace the ailing Fred. It's a strange and serendipitous happening that makes life interesting. Although it's sad to kennel a doting pet when away from home and even though I had previously vowed never to get another dependent companion after Fred was gone—and Sam's quite a handful—once again I'm possessed by a bewitching, adventurous, intelligent, perceptive Yorkie.

It's possible that Sammy thinks of humans as a weird-smelling, misshapen, strange variety of his breed. Pets accommodate their human family by altering their instincts and learning to show appreciation and affection. Dogs lick our faces to indicate submission through the same rituals used to show other animals that they are followers. Cats groom us in acceptance. We don't bite when stroking and we know how to open a can. We also can take on the pack mentality by eating, sleeping, playing, and resting with our pets. We are automatically pet leaders because of our superior size and intellect—and because we feed them. And for these reasons, we get to pick the names.

Numerology

For over thirty years, clients have called me for pet name descriptions and to ask for my opinion on compatibility based on their pet's breed or first names. This book has the answers.

To keep it simple, *From Ace to Zummo* focuses on cats and dogs. When selecting a name for your pet, select desirable behavior patterns by name number and compare breed and owner first name numbers. Sam's legal name is Semi-Sweet, and *Semi* was converted to *Sammy* instinctively. Some things get help with planning and others are meant to be.

Fred's #6 name was chosen with its numerology name description in mind. Sam, probably the gift of a protective angel, arrived with a #6 name. Both Sam (#6) and Fred (#6) are dedicated homebody names that, in my opinion, are choice because loved ones provide their reason for living.

Numerology uses numbers as symbols for traits of character and personality; when numbers are substituted for alphabet letters, they let you know what's in a name. By taking the numerical value assigned to each letter in a name and using a simple arithmetic system, you can learn what the animal with that name is capable of doing or is unprepared to cope with.

Numerology was popular with the Sumerians and Babylonians in 3600 B.C. and later modernized by the ancient Greek who coined the words *philosophy* and *mathematics*, Pythagoras. Although Pythagoras lived in the sixth century B.C. and the science of numbers is over eleven thousand years old, he is responsible for modernizing the number symbols assigned to alphabet letters that result in character analysis when applied to a name today.

Pythagoras

From about 580 B.C. through 500 B.C., the Greek mathematician-philosopher-politician-teacher Pythagoras revised and modernized the ancient 1-through-8 Chaldean-Sumerian numerology systems to add the number 9. During the Chaldean-Sumerian civilization, the number 8 described the height of that cul-

ture. Number 8 symbolized self-serving mental and physical strength: the accumulation of money, property, and power by force. Pythagoras saw the need for a new final number when the enlightened, refined Greek civilization developed and recognized humanitarian principles and polished cultural refinements in their lifestyle—unlike the barbaric Sumerians or Babylonians, which focused on survival alone.

Pythagoras believed that words did not adequately describe concepts and objects. He believed that the progression of numbers 1 through 9, used symbolically to detail how the human character evolves, best explain how we grow in a natural progression from selfishness to selflessness. These are the Pythagorean steps of evolvement:

#1: "I"—the ego, selfishness, assertiveness, aggressiveness, and independence

#2: "we"—union, emotional sensitivity, peace as a purpose, cooperation, and receptivity

#3: "us"—communication, sociability, humor, imagination, artistic talents, and appreciation of beauty

#4: "group perimeters, behavior boundaries, and product productivity"—practicality, dedication, manual dexterity, carefulness, discipline, exactitude, loyalty, thoroughness, and willingness to work

#5: "reproduction, spontaneous physical contact, sexual passion"—sensuality, sexuality, versatility, adaptability, flexibility, curiosity, and mental and physical freedom

#6: "family, group, and community relationships"—responsibility, domesticity, protectiveness, justice, stability, harmony, rhythm, and parental love

#7: "the spirit"—spiritual, intellectual, technical introspection, intuition, analysis, academic questioning, objective authority, and inner wisdom

#8: "power in group perimeters"—material ambition, financial freedom, physical strength, mental agility, efficiency, shrewdness, discrimination, and "might over right"

#9: "humanitarianism, culture, and romantic passions"—selflessness; spiritual, emotional, and physical healing; human understanding; compassion; generosity; quality and skill of performance; counseling with nobility of purpose; appreciation of culture and philosophy; and universal love

Day-to-Day

In *From Ace to Zummo,* your pet's name, a breed name, or a human name's Day-to-Day characteristics, talents, and means of self-expression are assigned the sum total of the numbers for all the letters in the first name. These assigned numbers appear next to the names included in the dictionary section of this book for easy reference.

The sum of the numbers ascribed to all the name letters describes average behavior, the meaning of the name Day-to-Day: Number 1 is an independent,

active, alert, creative, unemotional loner. Number 2 is a cooperative, easygoing, dependent, emotionally sensitive joiner. Number 3 is an entertaining, noisy, decorative, affectionate communicator. Number 4 is a practical, routine-oriented, dependable, unemotional worker. Number 5 is an adaptable, freedom-loving, fast-moving, changeable, sensual risk-taker. Number 6 is a serious, domestic, responsible, loving homebody and do-gooder. Number 7 is a spiritual, sedentary, aristocratic, reserved, well-mannered intellectual. Number 8 is a mental, physical, and social powerhouse and guardian. Number 9 is a peace-loving, humanitarian, empathetic, cultured service-provider that makes friends because he or she is a friend.

At First Glance

The sum of the numbers assigned to the consonant letters describes your pet, a cat or dog breed, or a human At First Glance; it is the first impression given. (Consonants include all alphabet letters that are not A, E, I, O, or U, and Y if there is no vowel in the syllable.)

The sum of the consonant numbers describes how your pet, a breed, or a human pique your interest or causes disinterest at first glance: Number 1 is a proud, active, alert, independent, and unusually patterned or colored loner. Number 2 is an unassuming, hesitant, gentle sweetie that is content to remain in the background until invited to join in. Number 3 is a cute, entertaining, noisy, decorative, youthful, playful charmer that takes center stage immediately. Number 4 is a sturdy, muscular, dark, slow-moving, cautious, quiet, self-disciplined pet or human and is natural and conventional for the breed. Number 5 is a frisky, unrestrained, amusing charmer that looks unconventional and makes immediate body contact. Number 6 is a serious, robust, parental and conventional do-gooder that is immediately attracted to children and other pets. Number 7 is an aristocratic, reserved, introspective, perfectly groomed observer. Number 8 is a mental and physical powerhouse that is confident, self-disciplined, and sociable. Number 9 is a polished, skillful, peaceful, relaxed communicator.

The Bottom Line

The sum of the numbers assigned to the vowel letters in a name describes The Bottom Line—the deepest yearnings, wants, desired comfort zone, or motiva-

tion of the pet, breed, or human. Vowels include the letters A, E, I, O, U, and Y if there is no vowel in the syllable. For example, in the last syllable of the name Marilyn (Mar-i-*lyn*), there is no vowel, but there is a *y*. Therefore, *y* is considered a vowel. Other examples include the *y* in the third syllable of Kennedy (Ken-ne-*dy*) and the *y* in the first syllable of Cynthia (*Cyn*-thi-a).

The sum of the numbers assigned to the vowels describes less obvious characteristics, or the "soul urge" of your pet, the breed, or the human: Number 1 wants independence, is a leader, and is uncomfortable following a human leader's commands. Number 2 wants a peaceful, cooperative, gentle, affectionate, dependent lifestyle and enjoys being spoiled and stroked. Number 3 wants attention and is comfortable center stage, enjoys being with people and playing with fun-loving humans and other pets. Number 4 wants a dependable routine and scheduled lifestyle that includes work and exercise. Number 5 wants freedom to investigate and play, loves the outdoors, is adaptable and clever, and is comfortable with unconventional humans. Number 6 wants good food, stability, comfort, and a home and family to love and protect. Number 7 wants quiet, peace, privacy, and time for rest, observation, and introspection. Number 8 wants physical and mental activity, enjoys challenges, is a shrewd protector, and is uncomfortable without vigorous, athletic exercise. Number 9 wants to meet everyone, learns skills and performs well, makes friends everywhere, and is comfortable providing service to anyone who is sick, lonely, emotionally needy, or disabled.

Quirks of Character

Quirks of Character are described by the number that is assigned to the last letter of a first name. The last letter in a name indicates habits and behavior patterns formed early in a pet's life or one's childhood that are surprising, "all too human," or possibly problematic. These are obsessive-compulsive tendencies, possibly established by improper, inappropriate youthful experiences, breeding, or the gene pool of inheritance. A pet is not conditioned to make expected or acceptable choices for one or all of a variety of unconventional or unacceptable extreme experiences. Just the way a pendulum swings from one extreme to the other, a pet only knows one extreme or the other. Centering the pendulum—the balanced way to act or react—is never learned, and a positive habit is never formed, possibly due to too careful handling or carelessness; impatience; overtraining or no training; too much or not enough

restriction; cruelty or abuse; criticism; instability; little or no affection or suppression of individuality; too much people contact or none at all; too much freedom, humiliation, deception, degradation; and various other possibilities. In short, the pet has never learned the right thing to do or puts itself in danger and needs positive motivation and patient retraining with a loving handler.

The number equivalent of the last letter in a name describes idiosyncrasies, surprising actions, and/or the extremes of obsessive-compulsive behavior referred to as Quirks of Character: Number 1 is either too aggressive or too submissive, too lazy or overly active, too independent or too dependent, too courageous or cowardly. Number 2 is either too sensitive to others or too self-absorbed, too needy or indifferent, and can be deceitful or subtly manipulative. Number 3 is either too noisy or too quiet, too extroverted or too introverted, too attentive to children or intolerant of children, too happy or too sad. Number 4 is too earthy and unmannerly, undignified, too trusting or disloyal, too dull or too energetic, too routine oriented or unable to learn routines. Number 5 is too irresponsible and unmanageable, too curious, too clever and mischievous, too sexual or disinterested in mating, careless, accident-prone, and may refuse to be housebroken, run away, or fear the unknown. Number 6 is too concerned and underfoot, too anxious or too disinterested, too close to children or intolerant of youngsters, too interested in food or unable to eat due to emotional reactions. Number 7 is too nervous, overly active or unwilling to move, too hesitant or too quick, too detached or too jealous, cold and unresponsive, melancholy, and moody. Number 8 is too powerful and careless, too discriminating of a guardian or an uncontrolled attacker, too friendly or unsociable; when not exercised vigorously, the flow of strength and energy is misdirected and the pet can be unstable and dangerous. Number 9 is greedy or too unselfish, too peaceful or too angry, too friendly or too unfriendly, too emotional or too uncaring, extremely secure or very insecure, and may refuse to let go of anything when playing or is fickle.

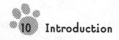

Do It Yourself

You can match the name number found next to each name in the dictionary (see page 51) to the breed number (see pages 13–21 for alphabetized cat and dog breed number lists) to reinforce a name's Day-to-Day personality traits.

For example, when you give a Boxer (breed #1) the name Peter (a number #1), the name Peter will attract the people and experiences that reinforce the Boxer's talents Day-to-Day. The sound of a spoken name sends out a unique vibration that attracts or repels people and experiences. When your pet's name number and breed number are the same, your pet will attract people and experiences that seem natural: Your pet will thrive and achieve all possible potential.

How to Determine Any Name Number

If a pet's breed, pet name, or human first name that interests you is not listed in this book, refer to the letter values chart below in order to determine the breed or name number. Add the letter values and reduce the sum to a single-digit numeral.

Letter Values

1	2	3	4	5	6	7	8	9
A	B	C	D	E	F	G	H	I
J	K	L	M	N	O	P	Q	R
S	T	U	V	W	X	Y	Z	

Example 1
Dog Breed—Boxer: B = 2, O = 6, X = 6, E = 5, R = 9.
Add: 2 + 6 + 6 + 5 + 9 = 28; 2 + 8 = 10; 1 + 0 = 1. A Boxer is #1.
Example 2
Cat Breed—Siamese: S = 1, I = 9, A = 1, M = 4, E = 5, S = 1, E = 5.
Add: 1 + 9 + 1 + 4 + 5 + 1 + 5 = 26; 2 + 6 = 8. A Siamese cat is #8.
Example 3
Pet Name—Ace: A = 1, C = 3, E = 5.
Add: 1 + 3 + 5 = 9. Pet name Ace is #9.
Example 4

Human Name—Mary: M = 4, A = 1, R = 9, Y = 7.
Add: 4 + 1 + 9 + 7 = 21; 2 + 1 = 3. Human name Mary is #3.

Human Name and Pet Name/Breed Compatability

A human first name number can be determined by using the Letter Values chart. Use the compatibility section at the end of each number's section (in the Number Meanings chapter) when comparing your pet's name, another pet name, pet breeds, and human names.

Pet, breed, and owner names may not have the same number, but that does not mean they are incompatible. A list of all number compatibilities—with a rating of "excellent" (three stars), "good" (two stars), or "friction" (one star)—is included at the end of each number section for reference.

Example:
Pet name—Zeke: Z = 8, E = 5, K = 2, E = 5.
Add: 8 + 5 + 2 + 5 = 20; 2 + 0 = 2. Pet name Zeke is #2.
Human Name—Michael: M = 4, I = 9, C = 3, H = 8, A = 1, E = 5, L = 3.
Add: 4 + 9 + 3 + 8 + 1 + 5 + 3 = 33; 3 + 3 = 6. Human name Michael is #6.
***Excellent; **Good with disciplines; *Friction!
#2 with #1 = ***, #2 with #2 = **, #2 with #3 = ***, #2 with #4 = ***, #2 with #5 = *, #2 with #6 = ***, #2 with #7 = ***, #2 with #8 = **, #2 with #9 = ***

Number 2 with #6 is an excellent combination. Number 2 is receptive, unassuming, and affectionate, and wants security. Number 6 is a responsible, loving, parental homebody that enjoys social interaction. Both numbers want harmonious relationships, and they charm each other as well as everyone else. Number 2 wants the security and comfort that #6 provides, and #6 wants the unconditional love and obvious gratitude that #2 offers—that's why #2 and #6 are compatible.

Meaning of Pet Name and Breed Name Numbers

The sum of the numbers assigned to the letters of a name describes one's natural talents, comfort zones, and usual means of self-expression.

Pet name and human name numbers do not have to be the same or even rated as excellent in the numbers sections. Name number descriptions give you insight into the traits exhibited daily, but the choice is yours: Decide

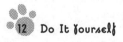

whether you prefer living with sameness or with more differences.

However, it is supportive for the animal to have matching descriptions of its personal name number and breed name number. When the pet name has the same Day-to-Day focus as that indicated by a breed or category name number description, there is less conflict for the pet. When the pet name and human first name are compatible, daily living is less stressful and more accommodating for both personalities.

You're the leader; the choice is yours.

Breed Numbers

If your pet is a mixed breed, add the different breed numbers and read the Day-to-Day description of the *sum* number. For example, for a cat that is a mix of Maine Coon (#8) and Manx (#7), add 8 to 7, which equals 15; then the sum of 1 and 5 is 6, so the Maine Coon–Manx mix number is #6. For a Yorkshire Terrier–Miniature Poodle mix, add 5 (for Yorkshire Terrier) to 6 (for Miniature Poodle), which totals 11, and 1 and 1 is 2. A Yorkshire Terrier–Miniature Poodle mix is therefore #2. (In the following lists of pet breeds, commonly-used descriptive names are also included.)

Cats

Abyssinian #5
American Bobtail #8
American Curl #1
American Shorthair #9
American Wirehair #2
Angora #2
Australian Mist #6
Balinese #4
Barn Cat #5
Bengal #5
Birman #3
Bombay #4
British Shorthair #3
Burmese #2
Burmilla #7
Calico #7
Cat #6
Chantilly (Tiffany #9) #5
Chartreux #1
Colorpoint Longhair #5
Colorpoint Shorthair #1
Cornish Rex #7
Cymric (Manx #7) #8
Devon Rex #8
Egyptian Mau #6
Havana Brown #2
Himalayan #3
House Cat #2
Japanese Bobtail #6
Javanese #5
Korat #2
LaPerm #2
Maine Coon #8
Manx (Cymric #8) #7
Munchkin #3
Nebelung #8

Norwegian Forest #9
Ocicat #6
Oriental #4
Persian #1
Pixie-Bob #1
Ragamuffing #4
Ragdoll #6
Rex #2
Russian Blue #6
Savannah #8
Scottish Fold #6
Selkirk Rex #6
Shorthair, American #9
Shorthair, British #3
Siamese #8
Siberian #5
Singapura #7
Snowshoe #1
Sokoke #4
Somali #6
Sphynx #7
Spotted Mist #7
Tabby #5
Tiffany (Chantilly #5) #9
Tonkinese #4
Turkish Angora #9
Turkish Van #8

Dogs

Affenpinscher #7
Afghan Hound #9
African Hunting Dog #9
Ainu Dog #8
Airedale Terrier #4
Akbash Dog #5
Akita #6
Alapaha Blue Blood Bulldog #4

Alaskan Husky #8
Alaskan Klee Kai #5
Alaskan Malamute #1
Alopekis #7
Alpine Dachsbracke #6
American Bandogge Mastiff #4
American Black and Tan Coonhound #4
American Blue Gascon Hound #9
American Bulldog #2
American Cocker Spaniel #6
American Eskimo Dog #9
American Foxhound #9
American Hairless Terrier #5
American Indian Dog #6
American Lo-Sze Pugg #3
American Mastiff (Panja #6) #3
American Pit Bull Terrier #6
American Staffordshire Terrier #8
American Staghound #2
American Toy Terrier (Amertoy #7) #1
American Water Spaniel #9
American White Shepherd #5
Anatolian Shepherd Dog (Karabash #7) #7
Anglos-Francais de Moyenne Venerie #2
Anglos-Francaises #1
Anglos-Francaises de Petite Venerie #9
Appenzell Mountain Dog #6
Argentine Dogo #8
Ariegeois #7
Armant #4
Arubian Cunucu Dog #4
Aryan Molossus #3
Australian Bandog #6
Australian Cattle Dog #5
Australian Kelpie #3
Australian Shepherd #1
Australian Terrier #2
Austrian Brandlbracke #5

Austrian Shorthaired Pinscher [5]

Azawakh [8]

Banjara Greyhound [2]

Barbet [3]

Basenji [6]

Basset Artésien Normand [2]

Basset Hound [2]

Bavarian Mountain Hound [3]

Beagle [5]

Beagle Harrier [1]

Bearded Collie [5]

Beauceron [3]

Bedlington Terrier [6]

Bedouin Shepherd Dog [8]

Belgian Griffon [8]

Belgian Mastiff [7]

Belgian Shepherd Groenendael [8]

Belgian Shepherd Laekenois [8]

Belgian Shepherd Malinois [9]

Belgian Shepherd Tervuren [4]

Belgian Shorthaired Pointer [2]

Belgrade Terrier [3]

Bergamasco [3]

Berger des Picard [8]

Berger des Pyrenees [1]

Berger du Languedoc [9]

Bernese Mountain Dog [3]

Bichon Frise [9]

Bichon Havanais (Havanese [3]) [9]

Black and Tan Coonhound [3]

Black Forest Hound [3]

Black Mouth Cur [4]

Black Russian Terrier [7]

Bleus de Gascogne [4]

Bloodhound [2]

Blue Gascon Hound [8]

Blue Lacy [9]

Bluetick Coonhound [3]

Boerboel [2]

Bohemian Terrier (Cesky Terrier [3]) [7]

Bolognese [4]

Border Collie [1]

Border Terrier [2]

Borzoi [4]

Boston Bull Terrier [9]

Bouvier des Flandres [1]

Boxer [1]

Boykin Spaniel [8]

Bracco Italiano [6]

Braque d'Ariege [5]

Braque d'Auvergne [8]

Braque du Bourbonnais [3]

Braque Dupuy [7]

Braque Saint-Germain [5]

Braque Francaises [6]

Brazilian Terrier [5]

Briard [7]

Brittany Spaniel [5]

Briquet [2]

Broholmer [7]

Brussels Griffon (Belgian Griffon [8]) [1]

Bull Boxer [3]

Bulldog [1]

Bullmastiff [4]

Bull Terrier [5]

Cairn Terrier [3]

Cajun Squirrel Dog [5]

Canaan Dog [6]

Canary Dog [7]

Cane Corso [3]

Canoe Dog [1]

Cao da Serra de Aires [2]

Cao da Serra Estrela [3]

Cao de Castro Laboreiro [1]

Cao de Fila de Sao Miguel [5]

Cardigan Welsh Corgi [5]

Carlin Pinscher #5

Carolina Dog #9

Carpathian Sheepdog #8

Catahoula Leopard Dog #8

Catalan Sheepdog #5

Caucasian Ovtcharka #9

Cavalier King Charles Spaniel #2

Cesky Fousek #5

Cesky Terrier #3

Chart Polski #6

Chesapeake Bay Retriever #6

Chien d'Artois #8

Chien de l'Atlas #5

Chiens Francaises #9

Chihuahua #8

Chin (Japanese Chin #6) #7

Chinese Crested Hairless #3

Chinese Crested Powderpuff #6

Chinese Shar-Pei #4

Chinook #3

Chortaj #3

Chow Chow #8

Cirneco dell 'Etna #5

Clumber Spaniel #6

Cockapoo #7

Cocker Spaniel #5

Collie #2

Continental Toy Spaniel (Papillon #5) #2

Corgi #7

Coton de Tuleur #2

Croatian Sheepdog #7

Curly-Coated Retriever #4

Czechoslovakian Wolfdog #3

Czesky Terrier (Cesky Terrier #3) #2

Dachshund #1

Dalmatian #3

Dandie Dinmont Terrier #3

Danish Broholmer #8

Danish Chicken Dog #8

Deutsche Bracke #8

Deutscher Wachtelhund #6

Dingo #4

Doberman Pinscher #2

Dog #8

Dogo Argentino #9

Dogue de Bordeaux #7

Dogue Brasileiro #7

Drentse Patrijshond #3

Drever #9

Dunker #1

Dutch Shepherd Dog #3

Dutch Smoushond #4

Elkhound #9

English Bulldog #3

English Cocker Spaniel #7

English Coonhound #3

English Foxhound #1

English Pointer (Pointer #7) #9

English Setter #8

English Shepherd #4

English Springer Spaniel #4

English Toy Spaniel (King Charles Spaniel #3) #3

Entelbucher Sennenhund #6

Epagneul Francais #8

Epagneul Pont-Audemer #6

Epagneuls Picardies #4

Eskimo Dog #8

Estonian Hound #6

Estrela Mountain Dog #6

Eurasier #6

Farm Collie (Scotch Collie #7) #4

Fauves de Bretagne #2

Feist (Rat Terrier #6) #5

Field Spaniel #4

Fila Brasileiro (Brazilian Mastiff #4) #1

Finnish Hound #6

Finnish Laphound [8]

Finnish Spitz [7]

Flat-Coated Retriever [9]

Foxhound [8]

Fox Terrier [3]

Fox Terrier, Toy [9]

French Brittany Spaniel [5]

French Bulldog [1]

French Mastiff [2]

Galgo Español [7]

Gascons-Saintongeois [9]

German Hunt Terrier [7]

German Longhaired Pointer [5]

German Pinscher [6]

German Sheeppoodle [7]

German Shepherd Dog [5]

German Shorthaired Pointer [1]

German Spitz [4]

German Wirehaired Pointer [3]

German Wolfspitz [6]

Giant Schnauzer [4]

Glen of Imaal Terrier [8]

Goldendoodle (retriever-poodle [7]) [4]

Golden Retriever [6]

Gordon Setter [7]

Grand Anglo-Francais [2]

Gran Mastin de Borinquen [6]

Great Dane [3]

Greater Swiss Mountain Dog [8]

Great Pyrenees [5]

Greek Harehound [5]

Greek Hound [9]

Greek Sheepdog [8]

Greenland Dog [7]

Greyhound [9]

Griffon Nivernais [6]

Griffons Vendéens [2]

Groenendael [1]

Grosser Munsterlander Vorstehhund [5]

Guatemalan Bull Terrier [1]

Hairless Terrier [4]

Halden Hound [7]

Hamiltonstovare [3]

Hanoverian Hound [7]

Harlequin Pinscher [8]

Harrier [5]

Havanese [3]

Hawaiian Poi Dog [6]

Hertha Pointer [4]

Himalayan Sheepdog [1]

Hokkaido Dog (Ainu Dog [8]) [1]

Hovawart [9]

Hungarian Kuvasz [4]

Hungarian Puli [7]

Husky [3]

Hygenhund [7]

Ibizan Hound [6]

Icelandic Sheepdog [4]

Inca Hairless Dog [9]

Irish Glen Imaal Terrier [5]

Irish Red and White Setter [9]

Irish Setter [6]

Irish Staffordshire Bull Terrier [9]

Irish Terrier [3]

Irish Water Spaniel [8]

Irish Wolfhound [1]

Italian Greyhound [3]

Italian Spinoni [9]

Jack Russell Terrier [8]

Japanese Spaniel (Japanese Chin [6]) [3]

Japanese Spitz [8]

Japanese Terrier [2]

Jindo [7]

Kai Dog [2]

Kangal Dog [9]

Kangaroo Dog [9]

Karabash (Anatolian Shepherd Dog #7) #7
Karakachan #6
Karelian Bear Dog #6
Karelian Bear Laika #5
Karelo-Finnish Laika #4
Keeshound #3
Kelb Tal-Fenek (Pharaoh Hound #3) #5
Kelpie, Australian #3
Kemmer Feist #7
Kerry Beagle #1
Kerry Blue Terrier #3
King Charles Spaniel (English Toy Spaniel #3) #3
Komondor #6
Kooikerhondje #5
Koolie #4
Krasky Ovcar #9
Kromfohrlander #5
Kuvasz #1
Kyi-Leo #5
Labradoodle (labrador-poodle #3) #8
Labrador Retriever #2
Lagotto Romagnolo #2
Lakeland Terrier #9
Lancashire Heeler #8
Landseer #6
Lapinporokoira #8
Lapphund #2
Large Munsterlander #9
Larson Lakeview Bulldogge #9
Latvian Hound #6
Leonberger #2
Leopard Cur #5
Levesque #7
Lhasa Apso #2
Lithuanian Hound #9
Louisiana Catahoula Leopard Dog #1
Lowchen (Little Lion Dog #1) #8
Lucas Terrier #5

Lundehund #4
Lurcher #4
Magyar Agar #2
Mahratta Greyhound #1
Majestic Tree Hound #1
Maltese #3
Manchester Terrier #1
Maremma Sheepdog #8
Markiesje #1
Mastiff #2
Mexican Hairless (Xoloitzcuintle #7) #7
Middle Asian Ovtcharka #1
Mi-Ki #6
Miniature American Mastiff #5
Miniature Australian Shepherd #3
Miniature Bull Terrier #7
Miniature Pinscher #4
Miniature Poodle #6
Miniature Schnauzer #9
Mioritic Sheepdog #4
Mongrel #3
Moscow Toy Terrier #7
Moscow Vodolaz #3
Moscow Watchdog #7
Mountain Cur #5
Mountain View Cur #1
Mucuchies #3
Mudi #2
Munsterlander Mastiff #4
Mutt #2
Nebolish Mastiff #5
Newfoundland #7
New Zealand Huntaway #2
New Zealand Sheepdog #4
Norbottenspets (Nordic Spitz #9) #4
Norfolk Terrier #4
Northeasterly Hauling Laika #7
Norwegian Buhund #5

Norwegian Elkhound [7]
Norwich Terrier [3]
Nova Scotia Duck-Tolling Retriever [7]
Old Danish Bird Dog [1]
Olde Boston Bulldogge [8]
Olde English Bulldogge [6]
Old English Mastiff [8]
Old English Sheepdog [4]
Original English Bulldogge [1]
Otterhound [5]
Owczarek Podhalanski [5]
Papillon [5]
Patterdale Terrier [6]
Pekepoo [2]
Pekinese [3]
Pembroke Welsh Corgi [6]
Perdigueiro Portugueso [5]
Perdiguero de Burgos [2]
Perdiguero Navarro [9]
Perro Cimarron [1]
Perro de Pastor Mallorquin [5]
Perro de Presa Canario [3]
Perro de Presa Mallorquin [2]
Perro Inca Orchid [3]
Perro Ratonero Andaluz [5]
Petit Basset Griffon Vendéen [1]
Petit Brabancon (Belgian Griffon [8]) [5]
Pharaoh Hound (Kelb Tal-Fenek [5]) [3]
Pit Bull [2]
Plott Hound [1]
Podenco Ibicenco [6]
Podengo Portuguesos Grande [4]
Podengo Portuguesos Medio [1]
Podengo Portuguesos Pequeno [3]
Pointer [7]
Poitevin [2]
Polish Hound [6]
Polski Owczarek Nizinny [7]

Polski Owczarek Podhalanski [6]
Pomeranian [7]
Poodle [4]
Porcelaine [8]
Portuguese Rabbit Dog [9]
Portuguese Water Dog [6]
Potsdam Greyhound [7]
Prazsky Krysavik [7]
Pudel Pointer [2]
Pug [8]
Puli [4]
Pumi [5]
Pyrenean Mastiff [1]
Pyrenean Mountain Dog [6]
Queensland Heeler [3]
Rafeiro do Alentejo [2]
Rampur Greyhound [6]
Rastreador Brasileiro [2]
Rat Terrier (Feist [5]) [6]
Redbone Coonhound [1]
Rhodesian Ridgeback [9]
Rottweiler [1]
Rough Collie [8]
Rumanian Sheepdog [8]
Russian Bear Schnauzer [8]
Russian Harlequin Hound [7]
Russian Hound [1]
Russian Spaniel [6]
Russian Tsvetnaya Bolonka [1]
Russian Wolfhound [3]
Russo-European Laika [5]
Saarlooswolfhond [8]
Sabuessos Españoles [1]
Sage Ashayeri [1]
Sage Koochee [4]
Sage Mazandarani [8]
Saint Bernard [8]
Saluki [1]

Samoyed [1]
Sanshu Dog [9]
Sarplaninac [9]
Schapendoes [1]
Schillerstovare [6]
Schipperke [2]
Schnauzer, Giant [4]
Schnauzer, Miniature [9]
Schnauzer, Standard [7]
Schnoodle (schnauzer-poodle [2]) [5]
Scotch Collie [7]
Scottish Deerhound [9]
Scottish Terrier (Scottie [1]) [8]
Sealydale Terrier [6]
Sealyham Terrier [6]
Segugios Italianos [4]
Setter, English [8]
Setter, Gordon [7]
Setter, Irish [6]
Shar-Pei [4]
Shepherd, White German [8]
Shetland Sheepdog (Sheltie [6]) [9]
Shiba Inu [2]
Shichon [4]
Shih Tzu [3]
Shika Inus [3]
Shikoku [4]
Shiloh Shepherd [1]
Siberian Husky [8]
Siberian Laika [4]
Silky Terrier [7]
Simaku [2]
Skye Terrier [9]
Sloughi [1]
Slovak Cuvac [4]
Smalandsstovare [3]
Small Munsterlander [5]
Smooth Collie [2]

Smooth Fox Terrier [3]
Soft-Coated Wheaten Terrier [7]
South African Boerboel [2]
South Russian Ovtcharka [4]
Spaniel [4]
Spanish Mastiff [7]
Spanish Water Dog [8]
Spinone Italiano [2]
Springer Spaniel [2]
Stabyhoun [8]
Staffordshire Bull Terrier [9]
Staghound [1]
Standard Poodle [4]
Standard Schnauzer [7]
Stichelhaar [5]
Strellufstover [5]
Stumpy-Tail Cattle Dog [9]
Sussex Spaniel [3]
Swedish Lapphund [8]
Swedish Vallhund [1]
Swiss Laufhund [5]
Swiss Shorthaired Pinscher [9]
Tasy [2]
Teddy Roosevelt Terrier [3]
Telomian [8]
Thai Ridgeback [8]
Tibetan Mastiff [1]
Tibetan Spaniel [3]
Tibetan Terrier [2]
Titan Terrier [4]
Tosa Inu [9]
Toy American Eskimo [7]
Toy Fox Terrier [9]
Toy German Spitz [1]
Toy Manchester Terrier [7]
Toy Munchkin [9]
Toy Poodle [1]
Transylvanian Hound [7]

Treeing Tennessee Brindle #5
Treeing Walker Coonhound #5
Tyroler Bracke #9
Valley Bulldog #6
Vasgotaspets #2
Victorian Bulldog #4
Villano de Las Encartaciones #1
Vizsla #8
Volpino Italiano #4
Vucciriscu #2
Weimaraner #8
Welsh Corgi #2
Welsh Sheepdog #2
Welsh Springer Spaniel #6
Welsh Terrier #7
West Highland White Terrier #9
Westphalian Dachsbracke #5
West Russian Coursing Hound #3
West Siberian Laika #7
Wetterhoun #5
Wheaten Terrier #7
Whippet #7
White German Shepherd #8
Wirehaired Fox Terrier #4
Wirehaired Pointing Griffon #9
Xoloitzcuintle (Mexican Hairless #7) #7
Yorkshire Terrier #5
Yugoslavian Hound #1

Number Meanings

#1

Name Day-to-Day

"Leave it to me, I'll do it my way," "Me first, me first!" "Don't come near me till I'm finished eating," says the #1 pet with an alpha personality. Routines or schedules that conflict with his plans are ignored. Number 1 refers everything to himself, is a proud performer that is humiliated easily, and works best alone. The independent #1 doesn't mind being different and walks in front of a human leader. This quick-acting, high-energy risk-taker confidently stares back when challenged and eats when he wants, plays when he's ready, and loves at will. Day-to-Day: #1 is determined, inventive, strong willed, and inner directed.

- #1 is comfortable alone
- #1 is self-reliant
- #1 is proud
- #1 is commanding and compelling
- #1 establishes a distinctive presence and wants to be boss
- #1 is an assertive communicator
- #1 is unlikely to feel separation anxiety
- #1 is distinctive and influential
- #1 is a mental being; wants more action and less affection
- #1 is intelligent; wants to be mentally and verbally stimulated
- #1 wants and responds to praise
- #1 is alert, energetic, and active
- #1 is full of spirit
- #1 is ready to risk
- #1 confidently takes the initiative
- #1 is persistent
- #1 accepts challenges
- #1 makes and enjoys appropriate changes
- #1 offers devotion, loyalty, commitment, and mutual respect
- #1 is impatient but teachable; learns good manners with a patient, gentle, authoritative leader and confronts a threatening trainer

Breed

Primary Trait: Independence

Secondary Traits: Active, alert, proud, courageous, assertive, aggressive, bold, daring, distinctive, forceful, inventive, quick acting, egocentric, mental and physical as opposed to emotional

Best Collar and Accessory Color: Red; but if name ends in A, J, or S, black is best

Planetary Association: Sun

Energy Level—Dog: Needs fast-moving, vigorous exercise (indoors and outdoors)

Energy Level—Cat: Active, assertive

Compatibility: Gets along best with adults

Best Toy—Dog: Frisbee, ball, rope, tug and chew toys

Best Toy—Cat: Animal-shaped squeaky toys, real mice, real lizards and bugs, bouncy balls, fluffy feather, cardboard tube

At First Glance
Independent, proud, dominant, active, alert, assertive, aggressive, distinctive, and appears to be a "first" for the breed, an "original," or different.

The Bottom Line
Wants to be independent, dominant, and active; wants to create his or her routine; wants to be praised for every accomplishment; and is comfortable alone.

Quirks of Character

If the name ends in A, J, or S, the tendency to be the only leader in a group has been challenged by too much restriction, instability, bullying, or not enough opportunity to test his or her courage at a young age. Judgment is out of balance because the pet or person has not learned when it is appropriate to do things alone and when to follow instructions. Habitual personality extremes that relate to independence, individuality, creativity, initiative, and perseverance form in youth and persist into adulthood; patient retraining is necessary.

Number 1 personality extremes indicate obsessive-compulsive behavior. Pets may alternate in varying degrees from one extreme to another yet be positively balanced at other times.

Is too aggressive or too submissive

Is too impatient or indecisive

Is too incautious or too cowardly

Is too noisy or too quiet

Is too tentative or too quick

Is too independent or too dependent

Is lazy or too active

Is too rigid or too changeable

Resents authority; very difficult to teach and resists commands

Is arrogant or lacks pride

Is always too busy; unable to bond or achieve intimacy

Is antagonistic

Is too bossy or too helpless

Urinates or defecates impulsively or stubbornly refuses to urinate or defecate during appropriate outings

Is too impulsive

Is selfish

Is greedy or too reluctant

Is insolent or spineless

Is too curious or lacks initiative

Is on-the-go or lethargic

Becomes obsessed with one idea

Fights or trembles when emotionally upset

Resists new ideas or follows anyone's lead

Refuses to play or teases and baits less aggressive pets or small children

Ignores playfulness or misinterprets the actions of small children as challenges

Paces; is constantly in motion and lacks direction

Compatibility with Other Pet Names, Breed Names, and Human Names

***Excellent; **Good with disciplines; *There is friction!

#1 with #1 = *, #1 with #2 = ***, #1 with #3 = **, #1 with #4 = *, #1 with #5 = ***, #1 with #6 = *, #1 with #7 = *, #1 with #8 = *, #1 with #9 = **

#2

Name Day-to-Day

"I'm vulnerable. You left me alone," "How can I trust you? I don't know you," "Don't give me stress, complications, or grief," says the easygoing #2 with the emotionally supportive, one-to-one responsive, cautious personality. Intimacy and personalization are as necessary as food to the #2, who builds bridges to ensure being babied, spoiled, and kept close at hand. Little toys and small favors are noticed and appreciated by a #2, who takes orders well and prefers to be cooperative. Day-to-Day: #2 tries to work with others, pays attention to the little things, and is obedient, peaceful, and unassuming.

- #2 is miserable alone
- #2 is not overtly aggressive
- #2 wants security, comfort, stability, and an easygoing lifestyle
- #2 is always willing to snuggle and be stroked
- #2 mirrors others' moods
- #2 is finicky, refined, and gentle
- #2 thrives on special handling
- #2 is uncomfortable with sudden changes
- #2 is selective when showing affection or dining
- #2 is the peacemaker when surrounded by disharmony
- #2 will trifle with a capture and walk away without making a kill
- #2 wants to be a partner and follows the alpha pet or human
- #2 holds back until leaders are satisfied
- #2 is patient, willing to learn obedience, and easy to house train
- #2 is hesitant with strangers
- #2 prefers watching TV on someone's lap to taking a vigorous walk
- #2 plays without showing dominance
- #2 is indifferent to provocation or intense eye contact

‡2 is often mystical and very psychic

‡2 works at staying clean and neat

‡2 prefers the company of women or subdominant pets

‡2 collects little things

‡2 won't stray because that would take too much effort

‡2 bonds for life

Breed

Primary Trait: Cooperative

Secondary Traits: Loving, charming, sensitive, gentle, considerate, unassuming, peaceful, "soft," patient, affectionate, easygoing, emotional as opposed to mental and physical

Best Collar and Accessory Color: Any tone of orange; but if name ends in B, K, or T, black is best

Planetary Association: Moon

Energy Level—Dog: Sedentary indoors and moderate outdoors

Energy Level—Cat: Slow, low

Compatibility: Gets along best with female adults; compatible with careful children, older youngsters, adults, and other quiet pets

Best Toy—Dog: TV, quiet toys, stuffed animals, chew stick

Best Toy—Cat: TV, quiet stuffed toys, catnip sack

At First Glance

Unassuming, quiet, shy, affectionate, receptive, cooperative, sensitive, happy to remain in the background, plain, and unpretentious.

The Bottom Line

Wants to be protected and loved; is sweet, docile, and vulnerable; is comfortable in close proximity to and serving a loved one in little ways.

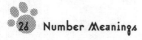

Quirks of Character

If the name ends in B, K, or T, the tendency to be adaptable and cooperative has been challenged by indifference, cruelty, past deceptions, or not enough opportunity to give or show affection at a young age. The pet has not learned when it is appropriate to be loving, intimate, gentle, or considerate with peers and leaders. Habitual personality extremes that relate to supersensitivity, aimlessness, and distrust form in youth and persist into adulthood; patient retraining is necessary.

Number 2 personality extremes indicate obsessive-compulsive behavior. Pets may alternate in varying degrees from one extreme to another yet be positively balanced at other times.

Is too rebellious or too accepting

Is too incautious or too fearful

Is too smothering or too indifferent

Is too edgy and spunky or too passive

Is too vulnerable or too defensive

Is too clinging or too detached

Is too anxious when alone or mischievously destructive

Is too alert or too relaxed

Is too finicky or too accepting

Is totally predictable or misleading, dishonest, and untrustworthy

Is subtly manipulative

Continually whines and wants to be babied

Is paranoid and assumes guilt

Creates situations that demand pacifying

Feels abandoned when left alone for short periods

Keeps others guessing to get attention

Has panic attacks and temper tantrums

Disobeys and attracts punishment to gain attention

Makes noise to mask anxiety

Compatibility with Other Pet Names, Breed Names, and Human Names

***Excellent; **Good with disciplines; *There is friction!

#2 with #1 = ***, #2 with #2 = **, #2 with #3 = ***, #2 with #4 = ***, #2 with #5 = *, #2 with #6 = ***, #2 with #7 = ***, #2 with #8 = **, #2 with #9 = ***

3

Name Day-to-Day

"Dress me up. Show me off. I'll twirl for you," "Of course I'm talking to you!" "Don't expect me to play with one toy all day," says the #3 with the fancy collar, saucy, charming personality, and cute habits. Attention and applause are as necessary as food to the extroverted #3, who teases, plays, talks, makes humans laugh, thinks life is a celebration, and always expects the best of everything. Discipline, routines, commands, and schedules are considered boring and too practical for #3. Day-to-Day: #3 has an extraordinary memory, develops a large vocabulary, and accumulates a variety of friends who appreciate entertainment.

#3 enjoys an audience

#3 is very vocal

#3 has an amazing memory

#3 feels beautiful

#3 is "turned on" to life

#3 craves the limelight

#3 remains youthful

#3 loves to be groomed and fussed over

#3 makes every feeding an event

#3 entertains and wants to be entertained

#3 lights up and dashes to the door to greet company

#3 is happy-go-lucky

#3 has a memorable voice

#3 has expressive eyes

#3 is multitalented

#3 is kind, happy, and optimistic

#3 is affectionate and loving

#3 loves crowds and is very sociable

#3 likes to travel and flirt

#3 favors children and other pets

#3 is imaginative

#3 has a sense of humor

#3 is charming, clever, and decorative

#3 wants and needs a variety of friends

Breed

Primary Trait: Communicative

Secondary Traits: Self-expressive, multitalented, sociable, people pleasing, attention getting, diversified, creative, extroverted, easygoing, emotional, mental and physical

Best Collar and Accessory Color: Yellow; but if name ends in C, L, or U, black is best

Planetary Association: Venus

Energy Level—Dog: Needs exercise and play (indoors and outdoors)

Energy Level—Cat: Sedentary alone and active with company

Compatibility: Gets along with fun-loving adults, children, and other pets

Best Toy—Dog: A variety of noisy balls, ropes, tugs and active toys, a mirror

Best Toy—Cat: Furry fake foxtail, animal-shaped playthings, and birds that dangle from a string, a mirror, cardboard tube

At First Glance
Attention getting, happy, friendly, talkative, cute, and youthful; a fashionable breed, with a decorative, golden coat, beautiful eyes, and a memorable voice.

The Bottom Line
Wants to be surrounded by onlookers who communicate, admire, and applaud; is comfortable with children, fun-loving adults, and other pets.

Quirks of Character
If the name ends in C, L, or U, the tendency to be extroverted and happy-go-lucky has been challenged by intolerance, criticism, and isolation or not enough opportunity to meet humans or socialize with other pets at a young age. The pet has not learned when it is appropriate to be playful, talkative,

happy, or friendly with peers and leaders. Habitual personality extremes that relate to introversion, disloyalty, and jealousy form in youth and persist into adulthood; patient retraining is necessary.

Number 3 personality extremes indicate obsessive-compulsive behavior. Pets may alternate in varying degrees from one extreme to another yet be positively balanced at other times.

Is too noisy or too quiet

Is too withdrawn or too outgoing

Is too reclusive or too underfoot

Is too detached or too attention grabbing

Is too intolerant or too agreeable

Is too impatient

Is too devil-may-care or too fearful

Is too restless and mischievous or too sedentary

Is too alert or too slow

Is too demanding or too inconspicuous

Worries too much or is unaware of danger signals

Is fearful of strangers or too friendly

Is too cowardly or is apt to tangle with a skunk

Is unable to concentrate or is fixed on one thing

Ignores behavior training and responsibility

Is aggressive when playing or too "spaced out" to play

Is fickle, flighty, and follows anyone offering food

Gets bored or depressed easily

Frequently changes personality

Is a prima donna or drab and lacks self-esteem

Seeks the sunlight or stays in the dark

Dislikes exercise or uses too much energy

Compatibility with Other Pet Names, Breed Names, and Human Names

***Excellent; **Good with disciplines; *There is friction!

#3 with #1 = **, #3 with #2 = ***, #3 with #3 = *, #3 with #4 = *, #3 with #5 = ***, #3 with #6 = ***, #3 with #7 = *, #3 with #8 = **, #3 with #9 = ***

#4

Name Day-to-Day

"Show me what you want me to do and I will do it," "I'm in the middle of my job and can't stop to cuddle," "Hey, don't change the rules," "You're talking too fast. Go slower," says the #4 with the routine-oriented, cautious personality, who is dependent on self-discipline and has physical endurance and inflexible habits. Work and regimentation are as necessary as food to the conscientious #4, who is a pragmatic, vigilant, humorless, earthy workaholic. Number 4 thinks life is a work-of-work and always expects to roll up his or her sleeves, dig in, do the job well, and be loved for dependability. Day-to-Day: #4 is careful, slow moving, thorough, loyal, and dependable.

#4 is steadfast

#4 is responds to routines and schedules

#4 labors for love

#4 is respectful and dutiful

#4 is a digger

#4 needs consistent physical exercise

#4 learns slowly but surely

#4 does not procrastinate

#4 listens to commands

#4 is motivated and purposeful

#4 always tries to do the best possible job

#4 is loyal

#4 implements others' ideas

#4 likes to get dirty

#4 is predictable

#4 is a mellow achiever

#4 is serious and dignified

#4 is patient and enduring

#4 loves nature

#4 serves the home, family, and territory

#4 is unemotional and practical

#4 is a rock of dependability

#4 has manual dexterity

#4 is a team worker

Breed

Primary Trait: Practical

Secondary Traits: Patient, enduring, physically strong, loyal, conscientious, routine oriented, hard working, devoted, dignified, physical as opposed to emotional or mental

Best Collar and Accessory Color: Green; but if name ends in D, M, or V, black is best

Planetary Association: Saturn

Energy Level—Dog: Needs routine and vigorous exercise (indoors and outdoors)

Energy Level—Cat: Quiet (indoors and outdoors)

Compatibility: Gets along best with disciplined youngsters and consistent adults

Best Toy—Dog: Tug, rope, Frisbee, ball, chew bone

Best Toy—Cat: Old or often-used quiet toys, catch and fetch toys, catnip sack

At First Glance

Sturdy, muscular, square, plain, and dark, with a natural coat and a dignified, quiet, cautious, slow-moving, respectful, self-disciplined approach.

The Bottom Line

Wants stability, patient handlers, dignity, practical work, established routines, and to know what is expected in order to do it dependably.

Quirks of Character

If the name ends in D, M, or V, the tendency to be trustworthy and dependable has been challenged by rigidity, crudeness, hatred, no behavior training, or lack of appreciation for his or her willingness to learn at a young age. The

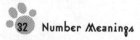

pet has not learned when it is appropriate to be self-disciplined, be careful, obey commands, or be motivated to maintain efforts with peers and leaders. Habitual personality extremes that relate to resistance to discipline, procrastination, and poor self-worth form in youth and persist into adulthood; patient retraining is necessary.

Number 4 personality extremes indicate obsessive-compulsive behavior. Pets may alternate in varying degrees from one extreme to another yet be positively balanced at other times.

Is too busy or too lazy

Is too focused or too nonproductive

Is too robotic and unfeeling or too intent on a destructive rampage

Is too rule-bound or generally "out-to-lunch"

Is too unfeeling or too jealous

Is too insensitive

Is too animalistic and undignified

Is too unmoving or too restless

Is too violent or too slow to anger

Is too impatient and stubborn

Is too shy or too aggressive

Is clumsy and unaware of strength

Is strong but acts weak

Is inattentive

Is undisciplined and efforts to be productive are fruitless

Is too brusque and too focused on duty

Is disrespectful and careless

Digs relentlessly

Is not gregarious or sociable

Is easily distracted

Refuses to be groomed

Lacks imagination and playfulness

Compatibility with Other Pet Names, Breed Names, and Human Names

***Excellent; **Good with disciplines; *There is friction!

#4 with #1 = *, #4 with #2 = ***, #4 with #3 = *, #4 with #4 = ***, #4 with #5 = *, #4 with #6 = ***, #4 with #7 = *, #4 with #8 = ***, #4 with #9 = *

#5

Name Day-to-Day

"I'll jump in the pool to see how it feels," "Show me. I'll mimic your actions," "Do we have to do that again?" "Don't fence me in!" says the #5 with the inventive, clever, sensual, freedom-loving personality. Number 5s depend on experimentation, learn from experience, have lusty sexual appetites and a short attention span. Variety and freedom are as necessary as food to the mentally and physically energetic #5, who is a versatile, changeable, charming, and amusing explorer. Number 5 thinks life is an open road and always expects to live in the fast lane while following a hunch or getting a lucky break. Day-to-Day: Magnetic, unrestricted, intellectually curious #5 adapts to varied situations.

#5 thinks travel is broadening
#5 learns easily
#5 learns from experience
#5 gets bored easily
#5 enjoys sexual stimulation
#5 charms a way out of trouble
#5 uplifts and inspires others
#5 is youthfully enthusiastic
#5 loves crowds and excitement
#5 is curious and resourceful
#5 makes changes easily
#5 is a talkative, enthusiastic wheeler-dealer
#5 is bright, sparkling, and funny
#5 is a mimic and a clown
#5 accepts household changes with ease
#5 needs companionship
#5 wants instant gratification
#5 has frequent mood swings
#5 looks for shortcuts
#5 loves physical contact
#5 dislikes routines and schedules
#5 is frisky and spontaneous
#5 is unpredictable

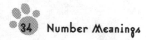

#5 improvises
#5 has short spurts of activity
#5 relieves tension by diversifying energies
#5 needs a variety of foods, toys, and playmates
#5 makes up the rules as he or she goes along

Breed

Primary Trait: Freedom loving

Secondary Traits: Versatile, adventurous, adaptable, flexible, curious, clever, active, understanding, sexual, sensual, seductive, amiable, and is physical, emotional, intuitive, and mental

Best Collar and Accessory Color: Turquoise, aquamarine; but if name ends in E, N, or W, black is best

Planetary Association: Mars

Energy Level—Dog: Need vigorous, changing, outdoor exercise

Energy Level—Cat: High; best when freedom outdoors is available

Compatibility: Gets along with children, adults, and other pets

Best Toy—Dog: Ball with bells, Frisbee, noisy toys, chew bone, a mirror

Best Toy—Cat: Variety of noisy action toys, catnip mouse, feather and string, Ping-Pong ball, cardboard tube

At First Glance

Is entertaining, friendly, talkative, unrestrained, curious, clever, and striking; has an attention-getting manner and an unusually colorful coat.

The Bottom Line

Wants mental and physical personal freedom, appreciates a variety of people and interests, and is comfortable outdoors, traveling, and learning from experience.

Quirks of Character

If the name ends in E, N, or W, the tendency to use freedom wisely and make appropriate changes has been challenged by inconsistency, abuse, regimentation, thoughtlessness, or physical restriction at a young age. The pet has not learned when it is appropriate to try something new or run free outdoors with peers and leaders. Habitual personality extremes that relate to housebreaking, following commands, responsibility, and escaping restraints form in youth and persist into adulthood; patient retraining is necessary.

Number 5 personality extremes indicate obsessive-compulsive behavior. Pets and humans may alternate in varying degrees from one extreme to another yet be positively balanced at other times.

Is too argumentative or too docile
Is too impulsive or too afraid to make a change
Is too challenging or too cowardly
Is too fascinated with sexuality or too disinterested
Is too loyal or too disloyal
Is too emotional or too unfeeling
Is too cool or too loving
Is too eager to please or too disrespectful
Is too selective or too accepting
Is too surprising or too dull
Is too inconsistent
Is too thoughtless
Is too fearful of change
Refuses to change habits
Is messy
Is nervous and temperamental
Is rebellious
Is compulsive
Is too frequently "out of control"
Is chaotic, reckless, frantic, erratic
Has no patience or follow-through
Has temper tantrums
Is sexually promiscuous
Courts danger and disaster
Panics and splits under pressure
Has energy that is too spasmodic
Constantly makes commotions

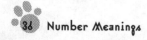

Compatibility with Other Pet Names, Breed Names, and Human Names

***Excellent; **Good with disciplines; *There is friction!

#5 with #1 = ***, #5 with #2 = *, #5 with #3 = ***, #5 with #4 = *, #5 with #5 = ***, #5 with #6 = *, #5 with #7 = *, #5 with #8 = **, #5 with #9 = ***

#6

Name Day-to-Day

"I'll step in and assume responsibility," "You make me comfortable and love me. Of course I'll follow you into the shower . . . I'll follow you everywhere," "There's no place like home," says the #6 with the socially interactive, understanding, parental personality. Number 6s depend on the exchange of family or group responsibility and make an effort to maintain harmony. A loving, crowded household to serve and protect is as necessary as food to the conscientious, musically talented, stable #6. Steadfast #6 is a concerned, burden-bearing, sympathetic, teacher and guardian, who thinks life centers on loved ones and always expects to make personal adjustments for the benefit of the group. Day-to-Day: Reliable, understanding, conventional #6 is a homebody.

#6 thinks home is where the heart is

#6 is kind and understanding

#6 makes friends by being a friend

#6 wants to express and receive love

#6 dislikes being alone

#6 needs reassurance and attention

#6 is trusting and trustworthy

#6 is a concerned family member

#6 steps in to break up an argument

#6 is a good parent

#6 is a good student or teacher

#6 cannot handle household tension or turmoil

#6 conforms to family routines and schedules

#6 is a foodaholic and favors the kitchen

#6 takes a backseat with strangers

#6 washes and helps nurture most any youngster

#6 doesn't like to play rough
#6 won't fuss when children play "dress up the pet"
#6 likes to curl up with a soft toy
#6 remembers every unpleasant visit to the vet
#6 enjoys chatting with friends and loved ones
#6 is a team player
#6 is a dignified, influential member of a group

Breed

Primary Trait: Nurturing

Secondary Traits: Home-loving, parental, compatible, responsible, compassionate, sympathetic, musical, serving, conscientious, emotional as opposed to mental or physical

Best Collar and Accessory Color: Blue; but if name ends in F, O, or X, black is best

Planetary Association: Jupiter

Energy Level—Dog: Needs small area for outdoor exercise; quiet indoors

Energy Level—Cat: Quiet and involved indoors; needs scratching post indoors; digs outdoors

Compatibility: Gets along best with children and young pets

Best Toy—Dog: Rope, ball, and edible chew toys

Best Toy—Cat: Soft, cuddly tossables, ball of yarn

At First Glance
Serious, quiet, interested, sympathetic, and parental; appears comfortable; wears a harmonious coat tinged with blue; has a rhythmic stride.

The Bottom Line
Wants a harmonious, steadfast, responsible, loving family to serve and is a

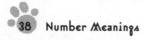

comfortable homebody, who centers interests on social interactions with loved ones.

Quirks of Character

If the name ends in F, O, or X, the tendency to value the comforts of home, to express love and gratitude, and to serve the needs of a family has been challenged by unfairness, suspicion, drudgery, and lack of protection and stability at a young age. The pet has not learned when it is appropriate to affectionately interact with leaders. Habitual personality extremes that relate to anxiety, depression, injustice, and group harmony form in youth and persist into adulthood; patient retraining is necessary.

Number 6 personality extremes indicate obsessive-compulsive behavior. Pets may alternate in varying degrees from one extreme to another yet be positively balanced at other times.

Is extremely family-oriented or too much of a loner

Is too protective or too neglectful

Is too loving or too hateful

Is too responsible or too unreliable

Is too understanding or too intolerant

Is too firm or too weak

Is too meddlesome or too disinterested

Is too suspicious or too trusting

Is too obstinate or too yielding

Is too serious or too flighty

Is too anxious or too calm

Is too smothering or too detached

Is too unselfish or too selfish

Is too conscientious or too careless

Is too stable or too unbalanced

Is too harmonious or too uncooperative

Is too self-satisfied or too discontented

Is a busybody or an extremely welcome friend

Is argumentative or extremely good natured

Is a homebody or a runaway

Compatibility with Other Pet Names, Breed Names, and Human Names

***Excellent; **Good with disciplines; *There is friction!
#6 with #1 = *, #6 with #2 = ***, #6 with #3 = ***, #6 with #4 = ***, #6 with #5 = *,
#6 with #6 = ***, #6 with #7 = *, #6 with #8 = ***, #6 with #9 = ***

#7

Name Day-to-Day

"I'll run and hide to escape the noise and confusion," "Just let me rest and watch you play," "Dig in the dirt? I never break my nails!" says the #7 with the introspective, regal, inscrutable, loner personality. Number 7s depend on their ability to sense or size up a situation before taking action and never get involved in others' problems or social activities. A quiet, peaceful, private space and considerate, refined leaders are as necessary as food to the reserved, intelligent, intuitive, shy, calm #7. Philosophical #7 is a secretive, investigative, finicky, wise aristocrat, who thinks life centers on logic and always expects to remain unemotional and distant from mundane activities. Day-to-Day: Calm, poised, analytic #7 enjoys being alone in a crowd.

‡7 is the Greta Garbo of pets

‡7 wants to be alone

‡7 reads between the lines

‡7 prefers to eat on fine china

‡7 avoids dirt and mess

‡7 tolerates young children at a distance

‡7 does not demand attention

‡7 avoids rough or careless handlers

‡7 does not force issues

‡7 bestows affection sparingly

‡7 prefers controlled situations

‡7 is too smart and cautious to fight

‡7 is a crafty hunter

‡7 finds secret hiding places

‡7 understands concepts

‡7 is psychic

#7 is a quiet, silent observer
#7 is an elitist
#7 is a perfectionist
#7 is selective
#7 initially trusts first impressions
#7 rethinks first impressions to be sure
#7 is curious and investigative
#7 keeps humans guessing
#7 is not the ideal parent
#7 is more studious than sexual
#7 is slow to warm
#7 is loved only after intimacy is established

Breed

Primary Trait: Analytical

Secondary Traits: Solitary, intuitive, intelligent, aristocratic, reserved, sedentary, observant, investigative, wise, meticulous, mental as opposed to emotional or physical

Best Collar and Accessory Color: Purple; but if name ends in G, P, or Y, black is best

Planetary Association: Mercury

Energy Level—Dog: Sedentary indoors and cautious outdoors

Energy Level—Cat: Languishing and inactive; prefers to be indoors

Compatibility: Gets along best with gentle, calm, quiet adults

Best Toy—Dog: TV, chew stick, a mirror

Best Toy—Cat: TV, piece of string, rubber band, a mirror, cardboard tube

At First Glance
Perfect in every way; wise, aristocratic, mystical, poised, introspective, quiet, peaceful, and content to observe the scene at a distance and alone

The Bottom Line
Is a comfortable observer; doesn't mind being alone in a crowd; wants peace, quiet, privacy; wants careful, refined, undemonstrative handlers; avoids noise, confusion, and unrestrained children.

Quirks of Character
If the name ends in G, P, or Y, the tendency to use logic, be peaceful, refined, spiritual, poised, calm, and comfortable alone has been challenged by humiliation, suppression, confusion, and actions by others that cause great fear and awareness of deceit at a young age. The pet has not learned to be alone and not fear loneliness or to enjoy privacy and not feel emotional poverty. Habitual personality extremes that relate to melancholy, nervousness, coldness, deceitfulness, skepticism, and negative attitudes form in youth and persist into adulthood; patient retraining is necessary.

Number 7 personality extremes indicate obsessive-compulsive behavior. Pets may alternate in varying degrees from one extreme to another yet be positively balanced at other times.

Is too aloof and superior
Is too questioning or too impulsive
Is too trusting or too skeptical
Is too finicky or too easily pleased
Is too secretive or too open
Is too cunning or too naïve
Is too patient or too hasty
Is too withdrawn or too eager
Is too somber or too sociable
Is too investigative or too accepting
Is too uncommunicative or too talkative
Is too refined or too earthy
Is too detached and silent
Is too reclusive and hermitlike
Is too irritable
Is too quiet
Is too easily spooked by intuition

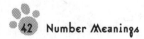

Is empty-headed and foolish or guarded

Is deceitful

Is too authoritative or too uncertain

Is confused by human behavior

Is too unreachable

Is overly suspicious

Is disinterested in learning

Is dispassionate and cold

Is too discerning or unperceptive

Compatibility with Other Pet Names, Breed Names, and Human Names

***Excellent; **Good with disciplines; *There is friction!

#7 with #1 = *, #7 with #2 = ***, #7 with #3 = *, #7 with #4 = *, #7 with #5 = *, #7 with #6 = *, #7 with #7 = ***, #7 with #8 = *, #7 with #9 = ***

#8

Name Day-to-Day

"I assume leadership and power and know when to draw the line," "First, I work and protect, and then I party," "Elect me the leader and we'll win," says the #8 with the mentally and physically powerful personality. Number 8s depend on their ability to be shrewd, efficient, self-disciplined, and discerning before taking action and never take advantage of less strong, less engaging, or less intelligent peers or leaders. A large space in which to exercise, athletic friends and leaders, an organized environment, and a position where ideas and judgment are respected are as necessary as food to the sociable, problem-solving, self-reliant #8. Discriminating #8 is a fair, authoritative, practical, polite, energetic powerhouse, who thinks life centers on work, exercise, good company, and physical and mental challenges. Day-to-Day: Dominant #8 uses good judgment.

#8 wants to compete and win

#8 is high powered

#8 is industrious

#8 is constructive

#8 is strong

#8 is decisive

#8 is businesslike

#8 is self-confident

#8 is self-reliant

#8 is spirited

#8 is shrewd

#8 is definite

#8 is determined

#8 is assertive

#8 is earnest

#8 is venturesome

#8 is quick witted

#8 is energetic and down-to-earth

#8 is a healthy skeptic

#8 is a good judge of character

#8 is a fair-minded leader

#8 is obedient, controlled, and dependable

#8 is a practical communicator

#8 has a commanding personality

#8 feels responsible

#8 has endurance

#8 has a balanced disposition

#8 confidently takes challenges

#8 is an enthusiastic participant

#8 has courage and imagination, and thinks positively

#8 is trustworthy and devoted to loved ones

#8 is routine-oriented and respects schedules

#8 thrives on vigorous work and play

#8 considers others when making decisions

Breed

Primary Trait: Material power

Secondary Traits: Mentally and physically powerful, energetic, businesslike, efficient, self-sufficient, self-confident, shrewd, sociable, consistent, resourceful, mental and physical as opposed to emotional

Best Collar and Accessory Color: Mauve, rose-pink-lavender; but if name ends in H, Q, or Z, black is best

Planetary Association: Sun

Energy Level—Dog: Needs vigorous indoor play and athletic exercise outdoors

Energy Level—Cat: High (indoors and outdoors)

Compatibility: Gets along best with older, stronger children and pets and athletic adults

Best Toy—Dog: Frisbee, ball, rope, tug and chew toys

Best Toy—Cat: Squeaky ball or toy, moving mice, rope

At First Glance

Mentally and physically energetic, self-disciplined, socially adept, businesslike, self-confident; is a strong powerhouse and a top-of-the-line, expensive, luxurious, fastidiously groomed example of the breed.

The Bottom Line

Wants to use strength, enthusiasm, courage, dependability, and mental and physical agility to face challenges; is comfortable working with the human leader's commands; appreciates athletic loved ones and community social interaction.

Quirks of Character

If the name ends in H, Q, or Z, bullying, abuse, strain, lack of direction, and improper use of leadership and power at a young age challenged businesslike tendencies, self-confidence, self-reliance, resourcefulness, and shrewdness. The pet has not learned to be discriminating, self-controlled, or self-reliant, or to direct physical and mental energy wisely. Habitual personality extremes that relate to carelessness, impatience, destructive actions, intolerance, and a desire for revenge form in youth and persist into adulthood; patient retraining is necessary.

Number 8 personality extremes indicate obsessive-compulsive behavior.

Pets may alternate in varying degrees from one extreme to another yet be positively balanced at other times.

Is too combative or too apathetic

Is too quick or procrastinating

Is too cool or hot-tempered

Is too demanding or indifferent

Is too energetic or spiritless

Abuses power or is too vulnerable

Is too adamant or too unsure

Is too cunning or too guileless

Acts bullying or too cowardly

Is egotistical or lacks confidence

Is too stubborn or too indecisive

Is very skillful or too undisciplined

Is too unyielding or too feeble

Is lazy or overambitious

Is a negligent or zealous protector

Is an overanxious or uncaring guardian

Is undisciplined or rule-bound

Is too defensive or defenseless

Is vindictive or oblivious

Is threatening or too timid

Is clumsy and inept

Has a one-track mind

Compatibility with Other Pet Names, Breed Names, and Human Names

***Excellent; **Good with disciplines; *There is friction!

#8 with #1 = *, #8 with #2 = **, #8 with #3 = **, #8 with #4 = ***, #8 with #5 = **, #8 with #6 = ***, #8 with #7 = *, #8 with #8 = *, #8 with #9 = ***

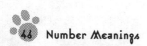

9

Name Day-to-Day

"I'll stay by your side as long as you need me," "You think I'm a human? Well, maybe I am," "Oops, he fell through the ice. I'll save him," says the #9 with a brave, generous heart; humanistic interests and approach; and a loving, socially interactive personality. Number 9s depend on their ability to understand human nature, work well with people, and see the "big picture." They are compassionate, empathetic, unselfish, imaginative, and inspirational to anyone who is needy, lonely, elderly, homebound, or disabled: #9s have a need to be needed. Friendship, affection, love, a natural environment, and meaningful purpose are as necessary as food to the peaceful, skillful, polished, humanitarian #9. Day-to-Day: Tolerant #9 is a wise, responsive, disciplined, generous, sociable, romantic, relaxed healer, who is a hero at heart and thinks life centers on human understanding, self-sacrifice, helping others, and making the world a better place.

#9 is one of the nicest beings

#9 has wisdom

#9 loves everybody unconditionally

#9 is an inspiration to others

#9 makes everything an emotional experience

#9 is sensitive, empathetic, and compassionate

#9 needs to have and give love

#9 is kind, patient, and forgiving

#9 is totally tolerant and understanding

#9 is intuitive

#9 is charming and attractive to all

#9 is skilled in discipline

#9 gives a polished performance

#9 is a good student and a gifted teacher

#9 daydreams for relaxation

#9 conceptualizes

#9 is polite and discreet

#9 looks at life through rose-colored glasses

#9 is a team player

#9 attracts notable personalities and dramatic experiences

#9 has a fine mind and a logical approach when solving problems
#9 networks the neighborhood
#9 knows how to get attention when necessary
#9 protects and serves
#9 enjoys roaming in a natural environment
#9 serves totally and never holds back
#9 makes the best of everything
#9 brings hope when despair is present
#9 is expectant and encouraging
#9 gets involved
#9 has a broad perspective

Breed

Primary Trait: Humanitarianism

Secondary Traits: Offers unconditional love, unselfishness, compassion, empathy, imagination, sympathy, skill, polish, bravery, emotional, mental, intuitive, physical

Best Collar and Accessory Color: Saffron (orange-yellow-gold); but if name ends in I or R, black is best

Planetary Association: The aura and influence of all planets

Energy Level—Dog: Needs outdoor exercise and space to roam

Energy Level—Cat: Needs outdoor space to roam

Compatibility: Gets along with children, adults, and other pets

Best Toy—Dog: TV, chew bone, chew toy, noiseless ball

Best Toy—Cat: Stuffed toys, noiseless balls, rope

At First Glance
Charismatic, magnetic, beautiful, virile, youthful, self-disciplined, peaceful, relaxed, properly groomed, polished, skillful, and attractive to all.

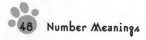

The Bottom Line

Wants to be of service; understands human nature; is an empathetic, compassionate, wise, brave, well-mannered, emotional, impressive personality, who is comfortable when trained to be at the side of anyone needy, lonely, sick, or disabled.

Quirks of Character

If the name ends in I or R, lack of love, intolerance, fickleness, and unexpected loss of a loved one at a young age challenged #9's generous nature, humanistic wisdom, ability to love unconditionally, and broad-scoped responsiveness. The pet has not learned to be unselfish, tolerant, skillfully disciplined, sympathetic, secure, or stable. Habitual personality extremes that relate to extreme emotionalism, bitterness, intolerance, egocentricity, and pettiness form in youth and persist into adulthood; patient retraining is necessary.

Number 9 personality extremes indicate obsessive-compulsive behavior. Pets may alternate in varying degrees from one extreme to another yet be positively balanced at other times.

Is too emotional or too passive

Is too involved or too apathetic

Is too enthusiastic or too half-hearted

Is too harsh or too soft

Is too serious or too capricious

Is too responsive or too cold

Is too immediate or too vacillating

Is too quiet or too talkative

Is too tolerant or too intolerant

Is very wise or unreasonable

Is unemotional or very passionate

Is dependable or unreliable

Is unreasonably faithful or fickle

Is too independent or too submissive

Is extraordinarily brave or cowardly

Is very demonstrative or too aloof

Is sweet or bitter

Is irresponsible or too committed

Is jealous or uncaring

Is wildly happy or joyless

Is petty or overly generous

Is too shy or too extroverted

Is too listless or too energized

Is totally cooperative or unbending

Is very empathetic or too detached

Is extremely animated or impassive

Is sociable or inhospitable

Is compassionate or unforgiving

Is extroverted or introverted

Is mindless or introspective

Is vindictive or amiable

Is greedy or unselfish

Is too aware of surroundings or "unconscious"

Lacks concentration or is obsessed with one project

Compatibility with Other Pet Names, Breed Names, and Human Names

***Excellent; **Good with disciplines; *There is friction!

#9 with #1 = **, #9 with #2 = ***, #9 with #3 = ***, #9 with #4 = *, #9 with #5 = ***, #9 with #6 = ***, #9 with #7 = ***, #9 with #8 = ***, #9 with #9 = ***

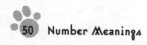

Name Dictionary

Guide to the Dictionary

This book of cat, dog, and people names is alphabetical and each name listed has a numerology reference number after it. The gender that is associated with a particular name is indicated by *M,* masculine; *F,* feminine; and *unisex* for both genders. Entries also include popularity ratings, country and language of origin, different meanings, general references, spelling variations, and suggested names for family, mates, and friends.

The opening text is followed by numerological personality descriptions. If you do not see a name you fancy in the in-depth name descriptions, go to the end of the entries for that alphabet letter to find additional names and their numerology numbers. Number meanings for the names that have only a number following are found in "Do It Yourself" at the beginning of the book.

Names that are rated one through thirty by the ASPCA (American Society for the Prevention of Cruelty to Animals) are accompanied by their ASPCA number rating. Some names, designated as "classic" when appropriate, serve as a standard and are established pet names.

Definitions, country, language and cultural origins, nicknames and names (including their numbers) that have a relationship are listed when appropriate.

The personality descriptions that follow the names described in-depth are divided into four sections: At First Glance (the first impression), Day-to-Day (general activity), The Bottom Line (inner motivation), and Quirks of Character (idiosyncrasies and obsessive-compulsive behavior). Complete explanations of the titles of the four sections are explained in "Do-It-Yourself" at the beginning of the book.

Ace (#9): *M*/(Greek) One, excellent, first in quality./(English) A boy's given name./A single dot or mark on a card or a die./Tennis, badminton, handball, etc.: A ball placement made on service that the opponent fails to touch and a point is thus scored./A very skilled person./A fighter pilot credited with destroying usually five or more enemy aircraft in flight./A one-dollar bill./Golf: A hole in one, driving one stroke of the club from the tee into the hole; to card an ace./Rare, a very small quantity, amount, or degree.

At First Glance: Is golden, decorative, and expresses beauty. First impression is friendly, attentive, and laid back. Appears to be conscientious and kind.

Day-to-Day: Relates sympathetically and understands human nature. Thrives when trained to serve anyone needy, lonely, or disabled. Is brave, sociable, and peaceful.

The Bottom Line: Wants social interaction. Prefers to belong to a pack; requires companionship and constant, strong relationships. Is a loving, responsible homebody.

Quirks of Character: Licks the ears of sexually attractive companions.

Ajax (#9): M/(Greek) Eagle./Classical mythology: Great Ajax (#9), from Telamonian Ajax, hero of the Trojan War.

At First Glance: Is regal, sleek, reserved, poised, and aloof. Tends to stand back and look things over; observes, analyzes, and acts after careful consideration.

Day-to-Day: Is devoted to needy people; wants to be helpful. Is very brave, skillful, peaceful, graceful, charming, and empathetic. Loves to roam outdoors and visit friends.

The Bottom Line: Thrives on intimacy and achieves best efforts when working one-on-one. Wants to give and get cooperation and prefers the company of women.

Quirks of Character: When surrounded by inharmonious conditions, forgets responsibilities and is eager to call any comforting, open door "home."

Albert (#4): M/(French) Aubert (#4)./(Old German) Noble, bright./Mate: Victoria (#7).

At First Glance: Is aristocratic, intelligent, investigative, introspective, reserved, quiet, and unemotional. Requires grooming and is perfect for the breed.

Day-to-Day: Is dependable, enduring, routine oriented, and loyal. Is a highly motivated, energized worker-builder. Is not quick-minded; learns by repetition and tests of strength.

The Bottom Line: Wants social interaction and a stable home. Guards and protects. Is sympathetic, dotes upon children, loves music, and is a foodaholic.

Quirks of Character: When upset, is sensitive, paranoid, and extremely needy.

Alexander (#3): M/(Greek) Defender of men, helper of men.

At First Glance: Appears trusting, wise, and classic for the breed. Wants to get to know everyone. Is a graceful, magnetic, peaceful, tolerant, skillful communicator.

Day-to-Day: Is charming, playful, conscientious, youthful, gentle, optimistic, poetic, and romantic. Loves toys and games; is a terrible tease and tries to make everyone happy.

The Bottom Line: Wants to be the focus of a fun-loving, unregimented, sociable, lively family. Is comfortable entertaining crowds of admirers and dislikes being alone.

Quirks of Character: Loses emotional control when anyone is in trouble.

Alfred (#1): M/(Old English) Wise./Teutonic/English/German/Danish/French.

At First Glance: Is natural, earthy, and conventional for the breed. Is sturdy, muscular, easy to groom; has a square frame. Appears to be dignified and respectful.

Day-to-Day: Is a creative, active, courageous, daring, investigative, bold loner. Takes direct action; is competitive, independent, assertive, and aggressive.

The Bottom Line: Wants stability and a loving atmosphere. Is parental, sympathetic, and responsible. Is comfortable with socially interactive, dependable humans.

Quirks of Character: Becomes rattled and destructive when schedules change.

Algernon (#5): M/(Old French) With mustache, with whiskers./English.

At First Glance: Is unpretentious, unassuming, unimpressive, gentle, shy, laid back, sensitive, easygoing, quiet, and mystical. Appears to be hesitant and approachable.

Day-to-Day: Is adventurous, unrestrained, frisky, charming, and clever. Is a sensual breeder who is affectionate and funny. Takes foolish challenges and learns from experience.

The Bottom Line: Wants a fun-loving, playful, undisciplined lifestyle. Gets bored easily, enjoys a variety of people, and has a good memory for vocabulary and tricks.

Quirks of Character: Becomes too impulsive, volatile, and troublesome if inactive.

Amber (#3): *F/(Old French) The amber jewel./Arabic.*

At First Glance: Is conventional, serious, robust; has a lush coat tinged with blue. Appears to be dignified, quiet, warm, friendly, maternal, and approachable.

Day-to-Day: Is fun to be with; is girlish, naïve, frisky, charming, and vocal. Always ready to play and hug. Loves attention and is entertaining, amusing, and companionable.

The Bottom Line: Is possessive and jealously guards home and food. Wants to be generous with peers and children. Is a homebody, comfortable with a daily routine.

Quirks of Character: Fails to conserve energy and is often exhausted.

Angus (#8): *M/(Celtic) Aengus (#4), Oengus (#9); the choice./(Irish), Oonghus (#9), Saint Aegnus (#4); god of love, youth, and beauty./Mythology: Angus Og (#3), god of love and beauty, patron deity of young men and women/(Scottish) Aengus (#4)./Nickname: Gus (#2).*

At First Glance: Appears unpretentious, conventional, respectful, hearty, even tempered, and stable. Is quiet, dignified, solid, muscular, strong, and self-disciplined.

Day-to-Day: Is mentally and physically alert, and highly energetic; has an inner drive to work and keep busy. Is businesslike, reasonable, deliberate, and purposeful.

The Bottom Line: Wants to live with dependable humans and is routine oriented. Is comfortable when he or she knows what to do; tries to do the "right" thing.

Quirks of Character: When reminded of insecurities, flees from imagined danger.

Annie (#7): *F/Nickname for all names that begin with Ann (#2)./(Hebrew) Hannah (#1); grace./Mate and friend: Daddy (#2) Warbucks (#8).*

At First Glance: Is active, proud, quick, and alert; appears different. Is not conventional or apprehensive; makes direct eye contact and will not back down.

Day-to-Day: Is reserved, aloof, and regal. Enjoys reflecting and resting in a quiet, peaceful atmosphere. Withdraws and hides when moody, upset by noise, or confused.

The Bottom Line: Is mature at birth and wants to be a valued member of

a socially interactive, affectionate, harmonious family. Enjoys relationships and needs company.

Quirks of Character: Is an impulsive escape artist when sexually stimulated.

Archibald (#4): M/(Teutonic, Old German), Erchanpald (#1)./(Modern German) Archimbald (#8); noble and genuinely bold.

At First Glance: Is plain, compact, "soft," graceful, charming, furry, receptive, and content to wait to be noticed. Has short hair, tinged with tones of orange.

Day-to-Day: Is influenced by a leader's expectations. Is quiet, cautious, supportive, respectful, and methodical. Is comfortable but not demonstrative with humans.

The Bottom Line: Wants companionship and demands little; gives loyalty, affection, and consistent attention. Is comfortable with gentle, sensitive, quiet humans.

Quirks of Character: Has passive-resistant behavior that prevents behavior training.

Arliss (#6): unisex/(Hebrew) (F) Arlise (#1), (M) Arlis (#5); pledge.

At First Glance: Is enthusiastic, clever, and unconventional for the breed. Appears to dislike restraints; is enthusiastic and promotes activity in surroundings.

Day-to-Day: Is a serious, mature, quiet, dignified, parental homebody. Is concerned about everything; can be particularly overbearing and possessive with loved ones.

The Bottom Line: Wants leadership and is assertive. Is motivated to be unregimented, unrestrained, and independent. Is comfortable alone and is a good hunter.

Quirks of Character: Is submissive when upset or reprimanded loudly.

Artie (#8): unisex/Nickname for Artemis (#4), Artemas (#5), Arthur (#5)./Art (#3) plus *ie* is a term of endearment.

At First Glance: Has an undistinguished, orange-tinged coat. Is hesitant and unassuming. Appears to be shy, "soft," cooperative, receptive, laid back, and easygoing.

Day-to-Day: Is mentally and physically strong; is a shrewd, energetic, commanding student and teacher. Is self-confident, self-controlled, athletic, and dominant.

The Bottom Line: Is the "cosmic parent"; a concerned, mature, serious, self-sacrificing group leader, involved in supervising home and territory.

Quirks of Character: Is too interested in mating rituals and sex.

Ashes (#7): *unisex*/Paleness, leftovers, coal, soot./(Scandinavian) Ashby (#1); ash-tree farm./(Old English) Ash-tree meadow./(Hebrew) Asher (#6); happy.

At First Glance: Stands alone and is different; has an unusually colorful coat. Appears to be self-assured, proud, competitive, assertive, and aggressive.

Day-to-Day: Is intelligent, investigative, moody, introspective, calm, and selective. Avoids noise and confusion. Is rarely affectionate and does not need companionship.

The Bottom Line: Strives for appreciation, wants to stay close to home, and enjoys being part of a family. Is comfortable loving and being loved.

Quirks of Character: Lacks initiative when threatened or upset.

Asta (#5): *F*/(Greek) The star./(Latin) Vulnerable./Nickname for Augusta (#9)./From Astraea (#2), the Greek and Roman goddess of justice.

At First Glance: Is colorful, bright, lively, and beautiful in form, coat, and face. Appears to be happy to see and greet everyone. Has an unforgettable voice and is chatty.

Day-to-Day: Is an adventurous rascal; is energetic, impulsive, and changeable. Easily forgets behavior training. Needs freedom to explore outdoors and is easily bored.

The Bottom Line: Is sensitive, devoted, friendly, affectionate, gentle, and patient with loved ones. Needs companionship and becomes spiteful when ignored or lonely.

Quirks of Character: Is submissive and cowardly with aggressive humans.

See the Number Meanings chapter to discover the traits described by the number that accompanies each name: Aardvark (#4), Aaron (#4) Abacus (#2), Abby (#3), Abdul (#4), Abdullah (#7), Abercrombie (#1), Abernathy (#4), Abie (#8), Abigail (#5), Aces (#1), Achilles (#6), Actor (#3), Adagio (#1), Addy (#7), Adelai (#5), Adelaide (#5), Adieu (#4), Adlib (#1), Adolfo (#8), Adonis (#8), Adrian (#2), Aesop (#2), Agamemnon (#2), Agassi (#2), Aida (#6), Aimee (#6), Akaysha (#3), Akiko (#4), Al (#4),

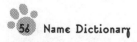

Alabama (#4), Alabaster (#7), Aladdin (#9), Alan (#1), Alaska (#9), Alba (#7), Albee (#7), Alberta (#5), Alberto (#1), Alden (#9), Aldo (#5), Alec (#3), Alexey (#9), Alexi (#6), Alexia (#7), Alf (#1), Alfie (#6), Alfonso (#1), Allegro (#7), Allen (#8), Almonds (#6), Aloha (1), Amadeus (#1), Amanda (#7), Amaretto (#3), Amazon (#7), Amigo (#9), Amtrak (#1), Amy (#3), Anabell (#2), Anastasia (#4), Anatol (#7), Andrea (#7), Android (#2), Andromeda (#3), Angel (#3), Angela (#4), Angelica (#7), Angelo (#9), Animal (#5), Antoine (#6), Antoinette (#6), Antonia (#2), Antony (#8), Aphrodite (#6), Apollo (#8), Apricot (#1), Aquarius (#8), Archie (#8), Aretha (#8), Arf (#7), Ariel (#9), Aristotle (#9), Arizona (#3), Armani (#2), Armstrong (#8), Arnold (#1), Arsenio (#9), Artemis (#4), Arthur (#5), Arty (#1), Asa (#3), Ashley (#7), Ashton (#5), Astaire (#1), Athena (#4), Atilla (#9), Atlas (#8), Auntie (#7), Aurora (#2), Aussie (#2), Autry (#4), Autumn (#9), Ava (#6), Avalanche (#4), Avalon (#2), Avanti (#4), Avenger (#9), Azura (#4), Azure (#8).

Babe (#1): *unisex*/(Early Middle English) Baban (#2); nursery word in origin./A baby or child./An innocent or inexperienced person./An especially attractive girl or woman./A term of familiar address to a woman./A novice or tenderfoot.

At First Glance: Is quiet, dignified, sturdy, muscular, square, traditional, and surefooted. Responds cautiously, heeds commands, and follows disciplines.

Day-to-Day: Is aggressive, assertive, unemotional, proud, independent, and fearless. Unafraid to be creative, attracts supporters, and is not inclined to run with the pack.

The Bottom Line: Is a homebody. Wants to be comfortable and loves to eat. Is comfortable and responsible with youngsters. May be overly protective and jealous.

Quirks of Character: Is adventurous, curious, impulsive, and accident-prone.

Bambi (#9): *F*/Classic./(F. Italian) diminutive for Bambino (#2); "little baby"; usually used in reference to the artwork of the infant Jesus./friend: Flower (#7).

At First Glance: Has a dominant, impressive personality. Is handsome, powerful, alert, energetic, luxurious, sociable, and businesslike. Appears to be a winner.

Day-to-Day: Is peaceful, easygoing, compassionate, and easily trained. Is friendly to all people and pets. Is a caring, calm, courageous, approachable service companion.

The Bottom Line: Wants to be active, creatively playful, and independent. Is comfortable alone and motivated to be assertive in appropriate situations.

Quirks of Character: Is uncaring and unfriendly if disloyalty is perceived.

Bandit (#5): *unisex*/Is number 17 of ASPCA top 30 names./A robber, an outlaw.

At First Glance: Is conventional, cautious, dignified, respectful, and strong. Has a durable, dark, thick, and healthy coat and a muscular, chunky, large-boned body.

Day-to-Day: Is interested in all activity and adventure. Is confident, unconventional, curious, and enthusiastic. Is a mimic and good company for easygoing, playful humans.

The Bottom Line: Is independent, assertive, active, creative, impatient, and unlikely to spend time on anyone's lap. Is clever, avoids disciplines, and wants autonomy.

Quirks of Character: Is too suspicious of women to bond or form an attachment.

Bear (#8): *unisex*/Is number 4 of ASPCA top 30 names./(Middle English) Bere (#3)./(Old English) Beran (#4)./(German) Bar (#3)./Any of the plantigrade, carnivorous (or omnivorous) mammals of the family *Ursidae,* having massive bodies, course heavy fur, relatively short limbs, and almost rudimentary tails./To endure./A gruff, burly, clumsy, bad-mannered, or rude person./A person who believes that general business conditions are becoming unfavorable.

At First Glance: Is unpretentious and plain; has a coat tinged with orange. Appears to be shy, quiet, hesitant, unassuming, and content to wait to be noticed.

Day-to-Day: Is a discerning, shrewd, businesslike, athletic, confident, and earthy guardian and worke. Has boundless energy and requires extensive exercise.

The Bottom Line: Wants to love and be loved. Is comfortable surrounded by socially interactive humans. Is a diligent, protective, and sympathetic "cosmic parent."

Quirks of Character: Is stingy with personal possessions.

Benny (#6): M/(Latin) Nickname for Benedict (#8); blessed./(Hebrew) nick-

name for Binyamin (#6) and Benjamin (#5); son of the right hand, fortunate, strong/Jacob (#4) and Rachel's (#2) youngest son; brother of Joseph (#1)./Slang for Benzedrine (#3), any amphetamine tablet/Pet name: Benji (#4).

At First Glance: Is extroverted, lighthearted, cute, sunny, golden, and good-looking. His approach attracts admirers and he loves all the attention that he can get.

Day-to-Day: Is a happy homebody who gives and expects love. Is protective, attentive, rhythmic, and responsible; needs close association with humans and friends.

The Bottom Line: Is attractive, funny, and vocally expressive. Is confident with humans, optimistic, youthful. Enjoys a variety of toys, games, and travel experiences.

Quirks of Character: When emotionally upset, retreats to a quiet, private space.

Billy (#6): *unisex*/(F&M, Anglo-Saxon) Nickname for Beverly (#6), "from the beaver's lea."/(M, Old High German) Nickname for William (#7); "will helmut."/(F, Old High German) Nickname for Wilhelmina (#7); "chosen protection."/A policeman's club or baton./(Scottish) Comrade./(Australian) Any container in which water may be boiled or carried and boiled over a campfire./(British) Textiles: a roving machine.

At First Glance: Is an impressive personality and an outstanding example of the breed. Should show well and appears to be expensive, self-sufficient, and intelligent.

Day-to-Day: Is devoted to home and family; is a faithful, protective, tolerant, sociable, affectionate, musical, sympathetic, helpful companion to adults and youngsters.

The Bottom Line: Wants time for rest, reflection, and privacy each day. Is comfortable with controlled, intelligent, investigative, refined, calm humans.

Quirks of Character: Is nervous and erratic in a noisy, confused situation.

Blacky (#9): *unisex*/(Middle English) nickname for Blak (#8), Black (#2); lacking hue and brightness; absorbing light without reflecting any of the rays composing it.

At First Glance: Appears to be too forceful. Is active and has unique coat coloration and design. Is not fearful of strangers and responds to encouraging words of greeting.

Day-to-Day: Is sympathetic and emotional; is happiest when needed and not confined indoors. Is eager to learn and can be extraordinary when trained to provide a humanitarian service.

The Bottom Line: Wants to assume leadership. Works well alone but is not a loner. Minds his or her own business. Is confident and protective; is happy when working.

Quirks of Character: Is intolerant of noisy, undisciplined, young children.

Blue (#4): *unisex*/(Middle English) Blewe (#2)./The hue between green and violet in the spectrum, the pure color of a clear sky: azure.

At First Glance: Is unconventional, colorful, and charming; has a lively disposition. Visitors are welcomed boisterously; playful humans are approached with enthusiasm.

Day-to-Day: Is respectful and obedient. A strong, silent, routine-oriented, and accommodating worker who obeys when exercised regularly and a routine has been established.

The Bottom Line: Wants to be active and exercised vigorously. Is an intelligent guardian and a clean, businesslike companion. Is comfortable with athletic humans.

Quirks of Character: Becomes disoriented when startled or surprised.

Boots (#8): *unisex*/Classic./(Middle English) Bote (#6)./A covering of leather, rubber, etc., for the feet and leg, usually reaching at least to the middle of the calf, and sometimes to the knee or higher.

At First Glance: Is striking, eager to please; is an enthusiastic self-promoter. Appears to be curious, happy, high-spirited, and clever.

Day-to-Day: Is powerful and requires extensive exercise. Is confident, courageous, active, alert, well balanced. A discriminating, sociable, and devoted friend and guardian.

The Bottom Line: Is a lively, attentive, and friendly communicator. Wants to be noticed. Is amusing, perpetually youthful, and an excellent children's companion.

Quirks of Character: Is self-insistent and stubborn when intimidated.

Bowser (#1): *unisex*/Classic./Nautical reference: Bowse, a trade name; Bowser boat, for a small boat having gasoline tanks for refueling seaplanes.

At First Glance: Appears to be expensive, impressive, dominating, controlled, agile, and physically powerful. Is alert, sociable, and determined.

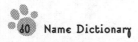

Day-to-Day: Is an independent leader who forms a partnership with one human or friend. Is mentally alert, active, inventive, and impatient.

The Bottom Line: May be inspired and inventive one minute and quiet and shy the next. Is a mystical pet who alternately charms and frustrates the human he or she loves the most.

Quirks of Character: Is uncommonly brave and self-sacrificing in a crisis.

Brandy (#1): *unisex*/Number 10 of ASPCA top 30 names./A spirit distilled from the fermented juice of grapes or of apples, peaches, plums, etc./Nickname: Brandi (#3), Brandie (#8)./(Teutonic) Brand (#3); a firebrand or flaming sword./(Anglo-Saxon) Brandon (#5); prince./(German) Brandt (#5)./(M, Irish, Welsh) Bran (#8), Brandubh (#7), Branduff (#9)./(F, Welsh) Branwen (#5); white, blessed raven./Mates: Soda (#3) and Alexander (#3).

At First Glance: Doesn't stand out in a crowd; appears to be sweet, shy, unassuming, peaceful, and reserved. Is friendly, sensitive, and receptive.

Day-to-Day: Is assertive, proud, and fast acting; has definite ideas. Is independent, active, mentally alert, bold, and inventive. Dislikes routines and tries to lead the leader.

The Bottom Line: Takes pride in possessions and tries to get the best deal when trading toys. Is energetic, powerful, and happiest when exercised by athletic handlers.

Quirks of Character: Is immobilized when surrounded by noise or confusion.

Brittany (#1): F/From Brittany, a Breton (#2)./A region in NW France./Brittany spaniel; a French breed of large spaniels developed as a game pointer, and having a reddish brown and white or orange and white coat./(M, Celtic) Britt (#6); speckled Briton./F, Britannia (#7); (eighteenth century) from Britain.

At First Glance: Is plain and undistinguished for breed but has a mystical quality. Appears to be quiet, unassuming, indecisive, and content to remain in the background.

Day-to-Day: Is an introvert-extrovert. Is reserved, proud, quick, and alert. Needs a secure home. Likes to explore alone, often ignores routines, and is often greedy or selfish.

The Bottom Line: Wants to be businesslike. Is extremely strong and energetic; is comfortable when exercised vigorously and given opportunities for leadership.

Quirks of Character: Hides and is nervous when emotionally upset.

Brownie (#5): *unisex*/(Old English) Brun (#1)./A dark shade with a yellowish or reddish hue./Folklore reference: a little brown goblin, especially one who helps secretly in household work./(U.S.) A small, chewy, chocolate cake or cookie, often containing nuts./A member of the junior division (ages 8–11) of the Girl Scouts or Girl Guides./Brand name of an inexpensive camera, c. 1900.

> *At First Glance:* Is golden, beautiful, expressive, trusting, entertaining, colorful, expectant, affectionate, and youthful. Appears to be happy and is very vocal.
>
> *Day-to-Day:* Is frisky, unrestrained, enthusiastic, and impulsive. Is courageous in a crisis and thrives in an atmosphere that offers variety, change, and freedom outdoors.
>
> *The Bottom Line:* Wants one partner to shower with affection. Is sensitive to reprimands; is subtly controlling and has difficulty adapting to new situations.
>
> *Quirks of Character:* Is extremely curious, accident prone, and easily bored.

Bubba (#1): *M*/(German) Bub (#7), short for Bube (#3); boy./Baby talk for "brother."/Bub slang: a term of address, usually condescending; brother; boy; buddy./(Yiddish) Grandmother.

> *At First Glance:* Is rotund, cautious, relaxed, lumbering, and slow acting. Appears to be stable, sturdy, congenial, comfortable looking, and receptive.
>
> *Day-to-Day:* Is an aggressive, active, independent, courageous rebel, who will defy the human leader's right to dominance. Is creative and alert when left alone.
>
> *The Bottom Line:* Wants to do the "right" thing. Is exacting, conscientious, loyal, unemotional, and hard working. May be destructive without exercise and daily routines.
>
> *Quirks of Character:* Is too assertive and aggressive without leadership.

Buddy (#2): *unisex*/Classic./Is number 9 of ASPCA top 30 names./(Anglo-Saxon) Budd (#4); messenger or commander./(Gaelic) Victorious./(U.S.) Comrade or chum; often used as a term of address./A familiar and often condescending term of address for a man or boy whose name is not known to the speaker./Childish version of the name Brother (#5).

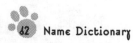

At First Glance: Is distinctive, different, and very active. Appears to be fearless, strong willed, dominant, unemotional, investigative, and very much an individual.

Day-to-Day: Is accommodating, docile, sweet, and friendly. A loving, charming, sensitive, emotional, unassuming companion who favors the company of a female leader.

The Bottom Line: Wants independence and has difficulty with behavior training. Has faith in himself and his own ideas. Is comfortable and active when left alone.

Quirks of Character: Has awe-inspiring intelligence and needs quiet time alone.

Bullet (#9): *unisex*/(French) *boulette* (*boule* [ball] + *ette*).

At First Glance: Is an unusual-looking, active loner. Appears to be an insistent, vigorous, independent, proud aggressor. Seems unapproachable at first meeting.

Day-to-Day: Is relaxed, easygoing, compassionate, loving, and devoted. Is happiest when providing a service or getting away from the household to roam freely.

The Bottom Line: Wants to work to use his or her high energy and needs to exercise vigorously and often. Is intelligent, trainable, and sociable; becomes bored without strenuous work.

Quirks of Character: When ignored, is spiteful, self-absorbed, and needy.

Buster (#4): M/Is number 30 of ASPCA top 30 names. /(U.S.) Somebody who breaks up something: *ghost busters*. /Something very big or unusual in a group. /A loud, raucous celebrant. /A familiar term to address a man or boy who attracts the speaker's annoyance or anger.

At First Glance: Striking, a mighty mix. Energetic, sensual, adaptable, enthusiastic, and a charming promoter that is capable of being "all thing to all people."

Day-to-Day: Is a dependable, stable, steady, quiet worker ideal for police and security patrol jobs.

The Bottom Line: Wants to be businesslike and is a dominant, intelligent, alert, well-balanced leader. Does not tolerate teasing and should be watched with children.

Quirks of Character: Is self-absorbed and unaffectionate when emotionally upset.

Name Dictionary **83**

Butch (#9): *M*/(Influenced by Scottish) Botch (#3), Butcher (#5)./To ruin or spoil; botch./To butcher, slaughter./Butch haircut: a short haircut for men or women that's similar to a crew cut./The partner in a lesbian relationship who assumes the role of the male.

> ***At First Glance:*** Is attentive, sturdy, robust, and parental; with a thick, lush, bluish tinged coat; appears to be overweight. Is drawn to children and is accommodating.
>
> ***Day-to-Day:*** Is easygoing; forms attachments but does not bond. Is affectionate and empathetic; understands human nature and finds common interests with everyone.
>
> ***The Bottom Line:*** Wants to do a variety of things and is entertaining, youthful, playful, and merry. Has a good memory. Talks or yowls at the slightest provocation.
>
> ***Quirks of Character:*** Is powerful and energetic; does not realize his strength.

See the Number Meanings chapter to discover the traits described by the number that accompanies each name: Babs (#6), Baby, ASPCA 12, (#3), Babyface (#9), Bacall (#4), Bacchus (#3), Bachelor (#1), Baily (#4), Baker (#1), Baldy (#8), Bambam (#5), Bambino (#2), Banditi (#3), Banger (#2), Banshee (#9), Banzai (#8), Barbarian (#3), Barbarino (#8), Barnaby (#9), Barnett (#8), Barney (#2), Barry (#1), Bart (#5), Bartholomew (#6), Bartley (#2), Barton (#7), Basha (#4), Bashful (#6), Basil (#7), Bathsheba (#3), Beagle (#5), Beamy (#1), Beardsley (#1), Beauregard (#1), Beauty (#2), Bedouin (#7), Belchy (#1), Benson (#6), Bessie (#5), Beta (#1), Bethany (#3), Betsy (#8), Beulah (#4), Bianca (#3) Bibi (#4), Biddy (#8), Bijou (#3), Bimbo (#5), Bingo (#2), Biscuit (#2), Bismark (#1), Bitchy (#4), Bits (#5), Blackie (#7), Blinky (#1), Blondie (#7), Blossom (#5), Bogey (#9), Bonaparte (#2), Bonbon (#8), Bones (#1), Boney (#7), Bonsai (#6), Booboo (#1), Boomer (#5), Boozer (#9), Boris (#9), Bosley (#6), Bowie (#9), Boxer (#1), Breezy (#9), Brenda (#8), Brendon (#9), Brewsky (#4), Bridget (#2), Bridie (#2), Bro (#8), Broadway (#8), Brodie (#8), Bromley (#9), Bronco (#4), Bronson (#7), Browser (#1), Bubbles (#9), Bubelah (#6), Buck (#1), Bucko (#7), Buddah (#4), Buffalo (#9), Bull (#2), Bullwinkle (#4), Bumper (#3), Bumpkin (#5), Bunko (#9), Bunny (#4), Burbank (#6), Butler (#6), Butterball (#5), Buttercup, (#9), Butterfly (#3), Butthead (#9), Button (#2), Buzzy (#1), Byron (#2).

Caesar (#2): *M*/(Latin) King./(U.S.) Caesare (#2); blue gray; hairy./A title of all Roman tyrants, dictators, emperors./(German) Kaiser (#9)./(Russian)

Czar (#3)./(F) Sherry (#3)./Mate: Cleopatra (#1)./Ex-wives: Cornelia (#5), Pompeia (#3).

At First Glance: Is solid, substantial, strong, muscular, with a dark, cottony coat on a square frame. Appears to be capable, conscientious, deliberate, patient, and likeable.

Day-to-Day: Is gentle, sedentary, playful, lovable, quiet, likes children, but is sensitive to rough handling, does not tolerate teasing, and demands personal attention.

The Bottom Line: Is intelligent, aristocratic, independent, sensitive to clamor; prefers to be an observer. Is comfortable with adults and wants to be trained gently.

Quirks of Character: When threatened, is volatile, impulsive, and dominating.

Candy (#2): *F*/(Middle English) *Sugre candy,* "candied sugar."/(Greek) Nickname for Candake (#3), Candace (#4); dazzling white, fire white, pure, sincere, a title of queens of ancient Egypt./Canace (#9), Kanake (#7); daughter of the wind./(Latin) Nickname for Candra (#5); moon, luminescent./Candida (#9)./(French) Candide (#4); dazzling white./(M, Turkish) Candan (#9); sincerely, heartily./(M, Scandinavian, Teutonic) Canute (#1); hill./Any of a variety of confections made with sugar, syrup, etc., combined with other ingredients./Slang: cocaine./To make sweet, palatable, or agreeable.

At First Glance: Is decorative, colorful, expressive, and charming; has beautiful eyes and a memorable voice. Appears to favor easygoing adults and playful children.

Day-to-Day: Is self-absorbed and strives for personal attention from a favored partner. Is sensitive, emotional, "soft," and easygoing. Wants love and never to be alone.

The Bottom Line: Wants to be dependable, businesslike, creative, productive, and sociable. Loves to collect toys and exercise vigorously. Is a shrewd guardian.

Quirks of Character: Is unpredictable; gets into trouble when impulsive or startled.

Casey (#8): *unisex*/(Celtic, Irish) Brave; derivative of Cathasach (#1); watchful./(English) Casey (#8); vigilant.

At First Glance: Is plain, unpretentious, shy, and unassuming. Appears to be gentle, cooperative, sweet, patient, and receptive when approached.

Day-to-Day: Is businesslike, alert, proud, dominating, self-disciplined, sociable, confident, exacting, mentally keen and shrewd, athletic, agile, and filled with energy.

The Bottom Line: Wants to be the parent. Is motivated to be quiet, harmonious, protective, responsible, and attentive to duties, the family, and community.

Quirks of Character: Wants privacy; dislikes to be disturbed or forced to move. Stays busy; Is purposeful, inflexible, wants to know the rules and obeys them.

Cat (#6): *unisex*/(Late Latin) *Cattus, catta.*/A domesticated carnivore, *Felis domestica* or *F. catus,* bred in a number of varieties./Also called: feline, grimalkin, tabby, gib, tomcat, tom, kitten, pussy./Archaic: catling./(F) Catia (#7), diminutive of Catherine (#2).

At First Glance: Is sensual and seductive, whether aloof or friendly. Appears to be adventurous, alert, curious, changeable, and moody; is alternately gentle and aggressive.

Day-to-Day: Is parental, protective, sympathetic, helpful, devoted to youngsters, and home loving. Enjoys being involved in all household and community activities.

The Bottom Line: Wants to do things independently. Prefers to take the lead and choose whether to be approachable or to be a loner; may be assertive or aggressive at will.

Quirks of Character: Is self-absorbed and deceptive when emotionally upset.

Champ (#5): *unisex*/Classic./(Latin) *Camp(us),* "field," "battlefield."/Informal: champion, one who has defeated opponents in a competition or series of competitions, so as to hold the first place./An animal that has won a certain number of points in officially recognized shows./One who fights for or defends any person or cause.

At First Glance: Is sturdy, square, and muscular. Appears to need to work off energy. Is conscientious, respectful, dignified, cautious, and unemotional.

Day-to-Day: Is friendly and adventurous; enjoys travel and new experiences. Needs to be with people and have freedom to do a variety of things. Prefers to be outdoors.

The Bottom Line: Wants independence. Is assertive, aggressive, self-insis-

tent, active, self-reliant, and devoted. Is comfortable with active humans.
Quirks of Character: Is selfish and dominating when upset.

Charley (#9): *unisex*/(Old High German) Nickname for (*M*) Charles (#3); full grown, strong, manly; and for (*F*) Charlotte (#3), Caroline (#5).

At First Glance: Is decorative, attractive, animated, amusing, and happy. Is filled with personality and friendliness. Appears to be a fashionable breed and eager to play.

Day-to-Day: Is a compassionate, expressive communicator. Is confident, peaceful, and comfortable in all situations. Is attentive to needy humans and friends.

The Bottom Line: Is devoted to home, family, and everyone in the immediate surroundings. Thrives on routines, good food, and working with others —never alone.

Quirks of Character: Becomes moody and aloof when left alone.

Checkers (#9): *unisex*/Classic./(Middle English) A checker chessboard./Checker (#8), a small, usually red or black disc of plastic or wood./To diversify in color or character; subject to alterations./People who check coats, baggage, etc./Cashiers in supermarkets or cafeterias.

At First Glance: Is proud, muscular, large, and dominating for the breed. Appears to be disciplined, sociable, and confident. Requires mental and physical activity.

Day-to-Day: Is an easygoing, polished, and skillful communicator. Is friendly to all and understanding of human nature. Thrives when performing service and being helpful.

The Bottom Line: Is mentally alert, active, and creative. Wants to be independent, courageous, and assertive. Is comfortable when left alone.

Quirks of Character: Jumps at virtually uncatchable things to exercise his or her body.

Chief (#4): *unisex*/Classic./(Latin) *Caput,* "head."/The head or leader of an organized body of men; the person highest in authority./Slang: boss or leader.

At First Glance: Is powerful and confident. Is a cut above the rest in breeding, balance, and alertness. Appears to be expensive, fastidiously groomed, and businesslike.

Day-to-Day: Is a cautious, respectful, dignified plodder. Is competitive and

thrives when exercised vigorously and adjusted to working within a structure of routines.

The Bottom Line: Is an adventurous mimic who is inclined to follow his curiosity. Thrives on excitement. Is difficult to restrain and learns caution by making mistakes.

Quirks of Character: Is smothering and underfoot when ignored by loved ones.

Chloe (#7): F/(Greek) Akin to *chloros*, "young green vegetation."/Young grass, blooming./A name for a beloved maiden.

At First Glance: Is restless, unconventional, curious, charming, entertaining, and unmanageable. Appears to be a striking and colorful rascal.

Day-to-Day: Is calm when secure. Is aloof, introspective, quiet, and dignified. Prefers solitude; becomes agitated and retreats when surrounded by high levels of traffic or noise.

The Bottom Line: Wants unconditional love. Thrives with a sensitive, calm, gentle female companion and enjoys nesting in a warm, welcoming lap.

Quirks of Character: Has difficulty adjusting to unexpected changes.

Clem (#6): *unisex*/Diminutive of names that begin with *Clem.*/Mates: (F) Clementine (#1), Clemency (#8), Clementia (#1); and (M) Clement (#9), Clemon (#8), Clemmie (#6).

At First Glance: Is an alert, fast-moving, unblinking, and independent loner. Has unusually bright coloration and unique patterning; is definitely different.

Day-to-Day: Is responsible, loving, devoted to home and family protection. Draws humans and friends into a close circle and is responsive to their moods and needs.

The Bottom Line: Wants freedom to explore the unknown and is funny, energetic, unconventional, enthusiastic, clever, and surprising.

Quirks of Character: Is routine oriented and unable to adjust to changes.

Cleo (#8): *unisex*/Egyptian theme./Nickname for (F) Cleopatra (#1), Cleota (#2), Cleone (#9); and for (M) Cleon (#4), Cleomenes (#1).

At First Glance: Is serious, sturdy, and rotund. Appears to be a parental, protective, welcoming communicator who makes humans feel comfortable.

Day-to-Day: Requires vigorous exercise and play. Has limitless energy and stamina combined with physical strength and a dominant personality.

The Bottom Line: Wants to be unobtrusive and is a subtle manipulator. Feels sensitive, gentle, and affectionate. Is mystical and devoted to one companion.

Quirks of Character: Becomes jealous and careless when ignored.

Comet (#2): *unisex*/(Greek) *Komet,* "long haired"; equivalent to *kome,* "hair of the head."/Astronomy reference: a celestial body that moves around the sun, usually in a highly eccentric orbit, and consists of a central mass surrounded by a misty envelope, which may extend to a stream away from the sun.

At First Glance: Is a magnetic, beautiful, polished, relaxed, friendly, classic example of the breed. Appears to be observant and charming.

Day-to-Day: Is a friendly, peaceful, adaptable, affectionate go-between who is sweet, shy, and indecisive. Prefers gentle handlers and dislikes rough play.

The Bottom Line: Wants to be spoiled and demands affection from a female partner. Has high, nervous energy and is easily frightened. Is comfortable being babied.

Quirks of Character: Is subtly manipulative when jealous.

Cookie (#4): *unisex*/(Middle English) *Kechel,* "little cake."/(German) *Kuchen.*/(U.S.) A small, sweet cake made from stiff dough, which has been dropped, rolled, or sliced and then baked./(Scottish) A bun./Informal: dear; sweetheart; a term of address, usually connoting affection./Slang: a person, as in "He's one smart cookie."

At First Glance: Is dazzling and out-of-the-ordinary. A bright, amusing, curious, people-lover who appears to wants short conversations and changing relationships.

Day-to-Day: Is cautious, quiet, dependable, energetic, strong, routine oriented, and dignified. Prefers a stable environment and is practical, earthy, and serious.

The Bottom Line: Is a discerning, courageous, agile, athletic guardian who is impulsive and likely to be promiscuous and produce unwanted litters.

Quirks of Character: His or her sexuality leads to raunchy, unconventional adventures.

Countess (#8): F/(Latin) Count, *comitem* + *ess.*/The wife or widow of a count in the nobility of continental Europe or of an earl in the British peerage./A woman having the rank of a count or earl in her own right./Mate: Count (#1).

At First Glance: Is beautiful, decorative, fashionable, happy, and cute. Has expressive eyes, a memorable voice, and a world of charm and personality.

Day-to-Day: Is a businesslike, intelligent, sociable, courageous, and mentally and physically strong guardian. Won't take a backseat to any human or friend.

The Bottom Line: Wants freedom outdoors and is unpredictable if too confined. Enjoys excitement and variety; is adaptable to change and surprises.

Quirks of Character: Is submissive when emotionally upset.

Cutie (#4): unisex/(chiefly U.S.) Informal: pleasingly pretty or dainty./Affected or mincingly pretty or clever; precious./Mentally keen, clever, shrewd.

At First Glance: Has a striking appearance and a friendly nature. Is impulsive, frisky, surprising, unconventional, and curious about humans and the environment.

Day-to-Day: Is a structured, respectful, strong worker. Is teachable, devoted, dependable, routine oriented, faithful, and earthy. Loves to dig for buried treasure.

The Bottom Line: Is athletic, plays hard, and approaches chores with enthusiasm, imagination, and a competitive spirit. Is comfortable with sociable, athletic humans.

Quirks of Character: Is bored when inactive and creates havoc when confined.

See the Number Meanings chapter to discover the traits described by the number that accompanies each name: Cabot (#5), Cadbury (#2), Cagney (#1), Calder (#7), Caldwell (#9), Calhoun (#2), Calico (#7), Callahan (#7), Callie (#6), Calloway (#2), Calvin (#7), Camden (#4), Camelot (#6), Cameron (#6), Campbell (#1), Capo (#8), Capone (#9), Capricorn (#7), Caramel (#8), Carlos (#5), Carlton (#2), Carly (#5), Carmel (#7), Carmen (#9), Carmichael (#1), Carolina (#1), Carson (#7), Carter (#2), Caruso (#5) Casanova (#4), Champagne (#5), Champion (#7), Channing (#7), Chaplin (#9), Charcoal (#7), Charlie (#2), ASPCA 24, Charo (#9), Chase (#9), Chatsworth (#9), Chaucer (#5), Chauncey (#8), Cheech (#5), Cheever (#3), Chekov (#1), Cher (#7), Cherry (#5), Chessie (#5), Chester (#6),

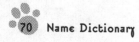

Chewy (#1), Cheyenne (#7), Chicky (#5), Chong (#2), Christopher (#4), Chuckles (#1), Cinderella (#2), Cisco (#4), Cissy (#3), Claire (#3), Clancy (#4), Clarabel (#9), Clarence (#7), Clarice (#6), Clayton (#9), Clementine (#1), Cleopatra (#1), Clifford (#1), Clint (#4), Clyde (#4), Cobra (#3), Cochise (#8), Coco (#9), Cody (#2), Cognac (#7), Colette (#8), Colombo (#3), Columbus (#7), Conan (#2), Connor (#7), Conrad (#1), Cooper (#9), Corbett (#2), Corky (#9), Cornelia (#5), Courtney (#4), Cousin (#9), Crackers (#6), Cricket (#6), Crissy (#3), Cristy (#4), Cruiser (#3), Crystal (#8), Cubby (#8), Cuddly (#6), Cupcake (#6), Cupid (#8), Curtis (#9), Cyclone (#5), Cyrano (#4), Cyril (#4), Cyrus (#5), Czar (#3).

Daisy (#4): F/(Anglo-Saxon, Old English) The day's eye./(English) From Candace (#4) or Margaret (#2)./(French) Marguerite (#9); daisy./A plant./Slang: someone or something of first-rate quality.

At First Glance: Is brightly colored and self-promoting. Is magnetic to the opposite sex, adventurous, clever, curious, funny, and very vocal.

Day-to-Day: Is a problem solver with workaholic energy. Is strong, wise, loyal, and comfortable following routines in a stable environment.

The Bottom Line: Wants to be accepted as a self-confident, self-disciplined athlete, who takes challenges and complete tasks.

Quirks of Character: Is a forecaster of storms and emotional unrest.

Dennis (#2): M/(Greek and Latin via French) *Dionysius* from *Dionysos;* god of Nysa, god of vegetation and wine./(Irish, English) Denis (#6)./(French) Denys (#4), Dione (#2)./(Spanish) Dionis (#7), Dionisio (#4)./(German) Dionys (#5)./Nickname: Denny (#8)./F. Denise (#2).

At First Glance: Is conventional, stable, and sociable; has a thick, easy-to-comb coat. Impresses onlookers as a comfortable, comforting, family companion.

Day-to-Day: Is gentle, quietly active, and sensitive. Is especially loving and affectionate to one special human and friendly with other pets.

The Bottom Line: Wants to see everything and is very inquisitive and surprising. May be mischievous and amuse humans with his antics. Delights in finding fence holes.

Quirks of Character: Has overly emotional, uncontrolled impulses.

Dixie (#6): F/(Latin, French) *Dix,* "the tenth," "ten."/Term of endearment.

At First Glance: Has an unusual appearance. Is alert and active; appears

to be independent, assertive, fast thinking, investigative, and proud.

Day-to-Day: Has an allegiance to home and family. Thrives when she has one special service to perform. Is maternal, comforting, dignified, and possessive.

The Bottom Line: Wants to be an entertaining personality. Learns from experience and needs freedom to roam. Is clever, charming, vocal, and self-promoting.

Quirks of Character: Adapts to changes easily and is an opportunist.

Doc (#4): M/(Latin) *docere*, "teach."/Informal: doctor.

At First Glance: Has aristocratic, intelligent eyes and a dignified, aloof air. Is neat, poised, and guarded. Appears to be withdrawn, suspicious, and unapproachable.

Day-to-Day: When secure, is conventional, practical, loyal, down-to-earth, planned, and practiced. Follows routines diligently and prefers an organized lifestyle.

The Bottom Line: Wants to be protective, is conscientious, and may be a sympathetic meddler who considers a peaceful home life to be his ideal.

Quirks of Character: When ignored, becomes a boisterous chatterbox.

Dog (#8): unisex/(Middle European) *Dogge.*/(Old English) *Docga.*/A domesticated carnivorous mammal, *Canis familiaris,* bred in a great many varieties./Any animal belonging to the family *Canidae,* including wolves, jackals, foxes, etc./Something worth less or of extremely poor quality./An utter failure; flop./Slang: an ugly, boring, or crude girl or woman.

At First Glance: Is refined and unassuming. Appears to be receptive, has eyes that emit a spiritual light, and is hesitant, high strung, and nervous.

Day-to-Day: Is a proud-spirited, high-minded, faithful, investigative, mentally and physically powerful presence who requires solitude, privacy, and activity.

The Bottom Line: Wants to have a family to love. Is parental, nurturing, musical, honest, fair, home loving, and protective. Likes personal comfort and wants peace.

Quirks of Character: When serenity is disturbed, is suspicious and erratic.

Dolly (#5): F/Diminutive of Dolores (#7), Dorothea (#5), Dorothy (#6), Theodora (#5)./Variations: Doll (#7), Dolley (#1), Dollie (#3)./Gift of god; sorrows./A toy representing a baby or other human being, particularly a child's

toy./A girl./A sweetheart./A pretty but expressionless or unintelligent woman./Slang: a very attractive girl or woman./A boy or man who is considered attractive by a woman.

At First Glance: Is an active, assertive, proud, confident, unusual-looking pet. Has a brightly colored coat and is uniquely patterned.

Day-to-Day: Is unconventional, unrestrained, entertaining, clever, curious, and spontaneous. Enjoys the outdoors and escapes when confined.

The Bottom Line: Is comfortable with practical, dignified, enduring, down-to-earth humans. Needs firm training, a consistent routine, and vigorous exercise.

Quirks of Character: Tends to be a hermit with boisterous humans.

Dougal (#6): M/(Scottish) Dark-haired stranger./(From Celtic) Douglas (#7)./(Irish) Dubhglas (#2); dark stranger, dark stream./(English) Color combination of black (or another dark color) plus blue, green, and gray.

At First Glance: Is unconventional, quick, approachable, curious, and talkative. Appears to like activity, people, and new experiences.

Day-to-Day: Prefers to be comfortable, well fed, and involved with a family and/or a neighborhood of friends to love, protect, and serve.

The Bottom Line: Feels independent. If necessary, is able to make transitions between nests and different leaders. Wants to be the first and the best at something.

Quirks of Character: Is careless about personal grooming.

Duchess (#7): F/(Latin) Dux, "leader."/(Middle English) Duchesse./The wife or widow of a duke./A woman who holds in her own right the sovereignty or titles of duchy.

At First Glance: Receives recognition. Is dominating, dynamic, mentally alert, expensively flashy, fastidiously groomed. Appears to have limitless endurance.

Day-to-Day: Is quiet, introspective, intuitive, analytical, inspirational, aloof, aristocratic, mystical, and irritable if the environment is noisy or confused.

The Bottom Line: Wants to be active and busy. Is strong, agile, and athletic; requires extensive exercise. Is comfortable with disciplined, strong humans.

Quirks of Character: Is an independent, creative, bossy loner when upset.

Duke (#5): *M/Classic./(Latin) Duc,* "leader."/(Anglo-Saxon) To draw or lead, as an army./(In continental Europe) The male ruler of a duchy; the sovereign of a small state./(British) A nobleman holding the highest hereditary title outside of the royal family, ranking immediately below a prince and above a marquis (c. 1300s).

At First Glance: Is steady, robust, comfortable, and welcoming. Appears to be paternal, protective, conventional, and ready to lend a helping hand.

Day-to-Day: Is seductive, enthusiastic, entertaining, spontaneous, sociable, self-promoting freedom lover. Prefers to be free to explore outdoors.

The Bottom Line: Is mentally and physically strong and socially dominant. Wants activity, exercise, vigorous play, and challenges.

Quirks of Character: Is sexual. Needs to be understood when impulsive.

Duncan (#3): *M/(Gaelic)* Of brown battle, brown chief or warrior, dark warrior.

At First Glance: Is commanding, expensive, businesslike, and sociable. Appears to be intelligent, strong, agile, and capable of earning a blue ribbon.

Day-to-Day: Is an imaginative, charming, attractive communicator who is entertaining and enjoys playing with children and other pets.

The Bottom Line: Wants stability. Is an earthy and devoted worker who enjoys routines and learns by rote. Thrives in a conventional, structured environment.

Quirks of Character: Has impulsive sexual urges. Runs off for an adventure.

Dustin (#6): *M/(Old High German)* Of the storm; the stormy or valiant fighter.

At First Glance: Appears to be charming and has beautiful, expressive eyes and a memorable voice. Entertains onlookers and loves to have an appreciative audience.

Day-to-Day: Is a conventional, trustworthy, helpful, sympathetic, music-loving, homebody who needs one special female to love and protect.

The Bottom Line: Is inwardly amused at everything and puts on a good show. Is affectionate, conscientious in regard to duty, and happy when making others happy.

Quirks of Character: Has lusty sexual appetites and the spirit of adventure.

Dusty (#8): *unisex*/Nickname for Dustin (#6)./Full of dust.

At First Glance: Is lean, unwrinkled, aristocratic, and impressive. Appears to be cautious, intelligent, intense, and mannerly. Prefers to observe the scene.

Day-to-Day: Is dominant, courageous, hardy, alert, and energetic. Has stamina and needs to be exercised as much as possible. Does not tolerate teasing well.

The Bottom Line: Is fairly willful and aggressive, but can be trained by a patient, strong leader. Is independent, reserved with strangers, and best with older children.

Quirks of Character: Is a bit of a snob. Enjoys being alone or with peers.

See the Number Meanings chapter to discover the traits described by the number that accompanies each name: Daffodil (#3), Dagmar (#8), Dahlia (#8), Daishi (#5), Dakota (#7), Dale (#4), Damian (#6), Dammit (#6), Damsel (#9), Danbury (#4), Dancer (#9), Dandee (#6), Danielle (#8), Danny (#4), Dante (#8), Danu (#4), Danza (#1), Daphne (#3), Daren (#6), Daria (#6), Darlene (#5), Darnel (#9), Darryl (#6), Darter (#3), Darwin (#6), Davenport (#7), Davis (#1), Davy (#7), Dawn (#6), Dean (#6), Deano (#3), Debbie (#9), Debussy (#5), Decan (#9), Decker (#1), DeeDee (#1), Delbert (#3), Delia (#4), Della (#7), Delman (#4), Delmonico (#9), Delores (#6), Delphi (#9), Delta (#6), Demetri (#2), Demitasse (#5), Demo (#1), Demon (#6), Deniro (#2), Denny (#8), Denton (#9), Denver (#5), Derby (#9), Derek (#7), Desdemona (#8), Desi (#1), Desiree (#2), Devon (#6), Di (#4), Diamond (#6), Diana (#2), Dick (#9), Dickey (#3), Diddley (#9), Didi (#8), Diego (#4), Digby (#2), Digger (#5), Dilbert (#7), Dillon (#3), Dilly (#8), Dimples (#6), Dina (#1), Dinger (#3), Dingo (#4), Dinker (#7), Dino (#6), Dirk (#6), Ditto (#5), Ditty (#6), Diva (#9), Dix (#1), Dizzy (#9), Dobie (#8), Dodger (#8), Dolan (#1), Dolby (#5), Doolittle (#4), Dom (#5), Domingo (#5), Dominic (#4), Domino (#7), Don (#6), Donahue (#5), Donald (#5), Donna (#3), Donovan (#4), Dooney (#6), Dora (#2), Doreen (#7), Doria (#2), Dorkis (#4), Doug (#2), Douglas (#7), Dozer (#5), Drake (#3), Draper (#8), Dreamer (#1), Dreyfus (#8), Dribbles (#8), Drooler (#6), Droopy (#3), Drummer (#2), Drummond (#3), Drusilla (#6), Dryden (#7), Drysdale (#7), Duane (#9), Duckie (#8), Ducky (#1), Duffy (#8), Dumas (#4), Dumbo (#1), Dunbar (#6), Dundee (#8), Dunhill (#8), Dupont (#9), Durango (#8), Durante (#2), Dushane (#9), Dutch (#2), Dutton (#4), Duval (#6), Dweezil (#3), Dylan (#2), Dynamite (#1), Dynamo (#9).

Ebony (#7): *unisex*/(Late Latin) *Hebeninus*, "of ebony."/(Greek) *Ebeninos*./A hard, heavy, durable wood, most highly prized when black, from various tropical trees of the genus *Diospyros*, of southern India and Ceylon, used for cabinetwork, ornamental objects, etc./A deep, lustrous, black.

At First Glance: Is detached, introspective, elegant, serious, mystical, and aloof. Has an aristocratic air. Appears to be a loner.

Day-to-Day: Enjoys moments of solitude and needs to have a safe, private area away from noise and confusion. Psychic abilities make him or her a fine protector.

The Bottom Line: Is emotionally responsive and wants to be of service to the needy. Is a brave defender who forgives and forgets the thoughtless acts of humans.

Quirks of Character: Is loyal to a family and does not attach to one individual.

Eddie (#9): *unisex*/Nickname for all names that begin with *Ed* (#9).

At First Glance: Is a magnificent example of the breed. Appears to take pride in appearance and performance; goes about being sociable in a businesslike manner.

Day-to-Day: Is a peaceful, polished, and skillful communicator. Instinctively serves the most needy humans and is unselfish and brave.

The Bottom Line: Is alert and courageous. Is comfortable, creative, and capable when alone. Will take independent action if the need arises.

Quirks of Character: Disappears when restlessly seeking a sensual adventure.

Effie (#4): *F*/(Hebrew, Irish) Equivalent to Mother Eve, the granddaughter of King Ler (#8), who became Shakespeare's King (#5) Lear (#9)./Aoife (#9); (Irish variant) Aoiffe (#6); the pleasant./(Scottish, German) Diminutive of Euphemia (#6), Efrica (#6), Effririca (#3)./(Fante, Ghana) Efia (#3); born on Friday./(Greek) Euphemia (#6); of good report.

At First Glance: Is beautiful, sunny, shiny, and filled with personality and good cheer. Appears to be amusing, open, and friendly with everyone.

Day-to-Day: Is a solid, dependable, dignified, cautious, dutiful companion. Enjoys routines, maintains schedules, and thrives in an orderly lifestyle.

The Bottom Line: Wants to be independent and should be given free time to roam alone. Is comfortable when active.

Quirks of Character: Is seductive and curious and find outlets for her impulses.

Elizabeth (#7): F/(Hebrew) El is oath, consecrated to God, oath of God./Saint's name, mother of John (#2) the Baptist (#6)./(Scottish, German, French) Elisabeth (#9).

At First Glance: Is friendly, honest, bright, magnetic, active, and out-of-the-ordinary. Appears to be clever and has a seductive charm that is attractive to all.

Day-to-Day: Prefers privacy and inactivity to noisy crowds. Needs vigorous exercise or play. Is intelligent, clear thinking, poised, restful, and highly intuitive.

The Bottom Line: Is sensitive, receptive, gentle, and quiet. When left alone too long, is affected physically by emotional stress. Thrives in partnership with one special human.

Quirks of Character: Is overly assertive when she wants to exert control.

Elmer (#8): M/(Old English, Teutonic) Nobly famous.

At First Glance: Is sleek, calm, cool, and collected. Is detached from the noise and reality around him. Appears to be aloof, quiet, peaceful, and withdrawn.

Day-to-Day: Has strength of character and physical stamina that is dependable and enduring. Is routine oriented, honest, and earthy.

The Bottom Line: Is most comfortable when acting independently. Has courage and assertiveness when he is able to take the lead. Vies for supremacy with the leader.

Quirks of Character: Is unusually sensitive to anyone who is ill, weak, or needy.

Elsa (#1): F/(Teutonic) The noble./(U.S. from French) Elsabeth (#9)./(Irish, Welsh) Eliza (#8)./(Scottish) Elizabeth (#7), Elspeth (#4); God is my oath./Variations: Alice (#3), Else (#5), Elsie (#5).

At First Glance: Is a traditional, muscular, conscientious plodder with a determined, serious attitude. Appears to be inclined to work rather than play.

Day-to-Day: Hears a different drummer and independently handles things her own way. Responds with strength and courage and prefers to take the lead.

The Bottom Line: Is protective and steps in with the attitude that she knows best. Is motivated to maintain harmonious relations in the family and community.

Quirks of Character: When emotionally upset, is forceful and thoughtless.

Elvis (#4): M/Form of Elwin (#9); (Anglo-Saxon) Elf friend./(Nordic) Wise.

At First Glance: His stance, stride, and form indicate power and authority. Is self-confident, strong, handsome, and energetic. Is alert, agile, and businesslike.

Day-to-Day: Has nervous energy that must be put to work. Is witty, cheerful, and always on the go. Is a stickler for routine, enjoys practice, and aims in one direction.

The Bottom Line: Wants adventure; without a variety of new people and sensual experiences, becomes bored, impatient, too curious, and self-destructive.

Quirks of Character: May lack courage and determination in times of crisis.

Emily (#1): F/(Latin) Winsome./(M, Teutonic) Emil (#3); the industrious./(Hebrew, Anglo-Saxon, Norse) Work, strength.

At First Glance: Is regal, aloof, quiet, reserved, sleek, and perfect for the breed. Appears to be introspective, observant, investigative, and mystical.

Day-to-Day: Is inventive, independent, and content when left alone. Is alert, energetic, assertive, and appropriately aggressive. Enjoys being a bossy authority.

The Bottom Line: Wants a variety of toys and loves to play. Has a good memory, builds a vocabulary, and is motivated to communicate her ideas and feelings.

Quirks of Character: Dislikes noise; retreats alone until the din dies down.

Emmett (#4): M/(Irish) Strength./(English) Work./May relate as a nickname to (Old German) *emmet*, "an ant," and to (F) Emma (#5).

At First Glance: Is golden, sunny, youthful, expressive, friendly, and vocal. Appears to have beautiful eyes, a memorable voice, and a world of charm.

Day-to-Day: Is a disciplined, dedicated worker who thrives on maintaining routines. Is loyal, emotionally balanced, and physically active.

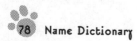

The Bottom Line: Is a loner in some respects and dislikes to be controlled. Is motivated to be a leader and may become aggressive and domineering when second in command.

Quirks of Character: If left alone for long periods, will be restless and spiteful.

Ernie (#6): unisex/Nickname for Ernest (#9) and Ernestine (#1)

At First Glance: Looks unconventional and appears to be a bright, sparkling, quick, clever, unrestrained, frisky risk-taker. Is a charming, amusing self-promoter.

Day-to-Day: Accepts responsibilities as a right and privilege. Gets involved in activities and brings love, understanding, and sympathy to all relationships.

The Bottom Line: Desires independence and does not follow routines and disciplines. Is determined, forceful, and comfortable when left alone.

Quirks of Character: Is quick to join anyone who goes out the door.

Eve (#5): F/Biblical reference: the first woman (Genesis 3:20)./(Old French) Aveline (#5); the hazel./(Greek) Zoe (#1); life./(Hebrew) Chava (#8), Eva (#1), Hava (#5), Haya (#8), Heve (#4), Jevera (#7); life./(Danish-Italian-German variant) Ewa (#2)./(Spanish) Eva (#1); life./(Irish) Aveline (#5), Eveleen (#5)./(Old Celtic) The pleasant, the hazel./(Polish) Ewa (#2); life./(Russian) Evva (#5); life./(Scottish) Evir (#9); life./(Spanish) Evita (#3); life./(Swahili, E. Africa) Eshe (#1); life./Mate: Adam (#1).

At First Glance: Is a solid, conservative, serious work breed. Applies muscle to the jobs that must be done. Appears to be hardy, dignified, patient, and enduring.

Day-to-Day: Is a mentally curious, sensual, active, versatile companion. Cleverly learns to understand and mouth words and mimic actions of humans and other pets.

The Bottom Line: Wants to be in control and asserts personality preferences with courage and originality. Is motivated to be an active leader.

Quirks of Character: Has difficulty submitting to routines or disciplines.

Evita (#3): F/(Spanish) Eve (#5).

At First Glance: Is an agreeable, dignified, concerned, friendly communicator. Appears to be a sympathetic, serious, proud, loving parent or guardian.

Day-to-Day: Is expressive in many ways and demands attention. Is vocal, playful, animated, and optimistic. Loves to be in the midst of groups of humans and other pets.

The Bottom Line: Assumes responsibility for the family's happiness and welfare. Is motivated to be of service and adapts her personality to maintain harmony.

Quirks of Character: Is aggressive when the human leader assumes control.

See the Number Meanings chapter to discover the traits described by the number that accompanies each name: Eartha (#8), Eastwood (#3), Ebba (#1), Ebenezer (#8), Eden (#1), Edgar (#8), Edison (#3), Edith (#1), Edsel (#9), Edward (#1), Edweena (#3), Edwin (#1), Efrem (#2), Egan (#9), Egbert (#3), Einstein (#5), Eldridge (#1), Eleanor (#7), Electra (#1), Eli (#8), Elias (#1), Elisha (#9), Elke (#6), Elle (#7), Ellen (#3), Ellery (#5), Ellie (#7), Ellington (#9), Ellis (#3), Elmira (#4), Eloise (#2), Elton (#3), Emerald (#4), Emerson (#8), Emmanuel (#3), Emmeline (#4), Emmet (#2), Emmy (#2), Emmylou (#5), Enoch (#9), Enola (#2), Erato (#5), Eric (#8), Erica (#9), Errol (#5), Essex (#9), Ethan (#3), Ethel (#5), Eton (#9), Eudora (#1), Eugene (#3), Eunice (#3), Eustace (#2), Eva (#1), Evans (#7), Evelyn (#2), Exeter (#5).

Fala (#2): *unisex*/(F. Native American, Choctaw) Crow./(M. Arabic) Falah (#1); success./A text or refrain in old songs.

At First Glance: Is polished, skillful, and attractive to all. Appears to be tolerant, patient, and obedient. Is welcomed by onlookers as an old friend and kindred spirit.

Day-to-Day: Is loyal, sensitive, and loving. Does not like rigid procedures; likes peace and harmony. Is an unobtrusive dependent who bonds with one human.

The Bottom Line: Is definitely not a loner; is motivated to seek companionship and is indifferent with strangers. Personal comfort is important. Adapts easily to changes.

Quirks of Character: Is rebellious when given commands by strangers.

Fang (#1): *unisex*/Classic./(Middle English, Old English) Something caught, to fasten./(German) Capture, booty./(Icelandic) Grasp, hold./(British dialect) To seize, grab./One of the long, sharp, hollow or grooved teeth of a venomous

snake, by which poison is injected./A canine tooth, a doglike tooth./The root of a tooth./One of the chelicerae of a spider./A pointed, tapering part of a thing.

At First Glance: Is a neat, beautiful, youthful, charismatic, graceful, responsive, and harmonious classic example of the breed. Appears to be very approachable.

Day-to-Day: Is alert, active, independent, impatient, and assertive. Prefers to be inventive. Is clever, self-centered, and content when left alone.

The Bottom Line: Prefers mental activity to physical labor and is often too busy to be affectionate. Is motivated to be assertive, forceful, and self-willed.

Quirks of Character: Responds thoughtfully and intelligently in a crisis.

Fido (#7): M/(U.S.) Classic./(possibly Latin) Fidel (#9); the faithful./Possibly an acronym: Fine Dog; or Forget It, Drive On./Coin collecting reference, acronym: Freaks, Irregulars, Defects, Oddities (coins having a minting error)./Aeronautics reference, acronym: Fog Investigation Dispersal Operations (a system for evaporating the fog above airfield runways by the heat from burners).

At First Glance: Is independent and different. Appears to be inquisitive, determined, and more interested in investigating the territory than meeting with humans.

Day-to-Day: Is highly intelligent. Is a talented observer who examines a situation before becoming involved. Is inclined to be aloof, introspective, and quiet.

The Bottom Line: Is motivated to protect and serve the family and the home. Wants to be involved in activities, responds to music, and is prone to overeating.

Quirks of Character: Generally steps in when there is friction or disharmony.

Fifi (#3): F/Classic./(M. Hebrew) Joseph (#1); he shall add./(F. French) Josephine (#2), Fifine (#4)./(M. Fante, Ghana) Born on Friday.

At First Glance: Is beautiful, decorative, and colorful, with an attractive personality. Appears to be playful, vocal, youthful, happy, and affectionate.

Day-to-Day: Is a hardworking social butterfly with a talent for keeping humans entertained. Is rarely depressed, loves to tease, and is never happy alone.

The Bottom Line: Is an emotional, loving, and generous companion who sees herself as a human. Is motivated to provide service and thrives in the country or near the shore.

Quirks of Character: Never meets a stranger and thinks that everyone needs her.

Flash (#1): *unisex*/Classic./(Middle English) *Flaschen,* "to sprinkle."/A brief, sudden burst of bright light./A sudden, brief outburst or display of wit, joy, etc./A very brief moment./Flashy; to be gaudy, tawdry, pretentious, superficial.

At First Glance: Is a noble, classically beautiful, polished, and graceful communicator. Appears to be magnetic, vibrant, tolerant, and approachable.

Day-to-Day: Is independent, quick, definite, assertive, and aggressive. Seeks self-gratification and is bossy. Prefers to do things alone and is creative.

The Bottom Line: Wants to be the leader of the pack. Is motivated to go it alone; is strong willed and courageous. Has the determination to overcome obstacles.

Quirks of Character: Is strong, lacks agility, and is clumsy.

Flopsy (#3): *unisex*/Classic./From *flop.*/To fall down or plop down suddenly, especially with noise; to drop or turn with a sudden bump or thud./Slang: to yield or break down suddenly; to fall; to flap, as in the wind./Informal: a failure.

At First Glance: Is handsome, expensive, powerful, dominant, and businesslike. Appears to be a self-confident, athletic, agile, and alert winner.

Day-to-Day: Is a funny, extremely charming, affable, sociable, loyal conversationalist. Is popular with all ages and seems to light up a room with personality.

The Bottom Line: Wants to be a stable worker and is motivated to follow routines and to adhere to behavior training. Is conscientious, cautious, energetic, and conservative.

Quirks of Character: Is gloomy without private time away from daily activity.

Fluffy (#3): *unisex*/Classic./Resembling or covered with light, downy particles, as of cotton./Having little or no intellectual weight./A light, frivolous thing: trifle.

At First Glance: Appears to be beautiful, youthful, and amusing, with expressive eyes and a memorable voice. Is talkative, colorful, happy, and friendly.

Day-to-Day: Is a scattered, clownish, and fickle friend. Shares love, toys, activities, and talents with everyone. Finds things to do and is always interested and entertained.

The Bottom Line: Refers everything to personal interests and desires. Is motivated to independently take the lead and wants to appear to be useful.

Quirks of Character: Subjects everything to analysis and is too hesitant.

Foxy (#7): *unisex*/(German) *Fuchs, fox.*/(English, Native American) Foxlike; cunning or crafty; clever./Discolored or foxed, like pages in a book./Yellowish or reddish brown, as of the color of the common red fox./Archaic: (especially of a painting) having excessively warm tones; containing too much red.

At First Glance: Is golden, decorative, beautiful, colorful, luxurious, and expressive. Appears to be affectionate, vocal, and attention getting.

Day-to-Day: Is strongly intuitive and introspective. Thrives in the country or by the seashore and is not suited to living in a small, noisy, crowded apartment.

The Bottom Line: Wants physical exercise and work. Is a dignified, stable, disciplined companion who relates to the earth and thrives in an orderly household.

Quirks of Character: Becomes irritable and nervous if the environment is noisy.

Frasier (#4): M/(Old French) Fraser (#4); the curly haired.

At First Glance: Has a regal bearing. Is reserved, quiet, calm, and aloof from the surroundings. Appears to be intelligent, proud, introspective, poised, and mystical.

Day-to-Day: Is a systematic, routine-oriented, disciplined, practical worker. Is dependable, serious, and physically strong. Needs consistent schedules.

The Bottom Line: Is motivated to enjoy household responsibilities and

wants to protect the territory and loved ones. Thrives when involved in all activities.

Quirks of Character: Understands human nature and is attractive to all.

Freddy (#8): *unisex*/(Old High German) Frederic (#5); powerful, rich, peace./Form of Frederick (#7), Frederica (#6), and all names that begin with *Fred* (#6).

At First Glance: Is unusual, colorful, and striking. Appears to be clever, youthful, enthusiastic, amusing, friendly, and frisky.

Day-to-Day: Is energetic, powerful, dominant, charming, and attractive to both sexes. Works and plays hard. Needs stability and outlets for tremendous energy.

The Bottom Line: Wants to make a game out of life; wants to entertain, talk, and amuse. Is motivated to be self-expressive and to be the life of the party.

Quirks of Character: Is scheming, jealous, and spiteful when serenity is upset.

Frenchy (#7): *unisex*/Characteristic or suggestive of the French./A Frenchman.

At First Glance: Is conventional for the breed: muscular, sturdy, strong, and square. Appears to be dignified, proud, competitive, and disciplined.

Day-to-Day: Is gentle, silent, observant, intuitive, and intelligent. Wants privacy and prefers to be alone in a crowd. Is uncomfortable with careless children.

The Bottom Line: Dislikes repetition, needs variety, and has courage, wisdom, and presence of mind in a crisis. Wants to maintain friendships in a serene lifestyle.

Quirks of Character: Requires periods of isolation to recoup physical energy.

Friday (#9): *unisex*/(Middle English, Old English) *Frigedaeg*, "Freya's day."/Freya (#1); lady./Norse mythology: goddess of beauty and love./(M, Anglo-Saxon) Frey (#9); lord./Sixth day of the week, following Thursday./Friend: Robinson (#7).

At First Glance: Is recognized as a dominant authority for the breed and capable of blue ribbons. Appears to be strong, energetic, sociable, and enduring.

Day-to-Day: Is an "old soul." Observes and senses the overview of the household and the territory; is an involved communicator, concerned about the welfare of all.

The Bottom Line: Wants to take the initiative to assert his or her individuality and is comfortable when independent. Is alert and active; needs outlets for mental energy.

Quirks of Character: Does not tolerate any form of bondage.

Frosty (#4): *unisex*/(German) From *frost,* akin to *freeze.*/To freeze or become covered with frost./Frost (#6); consisting of or covered with a covering of minute ice needles, formed from the atmosphere at night upon the ground and exposed objects when they have cooled by radiation below the dew point, and when the dew point is below the freezing point./Coldness of manner or temperament./Informal: coolness between persons./Resembling frost: white or gray; as of hair.

At First Glance: Is classically beautiful and charismatic. Appears to be understanding, approachable, and to have a bird's-eye view of the territory.

Day-to-Day: Is a dedicated doer. Is conscientious, routine oriented, serious, and energetic. Must be exercised regularly and is best suited to living in the country.

The Bottom Line: Is motivated to work and wants to be busy all the time. Enjoys digging, rolling in the earth, and following disciplines and routines.

Quirks of Character: Is a moody, suspicious loner when overtired or upset.

See the Number Meanings chapter to discover the traits described by the number that accompanies each name: Fabio (#6), Fagan (#2), Fairbanks (#9), Fairchild (#7), Fairfax (#2), Faith (#8), Fancy (#4), Fannie (#4), Fanny (#6), Farah (#7), Farfel (#3), Fargo (#2), Farley (#4), Farnsworth (#7), Fats (#1), Faulkner (#7), Fawn (#8), Fay (#5), FeeFee (#5), Feldman (#1), Felicia (#9), Felicity (#8), Fellah (#8), Feller (#4), Fellini (#4), Fendi (#2), Fenimore (#4), Fenton (#2), Fenwick (#8), Fergi (#9), Fergus (#4), Ferguson (#6), Fester (#1), Fiddler (#4), Filbert (#9), Findley (#3), Fink (#4), Finneus (#7), Finnigan (#2), Fiona (#9), Fischer (#5), Fitzgerald (#9), Fitzi (#7), Fitzpatrick (#4), Fleischmann (#5), Fletch (#9), Fletcher (#5), Fleur (#8), Flint (#7), Flipper (#1), Flora (#7), Florence (#6), Florie (#2), Floris (#7), Flossie (#4), Flossy (#6), Flurry (#1), Fogarty (#2), Fonda (#4), Forbes (#2), Ford (#7), Foreman (#9), Forest (#2), Foster (#2), Fowler (#7),

Foxie (#5), Frack (#3), Frampton (#4), Frances (#3), Francine (#7), Francis (#7), Franco (#3), Frank (#5), Frankenstein (#1), Frankie (#1), Franz (#2), Frieda (#7), Friskie (#5), Frisky (#7), Frizzy (#2), Fudd (#8), Fuddles (#8), Funnygirl (#9), Fussy (#9).

Gabe (#6): M/(Hebrew, French) Form of Gabriel (#9); messenger, Archangel of the Annunciation; God is my strength, God is strong, man of God./Islamic tradition: Gabriel was the angel who dictated the Koran to Mohammad (#5).

At First Glance: Is charismatic; a classic breed with golden coat and a virile, youthful, impressive personality. Appears to be well groomed, kindly, and impulsive.

Day-to-Day: Is paternal, steadfast, sympathetic, nosey, and rooted to the home. Thrives when involved. Loves to accompany humans and work with them.

The Bottom Line: Jealously guards and protects loved ones and wants to be a responsible member of the household.

Quirks of Character: Has wanderlust when sensual; disappears occasionally.

Gatsby (#2): M/(U.S. literature) *The Great Gatsby*, by F. (#6) Scott (#5) Fitzgerald (#9) (1896–1940), a novel set in the Roaring Twenties about a questionable millionaire, Jay (#9) Gatsby (#2), and his love for the elusive and unobtainable Daisy (#4).

At First Glance: Is colorful, attractive, and entertaining. Appears to be happy, hopeful, charming, friendly, vocal, and expressive.

Day-to-Day: Has a talent for subtle manipulation. Is quiet, shy, unassuming, and fussy about details. Thrives in a peaceful, cooperative, sensitive environment.

The Bottom Line: Wants power and is physically and mentally strong. Is motivated to be the boss.

Quirks of Character: Is emotionally aloof and intolerant when misunderstood.

George (#3): M/(Greek) Earth worker (farmer or husbandman)./A word formerly used in communications to represent the letter G (#7).

At First Glance: Is unconventional, striking, and noticed wherever he

goes. Appears to be enthusiastic, seductive, active, likeable, clever, quick, and amusing.

Day-to-Day: Is an attractive, friendly, animated, funny, talkative companion to all. Is interesting, happy, charming, and musical; has a good memory.

The Bottom Line: Is an intelligent and genteel extroverted introvert. Wants to have fun as well as have time to think and rest. Is motivated to investigate and act after analysis.

Quirks of Character: Is changeable when bored; learns from experience.

Gigi (#5): F/(French) Form of Georgine (#8) from George (#3) or Virginia (#8)./(Latin) Chaste.

At First Glance: Is unconventional, striking, adventurous, and undisciplined. Appears to be venturesome, entertaining, friendly, enthusiastic, and colorful.

Day-to-Day: Is always into something new and imaginative. Is curious about things and people. Loves to go where she meets strangers.

The Bottom Line: Wants to be of service and is a skillful, polished companion. Is motivated to help anyone in need; is dutiful, peaceful, intelligent, and brave.

Quirks of Character: Holds on to everything and cannot forget experiences.

Ginger (#6): F/Is number 11 of ASPCA top 30 names./Form of Regina (#9) or Virginia (#8)./(Latin) gingiber for zingiteris./Spicy; red head./The pungent, spicy rhizome of any of the reedlike plants of the genus Zingiber, especially of Z. officinale, grown in E. and W. Indies; used in cookery or medicine./A yellowish or reddish brown or sandy hair./Informal: piquancy; animation.

At First Glance: Is incomparable, distinctive, tinged reddish brown, and unlike any other. Appears to be assertive, aggressive, and independent.

Day-to-Day: Is friendly, cooperative, peaceful, and understanding. Loves music and has a fine voice. Is pleasure loving, charming, and generous. Dislikes being alone.

The Bottom Line: Is adventurous, seductive, and enthusiastic. Wants freedom; is motivated to leave home to meet new experiences. Is easily bored.

Quirks of Character: Is charismatic and attracts admirers wherever she goes.

Girl (#1): F/(Middle English) *Gurle;* child, young person./(Old English) *Gyrl,* as in *gyrlgyden;* virgin goddess./(Latin-German) *Gore;* young person./A female child or young person./A young unmarried woman./A female servant or employee./A man or boy's sweetheart./Informal: a friendly reference to a young woman.

At First Glance: Is individualistic, independent, energetic, and uncommon. Appears to be proud, dignified, and intent upon moving forward.

Day-to-Day: Has good judgment and takes responsibility. Is a vital, stimulating, resourceful, seductive, and daring companion.

The Bottom Line: Is motivated to serve the family and anyone in need. Wants room to roam and a peaceful environment.

Quirks of Character: Talks too much when happy, and too little when upset.

Goliath (#9): M/Biblical reference: I Samuel 17:48–51. The giant warrior of Gath (#9), as a representative of the Philistines, challenged the Israelites to send a champion against him to settle differences by single combat. Young David (#4), fortified by faith, accepted the challenge and killed Goliath with a stone from a sling.

At First Glance: Is indecisive, unassuming, thoughtful, and emotionally uncontrolled. Appears to be able to weigh and measure a situation.

Day-to-Day: Has a talent for seeing an overview of situations, understands human nature, and wants peace. Is imaginative, impressionable, devoted, and compassionate.

The Bottom Line: Is guarded and reserved; enjoys being alone. Wants to remain calm and is comfortable when celibate and undisturbed by humans.

Quirks of Character: Must be taught control; may be dangerous or destructive.

Gordon (#1): M/(Gaelic) Hero./(Old English) Cornered hill, round hill.

At First Glance: Is aristocratic, polished to perfection, and calm. Appears to have an alert, energetic mind and to be sensitive to noise and activity.

Day-to-Day: Is a mature, reserved individualistic companion. Is friendly and kind; values home as a secure base for happiness. Has a talent for influencing humans.

The Bottom Line: Is an introverted extrovert. Wants to be entertaining as well as have a private place for reflection. Is motivated to observe, meditate, and be very vocal.

Quirks of Character: Is a risk-taker and does not foresee the results of his actions.

Greta (#6:) *F/(German, Lithuanian, Lettish)* Abbreviation of Margaret (#2)./(Latin via Greek) A pearl.

At First Glance: Is a classic, graceful beauty. Is skillful, polished, magnetic, and charming. Appears to be understanding, emotional, and youthful

Day-to-Day: Is maternal, caring, unselfish, protective, and responsible. Loves music and is rhythmic. Is a homebody and "people person" who is not happy living alone.

The Bottom Line: Settles in and has difficulty adapting to a change in relationships. Is motivated to learn disciplines and to be comforting and comfortable.

Quirks of Character: Is extremely stubborn and is aggressive when repressed.

Gus (#2): *M/(Latin)* Form of *augere,* "marked by a majestic dignity or grandeur."/August (#8), Augustin (#4), Augustus (#3), Austin (#3); the high or august./(Swedish) Gustavus (#4); staff of the Goths./(F) Augustine (#9).

At First Glance: Is a handsome, expensive, dominant presence. Appears to be strong, willful, energetic, shrewd, athletic, and down-to-earth.

Day-to-Day: Is sensitive, inconspicuous, unassuming, and gentle. Is indecisive and high-strung. Best suited to a quiet, affectionate, one-human home.

The Bottom Line: When comfortable, is playful, amusing, and very talkative. Is motivated to be happy.

Quirks of Character: Does not know how to deal with a strong human leader.

Gypsy (#2): *unisex/*A roamer; from *gipcyan,* variant of *Egyptian,* from belief that gypsies originally came from Egypt./A member of a nomadic, Caucasaid people of generally swarthy complexion, who migrated originally from India, settling in various parts of Asia, Europe, and, most recently, North America./Informal: an independent, usually nonunion trucker, hauler, operator, etc./Slang: a chorus dancer, especially Broadway theater.

At First Glance: Is a comfortable, friendly communicator. Is robust, conventional, steady, and disciplined. Appears to be gentle, kind, and understanding.

Day-to-Day: Is often an inattentive dreamer. Is mystical, sensitive, vital, and nervous. Is a cooperative student, an affectionate friend, and a patient teacher.

The Bottom Line: Wants sexual freedom. Is competitive with children and other pets. Learns from experience and is an enthusiastic traveler.

Quirks of Character: Enjoys solitude; has an air of mystery and secrecy.

See the Number Meanings chapter to discover the traits described by the number that accompanies each name: Gable (#9), Gabor (#7), Gabriel (#9), Gabrielle (#8), Gage (#2), Galahad (#7), Gale (#7), Galen (#3), Gambler (#4), Gandhi (#5), Gangway (#6), Gannett (#9), Gardener (#9), Gardenia (#5), Garfield (#8), Garp (#6), Garrett (#8), Garrison (#2), Garroway (#9), Garth (#8), Garvey (#7), Gasman (#1), Gavin (#8), Gayle (#5), Geraldine (#3), Gertie (#1), Gertrude (#8), Gibson (#3), Gideon (#9), Gifford (#2), Gilda (#6), Giles (#7), Gillespie (#4), Gillis (#5), Gilmore (#7), Gilroy (#5), Gino (#9), Giorgio (#8), Giovanni (#1), Girard (#3), Gladstone (#7), Gladys (#5), Gleason (#1), Glenda (#7), Glenn (#7), Gloria (#8), Glover (#7), Goddard (#8), Golda (#3), Gomez (#3), Gorbie (#2), Gordo (#5), Gordy (#6), Grace (#7), Gracie (#7), Grady (#1), Graham (#4), Granger (#7), Grant (#6), Greeley (#5), Greer (#8), Gregory (#5), Gretchen (#8), Gretel (#4), Grier (#3), Griffin (#6), Griswald (#3), Gucci (#7), Guido (#2), Gumbo (#4), Gumdrop (#4), Gummo (#6), Gunther (#3), Guru (#4), Gussie (#8), Gustavo (#6), Gwendolyn (#2), Gyro (#2).

Hans (#6): *M/*(Germanic form of Hebrew) John (#2); God is gracious.

At First Glance: Is strikingly different and seductive. Appears to be curious, amusing, sociable, amiable, self-promoting, and undisciplined.

Day-to-Day: Has a talent for music. Is a devoted, protective, stable, conscientious homebody and a paternal, loving companion.

The Bottom Line: Is an extremely independent instigator. Is comfortable playing alone and wants to do things creatively.

Quirks of Character: Is selfish and possessive when leadership is threatened.

Happy (#3): *unisex/*From (F. Hebrew) Hepzibeth (#9); my delight is in her./Delighted, pleased, or glad, as over a particular thing./Favored by fortune; fortunate or lucky.

At First Glance: Is sturdy, stocky, stable, conventional, and square. Appears to be unemotional, energetic, strong, and trustworthy.

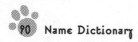

Day-to-Day: Is a multitalented, entertaining, imaginative, joyful, youthful, communicator: Enjoys being friendly, loving, popular, and kind.

The Bottom Line: Wants dominance and is a down-to-earth, self-reliant, polite, intelligent leader. Is comfortable when working and playing zealously.

Quirks of Character: Eats as if it were his or her last meal when emotionally upset

Harper (#3): *M/*(Middle English, Old English) *harpere;* one who plays a harp.

At First Glance: Approachable, sturdy, robust, and conventional. Appears to be affectionate, sympathetic, peaceful, and drawn to children.

Day-to-Day: Is cute, playful, amusing, and talkative. Is a joyful pet who uplifts humans and makes them feel optimistic and happy.

The Bottom Line: Wants to serve and protect the home and family. Is a happy foodaholic in a harmonious atmosphere where he can be devoted and loyal to loved ones.

Quirks of Character: Is highly intuitive and helpful with needy humans.

Harry (#7): *M/*(Teutonic) Home ruler./Nickname for Hal (#3), Harold (#4), Henry (#7).

At First Glance: Is luxurious, dominant, strong, athletic, and businesslike. Appears to be sensitive, responsible, self-confident, and fastidiously groomed.

Day-to-Day: Is quiet, introspective, and focused. Has a talent for thorough investigation and is a calm, silent observer; enjoys being alone. Is not emotional.

The Bottom Line: Is comfortable when vigorously exercised and working. Wants dominance and enjoys competition.

Quirks of Character: Is uneasy in crowds and reacts negatively to noises.

Heather (#2): *F/*(Middle English) *Hathir,* akin to Heath (#6)./(M & F. Anglo-Saxon) The heath or heather (pink, purplish flower).

At First Glance: Is classic, beautiful, poised, graceful, polished, skillful, and magnetic. Appears to be tolerant, romantic, noble, and friendly.

Day-to-Day: Is charming, businesslike, sensitive, high-strung, and affectionate. Is unassuming, vital, harmonious, and easygoing. Absorbs knowledge.

Name Dictionary 91

The Bottom Line: Wants to be helpful, is impractical, and prefers to have peer relationships. Is motivated to be creative and thrives with another pet for companionship.

Quirks of Character: Is an outstanding service pet in times of trouble or need.

Heidi (#8): F/From (German) Adalheid (#8), (English) Adelaide (#5).

At First Glance: Is golden, bright, sunny, friendly, cute, youthful, funny, luxurious, and beautiful. Appears to be an affectionate, entertaining, and attention getting.

Day-to-Day: Is businesslike, efficient, strong, athletic, and dependable. Has talent for solving problems and doing challenging, hard work.

The Bottom Line: Wants personal freedom and is an adventurer. Bores easily and gets into mischief. Does not submit to routines without strong discipline.

Quirks of Character: Spreads herself too thin in trying to be friendly to everyone.

Henry (#7): M/(Old High German) The ruler of an enclosure or private property./(German) Home rule./The name of many emperors, princes, and kings.

At First Glance: Is dark and conventional for the breed. Appears to be patient, respectful, serious, muscular, energetic, and strong.

Day-to-Day: Is calm, quiet, observant, introspective, and regal. Is a loner who enjoys privacy and dislikes being in the center of activity.

The Bottom Line: Wants to be happy and rarely takes routines and schedules seriously. Is motivated to be kind, affectionate, and expressive.

Quirks of Character: Is a closet extrovert who hides and thinks happy thoughts.

Herby (#4): M/Abounding in herbs or grass./Nickname for Herbert (#4).

At First Glance: Is one of a kind. Is a proud, alert, active, self-reliant leader. Appears to be impatient and independent.

Day-to-Day: Is dignified and stable. Learns by repetition and may be slow to follow rules of behavior training. After learning, is steadfast, exacting, and regimented.

The Bottom Line: Wants to play and is friendly to everyone. Is very vocal and has a good memory. Talks and entertains whenever he has an audience.

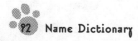

Quirks of Character: Becomes disoriented in noisy situations.

Herman (#5): M/(Latin) The armed./(Teutonic) Warrior.

At First Glance: Is a winner. Is dominant, powerful, expensive, energetic, and businesslike. Appears to be intelligent, approachable, and disciplined.
Day-to-Day: Is adventurous and changeable. Gets bored easily, needs a variety of toys, enjoys crowds of people, and adapts to new places easily.
The Bottom Line: Wants to be the center of an active, adoring home. Is protective, affectionate, and responsible; is eager to be of service.
Quirks of Character: Is a homebody who leaves to find sexual experiences.

Hilary (#1): *unisex*/(Latin) Cheerful./(Greek) The cheerful, merry, hilarious.

At First Glance: Is quiet, receptive, gentle, undistinguished, and "soft." Appears to be unassuming and indefinite.
Day-to-Day: Is fiercely independent, active, self-motivated, and assertive. Is impatient, proud, unemotional, and aggressive.
The Bottom Line: Wants to be dominant and is mentally and physically strong. Is shrewd and motivated to be a winner.
Quirks of Character: Lacks self-confidence when emotionally upset.

Homer (#5): (Hebrew) Literally, "heap."/(Greek) Pledge./Informal baseball reference: a home run.

At First Glance: Is attention getting and playful. Appears to be lively, funny, youthful, and extremely self-expressive.
Day-to-Day: Is clever, inventive, adaptable, changeable companion. Enjoys freedom to explore the unknown and gets bored very easily.
The Bottom Line: Wants unconditional love is becomes spiteful when ignored. Is motivated to bond with one human and is loyal to that relationship.
Quirks of Character: Is extremely empathetic to lonely, sick, or needy humans.

Honey (#4): *unisex*/(Middle English) *Hony:* a sweet viscid fluid, produced by bees from the nectar collected from flowers and stored in their nests or hives as food./A term of endearment for something or someone sweet, delicious, or delightful.

At First Glance: Is sweet, unassuming, gentle, calm, and affectionate. Appears to be sensitive, adaptable, charming, and cooperative.

Day-to-Day: Is an energetic, devoted, dignified, trustworthy worker who loves to dig, perform routines, and keep schedules.

The Bottom Line: Wants an easygoing relationship with everyone and special attention from one special female. Is motivated to tirelessly cling to the loved one.

Quirks of Character: Is extremely nervous and aloof in the wake of confusion.

Hugo (#6): M/(Latin, German) From Hugh (#8)./(Teutonic) Mind, Heart.

At First Glance: Is conventional for the breed, has harmonious colors, is robust and peaceful. Appears to be dignified, comfortable, and interested.

Day-to-Day: Has a talent for music and nurturing. Is protective, sympathetic, loving, responsible, creative, and sociable.

The Bottom Line: Wants to be of service to the family and the community. Is motivated to be a compassionate support for the elderly, infirm, or needy.

Quirks of Character: Is melancholy and depressed when left alone.

See the Number Meanings chapter to discover the traits described by the number that accompanies each name: Haddon (#1), Haggerty (#1), Hailey (#6), Hale (#8), Haley (#6), Hallie (#2), Halsey (#7), Halston (#8), Hamilton (#2), Hampton (#6), Hancock (#1), Handsome (#7), Hanna (#2), Hannah (#1), Hannibal (#7), Hansen (#7), Harden (#5), Harding (#7), Hardy (#2), Hari (#9), Harlan (#9), Harley (#6), Harlow (#5), Harrington (#7), Harris (#1), Hartley (#8), Haskell (#5), Hawk (#7), Hawkins (#4), Hawthorn (#8), Hayes (#4), Hayley (#4), Higgins (#1), Hingle (#2), Hobart (#1), Hobbit (#2), Hobie (#3), Hobson (#1), Hogan (#9), Hogie (#8), Holden (#4), Hollie (#7), Holly (#9), Hoosier (#8), Hoover (#2), Hope (#8), Hopkins (#2), Hopper (#6), Hortense (#5), Horton (#9), Hoss (#7), Houston (#4), Howie (#6), Hubert (#2), Huck (#7), Hudson (#7), Huggins (#4), Hulk (#7), Hunter (#5), Hutton (#8), Hyde (#6).

Igor (#4): M/Russian name for George (#3)./From the Scandinavian, Ingvarr (#8), a hero's name.

At First Glance: Is perfect for the breed. Is regal, quiet, calm, introspective, and classy. Appears to be refined, peaceful, and inquisitive.

Day-to-Day: Is a realistic, practical, devoted, sympathetic, loving, commu-

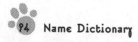

nity-minded companion. Is centered on the home and the family.

The Bottom Line: Wants roots and a stable home. Is motivated to protect, nurture, and provide service. Needs social interaction and responsibility.

Quirks of Character: Understands human nature and is unusually responsive.

Ike (#7): M/From Ikar (#3), a legendary Russian hero /(Hebrew) Diminutive of Isaac (#6); laughter./Nickname for U.S. President Dwight (#8) David (#4) Eisenhower (#4) (1890–1969).

At First Glance: Is unobtrusive, quiet, sensitive, hesitant, graceful, and receptive. Appears to be sweet, gentle, patient, and obedient.

Day-to-Day: Is an aristocratic, refined, quiet, calm, introspective observer. Is dignified, classy, and peaceful. Dislikes vigorous or earthy activities.

The Bottom Line: Has a lust for adventure and sexuality. Wants to make an escape for freedom at every opportunity, and if there is no opening, he will create one.

Quirks of Character: Gets bored easily; needs a variety of toys and experiences.

Imus (#8): M/Thought to be from the Hungarian, Imrie (#9)./Traces back to the Latin, Amery (#8), Amory (#9), Emory (#4), meaning loving one.

At First Glance: Is striking, colorful, and free from restraints. Appears to be a seductive, unconventional, active, friendly, and curious rascal.

Day-to-Day: Is a powerful, businesslike worker and a dominant leader. Easily learns discipline and control, and is a shrewd, independent guardian.

The Bottom Line: Wants affection and is an amusing, happy, entertaining attention-seeker. Makes work into play and communicates lavishly and loudly.

Quirks of Character: Is extremely submissive when loved ones are upset.

Inky (#5): unisex/(Latin) Ink (#7); enc(austum), a fluid or viscous substance for writing or printing./Resembling ink./Black as ink.

At First Glance: Is perfect for the breed; is peaceful, refined, calm, quiet, and self-examining. Appears to be silently observant and introspective.

Day-to-Day: Is a rambunctious, active, curious, sensual freedom-seeker. Has a talent for devising unconventional methods of escape from confining enclosures or situations.

The Bottom Line: Prefers privacy to crowds. Wants a quiet atmosphere and becomes withdrawn when confronted with bickering or upheaval.

Quirks of Character: Is often too preoccupied to bother with disciplines.

Irma (#5): *F*/(Latin) Noble./Nickname for Hermione (#6)./(Teutonic) Female warrior, war god./(Old High German) From Armina (#2), Irmina (#1), Ermintrude (#1), through (*M*, French) Armand (#6); regal.

At First Glance: Is energetic, stable, solid, and physically strong. Appears to be ready to dig right in to get things done. Is slow, sure, square, and respectful.

Day-to-Day: Has a self-promoting manner and makes everyone a friend or admirer. Is quick, clever, amusing; thrives on playing, exploring, and taking on new challenges.

The Bottom Line: Is comfortable alone and may be aggressive when the human leader assumes control and expects routines to be followed.

Quirks of Character: Is extremely submissive with a strong leader.

Isaac (#6): *M*/(Hebrew, Latin, French) Laughter./Nickname: Ike (#7)./Biblical reference: son of Abraham (#8) and Sarah (#2), father of Jacob (#4).

At First Glance: Is slow, sure, careful, and respectful. Appears to be conventional for the breed, quiet, dignified, neat, and unassuming.

Day-to-Day: Has a talent for parenting and is a zealous home and family protector. Tends to be underfoot in the kitchen; is a busybody and loves to eat.

The Bottom Line: Wants companionship and is unhappy alone. Is comfortable in an easygoing, quiet atmosphere with moments for solitude and rest.

Quirks of Character: Is a nonstop talker with an unforgettable voice.

Ivan (#1): *M*/(Russian, from Hebrew) John (#2); God is gracious.

At First Glance: Has a coat of strong, warm harmonious yellow-gold colors; is graceful, polished, skillful, and an impressive, classic example of the breed.

Day-to-Day: Looks for new ways to do things and loves new games and toys. Is an independent, courageous, self-sufficient, aggressive hunter.

The Bottom Line: Wants to do things quickly, is active and impatient. Is motivated to be a decisive, determined, assertive loner.

Quirks of Character: Has temper tantrums when restrained or denied freedom.

Ivy (#2): *unisex/(F)* A plant./(M) Variant of Ivaan (#2), not Ivan (#1), John (#2)./Also called English ivy, a climbing vine; *Hedera helix.* smooth, shiny evergreen leaves, with small yellowish flowers and black berries, grown as an ornamental.

At First Glance: Appears sturdy, serious, orderly, and conventional for the breed. Is cautious, dignified, quiet, and unemotional.

Day-to-Day: Is detail conscious and finicky; tries to create a peaceful atmosphere. Is careful, sensitive, interested in the quieter things. Prefers to be sedentary.

The Bottom Line: Wants quiet and privacy; likes doing things alone. Is observant, intelligent, introspective, investigative, poised, peaceful, and crafty.

Quirks of Character: Problems arise if too many demands are made upon him or her.

Izzy (#5): *M/*(Hebrew) Diminutive of Isaac (#6); laughter./(Greek) Diminutive of Isadore (#8); gift of Isis (#2)./(Hebrew) Diminutive of Israel (#1); contender with God, he who wrestles with God.

At First Glance: Is reserved, regal, quiet, analytical, poised, introspective, and guarded. Appears to be peaceful, dignified, and content to be alone.

Day-to-Day: Is an unpredictable and frustrating rascal. Is frisky, unrestrained, colorful, clever, attention getting, daring, curious, and venturesome.

The Bottom Line: Wants to search for his own answers and is a loner. Feels comfortable in a peaceful, adult, slow-moving household.

Quirks of Character: When emotionally upset, is uncaring and withdrawn.

See the Number Meanings chapter to discover the traits described by the number that accompanies each name: Ibsen (#4), Ichabod (#6), Icky (#3), Ida (#5), Idabel (#6), Iggy (#3), Ignatz (#5), Ilona (#6), Ilse (#9), Immanuel (#7), Immy (#6), Imogen (#9), Imp (#2), Ina (#6), Inca (#9), India (#1), Ines (#2), Inez, (#9), Ingmar (#8), Ingram (#8), Iona (#3), Ira (#1), Ireland (#9), Irene (#6), Irish (#9), Irving (#7), Irwin (#1), Isabel (#3), Ishta (#3), Isley (#7), Ivana (#2), Ivanhoe (#2), Ives (#1).

Jacob (#4): M/(Danish, Dutch, French, Hebrew, Portuguese) Variant of James (#3)./(Hebrew) From Yaakov (#3); to hold the heel, or supplanter. Biblical reference: Jacob (later called Israel [#1]) was born holding his twin brother Esau's (#1) heel; he was the son of Isaac (#6) and Rebecca (#1); and his sons Reuben (#2), Simeon (#3), Judah (#8), Zebulun (#2), Issachar (#6), Dan (#1), Gad (#3), Asher (#6), Naphtali (#9), and Benjamin (#5) plus the two sons of Jacob's son Joseph (#1), Ephraim (#7) and Manasseh (#8), founded the twelve tribes of Israel./Nickname: Jacco (#5).

At First Glance: Is comfortable and robust, not messy. Is conventional for the breed and dutiful. Appears to be understanding, approachable, and focused on children.

Day-to-Day: Assumes that he is in charge of patrolling his territory. Has strength and energy; thrives when busy, disciplined, and kept to a consistent schedule.

The Bottom Line: Wants to study and understand everything. Is comfortable when given time for introspection before taking action and not expected to respond quickly.

Quirks of Character: When insecure, is dependent and follows others.

Jake (#9): M/Is number 16 of ASPCA top 30 names./Form of Jacob (#4)./(U.S.) Slang: homemade or bootleg liquor made during Prohibition./Slang: satisfactory, all right, as in "It's jake with me."

At First Glance: Has beautiful eyes and a memorable voice. Is charming, sociable, entertaining, noisy. Appears to be youthful, trusting, and very expressive.

Day-to-Day: Grows to be a skillful, polished, brave, tolerant, unselfish, classic beauty. Has a talent for understanding human qualities and is emotionally responsive.

The Bottom Line: Is comfortable with a large, affectionate, active family, and has a strong sense for responsibility for their welfare.

Quirks of Character: Is restless and undependable when sexually stimulated.

Jeremy (#4): M/(Hebrew) Exalted of the Lord./Anglicized form of Jeremiah (#6).

At First Glance: Is enthusiastic, colorful, striking, and unconventional. Appears to be self-promoting, curious, fast moving, and undisciplined.

Day-to-Day: Is a dutiful, routine-minded, predictable worker, whose major

talent is to be dependable. Thrives when allowed to plod along and do what is expected of him.

The Bottom Line: Has a dominant streak and is powerful. Is comfortable when taught to do the jobs that must be done and left to do them in his businesslike manner.

Quirks of Character: Wants love but does not show affection often.

Jerry (#4): *unisex*/Nickname for (M) Gerald (#2), Gerard (#8), Jeremiah (#6), Jerome (#3); (F) Geraldine (#3), Jeronima (#4), Jerusha (#1)./Building trades slang: inferior materials or workmanship./British slang: a chamber pot./Slang: a German, or Germans, collectively.

At First Glance: Is unusual, independent, and determined. Appears to be self-sufficient, active, alert, assertive, and intent upon going his or her own way.

Day-to-Day: Is a Johnny-on-the-spot: a reliable and routine-dependent companion. Takes his or her work seriously; wants to know what is expected and does it.

The Bottom Line: Is generally satisfied with whatever he or she gets. Enjoys children and other pets. Doesn't like being alone and likes to do the things that make others happy.

Quirks of Character: Takes things apart to see what make them tick.

Jet (#8): *unisex*/Hard, compact, black coal (lignite) that takes a brilliant shine; polish used for ornaments./A glossy black color./To shoot forward, as a "jet stream."/To strut or walk with a haughty gait; to be insolent.

At First Glance: Is sunny, sociable, entertaining, and very vocal. Has beautiful, expressive eyes and an unforgettable voice. Appears to be an attention getter.

Day-to-Day: Is a powerful, disciplined, energetic, intelligent worker. Has good judgment; knows when to protect loved ones and when to play.

The Bottom Line: Has wanderlust, is flexible, and adapts to change quickly. Is comfortable in a fast-moving, crowded environment.

Quirks of Character: Has a sensitive, emotional nature; is easily hurt.

Jinx (#3): *unisex*/A person, thing, or incident that is supposed to bring bad luck.

At First Glance: Attracts attention. Is sociable, happy, entertaining, decorative, golden, and bright. Appears to be playful, talkative, and trusting.

Day-to-Day: Is rarely quiet; is often very noisy. Has a formidable memory, loves to entertain, and likes humans, pets, lots of friends, and all social gatherings.

The Bottom Line: Is comfortable with everyone and thrives when being of service to the elderly, needy, or infirm. Remains youthful and is brave, loyal, and compassionate.

Quirks of Character: Dotes on loved ones and is possessive and jealous.

Joey (#1): *unisex*/Nickname for Joe (#3)./A clown./(British) A threepenny piece./(Australian) A young child; a young animal, especially a kangaroo.

At First Glance: Is a powerful, sociable, energetic, disciplined, determined personality. Appears to need extensive exercise and room for athletic play.

Day-to-Day: Is a loner who challenges the authority of the human leader. Has courage, is creative with routines, and is strong willed, very active, and self-centered.

The Bottom Line: Wants one human female to adore; is conscious of everything she does and shadows her wherever she goes.

Quirks of Character: Will not play with loud, squeaky toys or crude, noisy humans.

Johnny (#5): *unisex*/Nickname for (Hebrew) John (#2)./Slang: a short, collarless gown that is open in the back and worn by hospital patients.

At First Glance: Is forceful, determined, active, and disinterested in disciplines. Appears to be independent, fearless, and thoughtless.

Day-to-Day: Cannot abide by the rules or follow constant procedures. Has a talent for finding escape routes and has a charming personality that attracts forgiveness.

The Bottom Line: Wants security and needs to use energy wisely. Is slow to learn but will follow procedures when taught. Is routine oriented and will bow to the wishes of the human leader.

Quirks of Character: Is withdrawn, shy, and reserved when emotionally upset.

Joker (#5): *unisex*/A person who provokes laughter or amusement; a prankster or anyone who thinks himself funny; a wise guy or smart aleck./One of two extra playing cards in a deck./An unexpected final fact, factor, or condition that changes or reverses a situation or result completely./Any method or trick for getting the better of another.

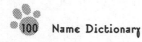

At First Glance: Is happy, optimistic, decorative, and entertaining. Appears to be a kind, conscientious, friendly, chatty clown.

Day-to-Day: Thrives when unrestrained and free to wander. Wants to be active and is fascinated by new things. Changes allegiances easily and makes friends instantly.

The Bottom Line: Wants a cooperative household peopled with sensitive, gentle loved ones and acts needy when ignored. Is spiteful when criticized and may piddle a puddle to get even.

Quirks of Character: Is cold and uncaring in response to disloyalty.

Jonah (#3): M/(Hebrew) Yonah (#9); dove./Any person or thing regarded as bringing bad luck. Biblical: A minor prophet who was swallowed by a large fish, rumored to be a whale, and remained in the belly of the fish for three days before being swept ashore unhurt.

At First Glance: Is teeming with energy, enthusiasm, and curiosity. Appears to be incautious. Looks over all the possibilities and tries to touch on each one.

Day-to-Day: Is a born people-person and thrives with large groups of expressive, affectionate, playful humans. Does not like behavior training or responsibilities.

The Bottom Line: Closes himself off when overtired. Is an introverted extrovert who needs private space and quiet to recoup energy.

Quirks of Character: Does not realize the extent of his strength and agility.

Junior (#6): M/Nickname for the younger of two men with the same name./A person who is younger than another./A person who is newer or of lower rank.

At First Glance: Is stocky, robust, rhythmic, and conventional for the breed. Appears to have tinges of blue in the coat and a comfortable manner.

Day-to-Day: Has musical talents and loves to sing. Is a parental, responsible, emotional homebody who has a need for harmony and a peaceful environment.

The Bottom Line: Needs to be needed. Welcomes guests as friends and is a trusting, compassionate, empathetic, loving communicator.

Quirks of Character: Understands humans and is often a mind reader.

Justin (#3): *M*/(Latin, French, German) The just./(Roman) Justinus (#7), derived from Justus (#2).

> *At First Glance:* Is classic, polished, skillful, graceful, youthful, and handsome. Appears to be tolerant, peaceful, loving, and approachable.
>
> *Day-to-Day:* Is a multitalented communicator and a very amusing clown. Has an excellent memory, acquires a large vocabulary, and demands attention.
>
> *The Bottom Line:* Is comfortable in a lively, crowded, loosely disciplined home. Dislikes to labor over anything and prefers to be less practical and more playful.
>
> *Quirks of Character:* Loves his home but escapes occasionally for adventure.

See the Number Meanings chapter to discover the traits described by the number that accompanies each name: Jackelyn (#9), Jackie (#3), Jacko (#4), Jaime (#2), Jan (#7), Janet (#5), Janice (#6), Janie (#3), Jannings (#7), Janus (#2), Jared (#2), Jarvis (#7), Jason (#5), Jay (#9), Jean (#3), Jeanette (#8), Jeannie (#4), Jed (#1), Jefferson (#8), Jeffrey (#3), Jelly (#1), Jena (#3), Jenkins (#1), Jennings (#2), Jensen (#4), Jerold (#1), Jerome (#3), Jerrie (#2), Jersey (#1), Jess (#8), Jesse (#4), Jessica (#3), Jessie (#4), Jessup (#9), Jester (#5), Jethro (#4), Jewel (#1), Jillian (#4), Jimmie (#5), Jingo (#1), Jo (#7), Joanie (#9), Jodi (#2), Joe (#3), Joel (#6), John (#2), Johnson (#5), Jojo (#5), Jolly (#2), Jonas (#5), Jonathan (#2), Jones (#9), Jonesie (#5), Jordan (#8), Jordie (#7), Jose (#4), Joseph (#1), Josette (#4), Joshua (#2), Josie (#4), Joslyn (#5), Joy (#5), Joyce (#4), Juan (#1), Juanita (#4), Judah (#8), Judd (#3), Judge (#2), Judith (#9), Judy (#6), Julep (#1), Jules (#4), Julia (#8), Julio (#4), July (#5), June (#5), Justina (#4), Justine (#8), Justus (#2).

Karma (#8): *unisex*/Fate; destiny./Good or bad emanations imagined or felt to be caused by someone or something./(Hinduism, Buddhism) Action, seen as bringing upon oneself inevitable results, good or bad, either in this life or in a reincarnation.

> *At First Glance:* Is fluffy, comfortable, robust, and affectionate. Appears to be sympathetic, steady, and drawn to play with children.
>
> *Day-to-Day:* Is a dominant, businesslike, territorial, fierce worker. Prefers disciplines and a controlled environment. Needs regular, high-powered, athletic exercise.
>
> *The Bottom Line:* Wants affection in large doses and clings to and follows

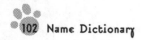

one special human female. Is comfortable in an easygoing, quiet, peaceful home.

Quirks of Character: Is extremely assertive and demanding when hungry.

Keanu (#7): M/(Hawaiian) Cool breeze over the mountains./(Possibly Kikuyu, Kenya) Keanjaho (#2); mountain of beans.

At First Glance: Is quiet, introspective, unruffled, cool, calm, and regal. Appears to be investigative, questioning, and aloof.

Day-to-Day: Prefers to listen and observe; takes action only when sure of the results. Is a loner who thrives near the ocean in a serene environment, surrounded by gentle adults.

The Bottom Line: Wants love and finds it by helping or entertaining everyone. Is comfortable with many friends and rarely bonds with a human or other pet.

Quirks of Character: Wants little responsibility; makes light of everything.

Kelly (#2): unisex/(Celtic, Gaelic) church, a warrior, or wood; from Ceallach (#9), O'Ceallaugh (#4)./(F) Farm by the spring.

At First Glance: Appears to be powerful, mentally alert, energetic, handsome, and self-confident. Is sociable, athletic, agile, and self-disciplined.

Day-to-Day: Dislikes being alone and needs a mate or human companion. Is sensitive, calm, receptive with strangers, and spiteful when ignored.

The Bottom Line: Wants attention and is affectionate, amusing, affable, happy, and very vocal. Has a good memory and builds a large vocabulary.

Quirks of Character: Is cautious; will not be aggressive unless threatened.

Kerry (#5): unisex/(Celtic) The dark./(Anglo-Saxon) The leader./(F) Pure; unsullied.

At First Glance: Is a neat, quiet, cooperative, shy follower. Appears to be hesitant, sensitive, finicky, and content to remain in the background.

Day-to-Day: Enjoys being around humans and is an excellent travel buddy; is clever and mischievous; bores easily. Is curious, adaptable, and virtually impossible to train.

The Bottom Line: Wants to play, talks, jumps incessantly, and is difficult to housebreak. Is comfortable with children and other pets; is affectionate and amusing.

Quirks of Character: Needs peaceful surroundings. Is irritable surrounded by noise and confusion.

Kevin (#7): M/(Celtic), Kind./(Gaelic), *Caomh*, "the gentle and beloved"; from Caoimhen (#5)./(Irish) Little gentle one.

At First Glance: Is calm, neat, unassuming, sensitive, keen, and quietly observant. Appears to be receptive, considerate, cooperative, and shy if approached forcefully.

Day-to-Day: Is an intelligent, observant investigator and a perfectionist. Needs a serene environment and time for rest. Is not recommended for young children.

The Bottom Line: Wants to be mentally busy and gets bored with toys or if too confined. Must be trained to focus on commands and routines; is difficult to housebreak.

Quirks of Character: Is a rule breaker and an escape artist.

Killer (#4): unisex/Classic./One who has a forceful, violent, or striking impact./One who is extremely difficult to deal with and who may cause death or destruction.

At First Glance: Is a dynamic, handsome, expensively groomed figure and a dominant personality. Is self-assured, physically and mentally alert, and sociable.

Day-to-Day: Is dependable, conscientious, serious, self-disciplined, and cautious. Learns routines, sticks to schedules, and requires consistent exercise.

The Bottom Line: Wants stimulating friends and activity. Is dull and listless without a change of toys and the opportunity to run free occasionally.

Quirks of Character: Will bravely defend after signaling when danger threatens.

King (#5): M/Classic./A male sovereign or monarch./A man who holds by life tenure, and usually by hereditary right; the chief authority over a country and people./A playing card./A chief piece in the game of chess./A fertile male termite./God or Christ.

At First Glance: Is striking, colorful, bold, inquisitive, noisy, and quick. Appears to be self-promoting, restless, sensual, and seductive.

Day-to-Day: Has talent for adapting to every variety of human, pet, and environment. Thrives in a constantly changing household with unconventional humans.

The Bottom Line: Wants to roam the country or seashore and to have a peer relationship with humans. Is compassionate and instinctively knows when he is needed.

Quirks of Character: Is a watchful, nonaggressive loner.

Kissy (#2): *unisex*/From Kiss (#4), a nickname for a person or pet who frequently touches or caresses with the lips as an expression of affection, greeting, respect, or amorousness.

At First Glance: Is energetic, strong, muscular, slow moving, cautious, and conventional for the breed. Appears to be serious, respectful, and down-to-earth.

Day-to-Day: Needs company and consistent affection. Is unassuming, friendly, and shy; prefers to stay in the background as an undisciplined onlooker.

The Bottom Line: Wants privacy, quiet, and small groups of humans. Is comfortable in a serene household and is aloof from noisy children and clumsy adults.

Quirks of Character: Is highly intelligent and aggressive only when defending.

Kitten (#7): *unisex*/Classic./A young cat.

At First Glance: Is shy, sensitive, hesitant, "soft," and may be too insecure to be approached. Seems to be reserved and unassuming.

Day-to-Day: Needs quiet, privacy, and a secure space for observation. Likes to think things out. Wants love but rarely shows of affection. Is nervous in noisy, crowded areas.

The Bottom Line: When comfortable, is a curious, risk-taker who learns from experience and wants to be a friendly, entertaining, vocal, surprising, sensual companion.

Quirks of Character: Loves home but travels to hunt or to have lustful adventures.

Kitty (#4): *unisex*/Is number 7 of ASPCA top 30 names./A kitten./Nickname for a cat or (F. Greek) Catherine (#2), Katherine (#1); pure./A fund contributed jointly, for communal use by a group of people./A widow.

At First Glance: Is fluffy but not fat, and has harmonious colors in a coat tinged with blue. Is conventional and appears to be concerned, sympathetic, and parental.

Day-to-Day: Is a talented and strong digger, conscientious hunter, and loyal domestic worker. Thrives in a disciplined environment that runs on routines and schedules.

The Bottom Line: Wants private time and personal space to observe and plan investigations. Dislikes crowds and clamorous activity. Is comfortable alone.

Quirks of Character: Is aloof, skeptical, and crafty when threatened.

See the Number Meanings chapter to discover the traits described by the number that accompanies each name: Kafka (#3), Kaiser (#9), Kali (#6), Kama (#8), Kanga (#7), Kansas (#2), Kaplan (#1), Kappa (#9), Kara (#4), Kareem (#8), Karen (#4), Karl (#6), Karla (#7), Kashmir (#7), Kasper (#7), Kat (#5), Kate (#1), Kathie (#9), Katie (#1), Katz (#4), Kay (#1), Keach (#1), Keats (#2), Keith (#8), Kellogg (#6), Kelsey (#5), Kelvin (#1), Ken (#3), Kendal (#2), Kendra (#8), Kenji (#4), Kenmore (#9), Kennedy (#6), Kenneth (#5), Kenny (#6), Keno (#9), Kenton (#7), Kentucky (#2), Kenya (#2), Kerby (#7), Ketchum (#9), Kid (#6), Kidder (#6), Kiddo (#7), Kiki (#4), Kiley (#8), Kilroy (#9), Kim (#6), Kimberley (#1), Kingsley (#3), Kinski (#1), Kipling (#6), Kippy (#5), Kira (#3), Kirby (#2), Kirsten (#6), Kishka (#5), Kisses (#1), Kita (#5), Klein (#6), Klinger (#4), Knudsen (#7), Kody (#1), Koko (#7), Kong (#2), Kooky (#5), Kramer (#3), Kris (#3), Krissie (#9), Krista (#6), Kruger (#8), Krupa (#4), Kurt (#7).

Laddie (#8): M/Nickname for (Middle English) Ladd (#3); a boy or youth./(Scottish) A boy sweetheart.

At First Glance: Is shy, quiet, gentle, adaptable, charming, and unassuming. Appears to be receptive, cooperative, friendly, and considerate.

Day-to-Day: Is self-reliant, controlled, discriminating, and physically and mentally alert and powerful. Needs firm training and vigorous exercise.

The Bottom Line: Is stable. Wants to love, enjoy, and protect a loving home and family. Is comfortable in a peaceful environment where he is helpful and responsible.

Quirks of Character: Has a very active libido and is self-indulgent.

Lady (#6): F/Is number 3 of ASPCA top 30 names./Any woman who is polite, refined, and well spoken, or who is in a high economic or social position./Slang: a female lover or steady companion.

At First Glance: Is regal, aloof, calm, quiet, observant, and reserved.

Appears to be peaceful, poised, trusting, stoic, and in a world all her own.

Day-to-Day: Has a talent for mothering everyone and wants to be involved in all activity. Dotes on children and thrives in an affectionate, musical household.

The Bottom Line: Is businesslike, self-reliant, confident, and discriminating. Wants to be the alpha of a group and requires a strong leader who has experience with powerful personalities.

Quirks of Character: Is nervous, cold, and deceitful when emotionally upset.

Lassie (#2): F/Classic./(Scottish) A young girl; a young, unmarried woman, little maid./An amazing and beloved dog star of the 1943 film *Lassie Come Home*, and star of the Emmy-award-winning TV spinoff, *Lassie*.

At First Glance: Appears to be eager for adventure and trouble. Is striking, multicolored, energetic, sociable, self-promoting, and unrestrained.

Day-to-Day: Follows her leader's every move and expects lavish shows of affection. Learns easily; is gentle and sweet; and responds to positive-reinforcement training.

The Bottom Line: Wants to be a family companion and to be included in all activity. Is comfortable thinking that everything needs to be tended and protected.

Quirks of Character: Gets snappish when surprised, frightened, or overteased.

Leader (#9): unisex/Someone or something that leads or guides others.

At First Glance: Is aristocratic, quiet, calm, shy, observant, and unapproachable. Appears to be obedient, timid, and reserved with strangers.

Day-to-Day: Is a courageous, faithful, trusting, loving, gentle companion who makes friends everywhere. Thrives when able to roam; adapts to all terrain.

The Bottom Line: Is very sensitive and emotional. Learns easily when taught gently and bonds with one female human. Is neurotic if overprotected.

Quirks of Character: Has a bird's-eye view of the world and is a roamer.

Lenny (#7): M/Nickname for (Germanic) Leonard (#6); lion brave, lion hard.

At First Glance: Is sturdy, square, strong, and friendly to humans he knows. Appears to be respectful, self-disciplined, down-to-earth, and conventional for the breed.

Day-to-Day: Is possessive of his space, investigative, and guarded with new friends. Is a talented, observant tracker; prefers a quiet environment and is uncomfortable alone.

The Bottom Line: Wants little responsibility and a variety of toys; is active indoors and out. Obedience training is necessary or he will not focus on routines or schedules.

Quirks of Character: Rarely hurries and stops to think before taking action.

Leo (#5): *M*/(Latin) Lion (#5)./A constellation and the fifth sign of the zodiac.

At First Glance: Is beautiful, decorative, golden, and attention getting. Appears to take things as they come, is tolerant, and makes humans smile.

Day-to-Day: Is a great diagnostician; always knows who to invite in and who to keep out. Thrives when free from routines and is bored by anything repetitious.

The Bottom Line: Wants to be cooperative and tries to please everyone. Is shy, unassuming, and receptive. Prefers company and becomes insecure when left alone.

Quirks of Character: Is protective and jealous when strangers are near loved ones.

Leroy (#3): *M*/(French) The king.

At First Glance: One of a kind or a first for the breed. Appears to be an independent, unemotional, proud, assertive, and strong-willed loner.

Day-to-Day: Is a talented tease who is rarely quiet and is often noisy. Thrives when the center of a youthful, active family. Generally is spoiled by admirers.

The Bottom Line: Wants unconditional love and personal attention. Is comfortable when treated gently and patiently and never left alone.

Quirks of Character: Needs daily rest periods or becomes moody and jealous.

Lexy (#3): *unisex*/(Latin) *lex, leges,* "law."/Variant of (*F,* Greek) Alexandra (#8), from Alexandre (#3). Nickname for Alexandra (#8)./Nickname for (*M,* Greek) Alexander (#3); defender of men.

At First Glance: Is a classic, polished, peaceful, easygoing, tolerant, youthful, approachable performer who is magnetic and artistically beautiful for the breed.

Day-to-Day: Is conscientious and imaginative; remembers every learned command until death. Loves to get attention for performing tricks and entertaining.

The Bottom Line: Loves people, hates to be without an audience, and is a charming, social butterfly. Wants to show off and is a cute, friendly, talkative companion.

Quirks of Character: Is nervous when confronted with confusion and bickering.

Lily (#4): F/The name of a flower symbolic for purity./Pale, fragile, weak.

At First Glance: Appears to be well fed, dignified, interested, and conventional for the breed. Is comfortable with humans, especially children.

Day-to-Day: Is a strong, regimented, dependable, responsible, disciplined worker. Thrives in a traditional lifestyle with down-to-earth, practical, dependable humans.

The Bottom Line: Is cautious; intelligently investigates before taking action. Is most comfortable when allowed time for daily rest and given a quiet, private space in which to be alone.

Quirks of Character: Is reserved and uncomfortable with crude handlers.

Linus (#3): M/(Latin) Flax./(Greek) Flax, or the flaxen haired./Son of Apollo (#8).

At First Glance: Is a harmoniously multicolored, noble, classic example of the breed. Appears to be groomed, polished, skillful, peaceful, and approachable.

Day-to-Day: Is an amusing, talkative, playful, kind, youthful multitalent. Loves children and games. Thrives with humans who talk to him and appreciate his personality.

The Bottom Line: Wants to be free of responsibilities, schedules, and restraints. Is comfortable when everyone is smiling and he is the center of attraction.

Quirks of Character: Is sensitive to forceful controls and responds with anger.

Lizzy (#8): F/Nickname for (Hebrew) Elizabeth (#7); oath of God.

Name Dictionary 107

At First Glance: Is different, one of a kind, or the first of a breed. Appears to be independent, proud, active, assertive, and determined.

Day-to-Day: Is a talented problem-solver with superior energy, strength, and intelligence. Requires vigorous exercise, is self-disciplined and sociable.

The Bottom Line: Wants a quiet atmosphere, private time for reflection, and leaders who know their job. Is comfortable alone and with small groups of adults.

Quirks of Character: Is intolerant and impatient with children.

Louis (#4): M/(French) Ludwig (#4), from (Germanic) *hlud,* "famed warrior."

At First Glance: Is strong, muscular, energetic, square, and conventional for the breed. Appears to be slow moving, cautious, respectful, and dignified.

Day-to-Day: Keeps everything orderly and is routine oriented. Enjoys digging, hiking, camping, and keeping busy doing physically taxing chores.

The Bottom Line: Likes to roam and takes pleasure being with humans and other pets. Wants to be needed and wanted; is very unselfish and emotional with loved ones.

Quirks of Character: Is incautious and will not back down from a fight.

Lovey (#7): *unisex*/(British) Sweetheart; a term of endearment./(F) Nickname for Love (#9).

At First Glance: Is unconventional, striking, colorful, and unrestrained. Appears to like humans and to be curious, vocal, frisky, entertaining, and flighty.

Day-to-Day: Is a talented investigator and tracker. Thrives with calm, quiet adults who understand motivational training. Needs to have privacy and time to rest.

The Bottom Line: Is comfortable with gentle, sensitive, inactive humans. Dislikes getting dirty or participating in rough games. Appreciates affection and responds with cooperation.

Quirks of Character: Is highly intelligent and outsmarts an inept leader.

Lucky (#9): *unisex*/Is number 20 of ASPCA top 30 names./(Scottish) Nickname applied to an elderly grandmother, a wife, or a barmaid./A person who is marked by good luck or brings good luck to others.

At First Glance: Appears to be self-reliant, confident, powerful, sociable, energetic, and luxuriously expensive. Is businesslike and extremely alert.

Day-to-Day: Is a talented service worker. Wants to be able to roam the countryside or shore, to see the world, to meet as many humans as possible, and to be helpful.

The Bottom Line: Wants autonomy and is comfortable alone doing things creatively. Is unable to follow routines and challenges authority courageously.

Quirks of Character: Will not attack or defend unless sure of the outcome.

Lucy (#7): F/From (M. Latin-Roman) Lucius (#4); light.

At First Glance: Is interested, comfortable, and dutiful. Has a lush, thick coat tinged with blue. Is a responsive and parental communicator.

Day-to-Day: Is quiet, calm, introspective, and intelligent. Enjoys investigating everything slowly and carefully; needs time for reflection, rest, and privacy.

The Bottom Line: Wants to be independent and to work alone within the family structure. Is comfortable showing others the way; is not a follower.

Quirks of Character: Reacts slowly and is never sure she's doing the right thing.

Luke (#4): M/From (Greek) Loukas (#7); of the Lucania region.

At First Glance: Is frisky, unrestrained, self-promoting, and curious, with a striking coat and unconventional features. Appears to be active, excited, and enthusiastic.

Day-to-Day: Is a talented, strong, loyal, dedicated worker who likes routines and schedules. Needs to be trained patiently, exercised consistently, and kept busy.

The Bottom Line: Wants to use his power and energy. Is comfortable with active, athletic, businesslike, authoritative humans and subdominant pets.

Quirks of Character: Has an active libido; runs off for lustful adventures.

Lulu (#3): F/Nickname for names that begin with *Lu.*/(F. French) Nickname for Louise (#9), from Louis (#4).

At First Glance: Appears to be maternal, friendly, robust, vocal, and rhythmic. Is comfortable with humans and very affectionate with children.

Day-to-Day: Is a talented, amusing entertainer; loves to play. Has a good memory for disciplines and tricks. Avoids work and enjoys a variety of interests.

The Bottom Line: Wants to be the center of an adoring family and a welcome member of the community; wants to be needed. Steals snacks whenever possible.

Quirks of Character: Is a chatty, flitting pest when nervous or upset.

See the Number Meanings chapter to discover the traits described by the number that accompanies each name: Lad (#8), Laker (#2), Lala (#8), Lally (#8), Lamar (#9), Lambchop (#7), Lambert (#8), Lambie (#6), Lance (#8), Lancelot (#1), Langley (#4), Langston (#3), Lanie (#5), Lansing (#4), Lanza (#9), Larissa (#7), Lars (#5), Larsen (#6), Latitia (#9), Latka (#9), Latoya (#2), Lauder (#7), Laughton (#8), Lauper (#1), Laura (#8), Laureen (#4), Laurel (#6), Lawton (#4), Lazarus (#8), Leary (#7), Leda (#4), Leland (#3), Lena (#5), Lenin (#9), Lennon (#2), Leno (#1), Lenore (#6), Leo (#5), Leon (#1), Leona (#2), Leonard (#6), Lesley (#6), Leslie (#8), Lester (#7), Letty (#1), Levant (#2), Levi (#3), Lewis (#5), Lex (#5), Lexis (#6), Lia (#4), Liam (#8), Libby (#5), Libra (#6), Licorice (#2), Lightning (#1), Lilac (#1), Lili (#6), Lincoln (#7), Linda (#4), Linden (#4), Lindsay (#3), Lion (#5), Lippi (#8), Lisa (#5), Livingston (#6), Livy (#5), Liz (#2), Lizzi (#1), Lloyd (#5), Lobo (#8), Loco (#9), Lodi (#4), Logan (#4), Lois (#1), Loki (#2), Lola (#4), Lolli (#6), Lolly (#4), Lomax (#2), London (#2), Loni (#5), Lopez (#2), Lord (#4), Lorelei (#4), Loren (#1), Lorenzo (#6), Loretta (#1), Lotha (#2), Lotus (#6), Louella (6), Louie (#8), Loupi (#1), Love (#9), Lover (#9), Luca (#1), Lucci (#3), Lucia (#1), Lucifer (#2), Lucille (#2), Lucretia (#8), Ludwig (#4), Luigi (#4), Lynn (#2), Lynx (#3).

Mac (#8): M/Fellow (#1), Bud (#7); an informal address for anyone other than the speaker./Nickname for any name beginning with *Mac*.

At First Glance: Appears to be introspective, regal, proud, quiet, reserved, and peaceful. Is calm and investigative without getting involved with humans.

Day-to-Day: Is a mentally and physically powerful, energetic, talented problem-solver who thrives on vigorous exercise in an athletic, disciplined environment.

The Bottom Line: Is the alpha of a group and wants to be autonomous. Is sociable unless leadership is threatened; should be watched with small children.

Quirks of Character: Interprets reprimands as disloyalty. Is sullen when upset.

Maggie (#6): F/Is number 23 in ASPCA top 30 names./Nickname for (Greek) Margaron (#6), Margaret (#2).

At First Glance: Appears to be interested in and comfortable with everyone. Is warm, friendly, charming, emotional, unselfish, and tolerant.

Day-to-Day: Is a maternal peacemaker who cannot live with disharmony in relationships. Loves to eat and spends most time in the kitchen.

The Bottom Line: Wants loving neighbors and children to nurture and protect. Is comfortable when serving, protecting, and giving her maternal instincts free rein.

Quirks of Character: Needs freedom to follow her spontaneous enthusiasms.

Max (#2): unisex/Is number 1 in ASPCA top 30 names./Nickname for (M) Maximilian (#6), Maxwell (#9), and (F) Maxine (#3).

At First Glance: Is independent, active, proud, and different. Is a first for the breed or a new creation, with decided colors and unique patterning. Appears to be on the alert.

Day-to-Day: Has nervous energy and is sensitive to reprimands. Is sweet, shy, selective, loving, kind, and thoughtful. Collects everything and bonds with one special female.

The Bottom Line: Wants autonomy and dominance. Is comfortable playing alone; is impatient and hasty. Attempts to be useful and anticipates lavish praise.

Quirks of Character: Is overly protective of family, household, and territory.

Meow (#2): unisex/Classic./(Greek) Miauen (#9)./The sound a cat makes./Informal: a malicious, spiteful, or catty remark.

At First Glance: Is polished, graceful, easygoing, and classic for the breed. Appears to be trusting, interested, youthful, friendly, and wise.

Day-to-Day: Has incomparable charm and is cooperative. Thrives with the close companionship of an affectionate female, is supersensitive, and dislikes being left alone.

The Bottom Line: Is unassuming, sweet, and receptive. Attracts friends, learns easily, and is uncomfortable with rigid disciplines. Is musical and collects small objects.

Quirks of Character: Is quick, curious, and impatient; gets bored easily.

Merlin (#8): M/(Medieval Latin) Merlinus (#3)./(Welsh) Myrddin (#6); sea fortress./Wizard-prophet of Arthurian legend.

At First Glance: Has a sunny, golden coat, with a happy matching personality. Appears to be kind, friendly, playful, vocal, carefree, and entertaining.

Day-to-Day: Is a businesslike, self-disciplined, confident, strong, agile, athletic powerhouse of efficiency. Thrives with active humans who enjoy vigorous exercise.

The Bottom Line: Wants freedom to follow his curiosity; is a sensual, sexual seeker. Is comfortable with changes, adapts easily, and is a good traveler.

Quirks of Character: Loves home but is adept at getting away from restrictions.

Mickey (#3): M/Nickname for Mick (#9), (Hebrew) Michael (#6); who is like God.

At First Glance: Is a poised, aristocratic, introspective, quiet, calm, polished example of the breed. Appears to be observant, mystical, and content to be alone.

Day-to-Day: Loves to play and be the center of attention. Is demanding, frisky, vocal, happy, entertaining, highly responsive, and friendly to everyone.

The Bottom Line: Wants a variety of toys and new adventures. Finds trouble; is restless and bores easily. Is comfortable when unconfined and free of routines.

Quirks of Character: Hides and is secretive when upset by noise and confusion.

Midnight (#3): unisex/Twelve o'clock at night; middle of the night or darkness; resembling night.

At First Glance: Is frisky, sociable, cute, amusing, and beautiful. Appears to be an optimistic, demanding, natural-born ham who intuitively takes center stage.

Day-to-Day: Awakens from and goes to sleep happy, playful, and talkative. Loves to sit in the sun and preen. Mingles with guests, looking for affection; is a fun-loving tease.

The Bottom Line: Wants to be useful and is responsive to anyone in need of help, sympathy, or service. Is very tolerant with youngsters; forgives and forgets easily.

Quirks of Character: When emotionally upset, is spiteful and manipulative.

Mike (#2): M/Nickname for Michael (#6), (Hebrew) Mikhael (#5); who is like God.

At First Glance: Has a lush coat trimmed with blue, and a robust, well-fed, comfortable appearance. Is congenial, quiet, dignified, and attracted to children.

Day-to-Day: Bonds with one special female but is generally cooperative with all. Is shy with boisterous strangers; is affectionate, quiet, calm, sweet, sensitive, gentle, and unassuming.

The Bottom Line: Wants to explore the territory and dislikes being mentally or physically confined. Is comfortable in an unconventional household with active humans.

Quirks of Character: Is extremely sensual; is difficult to housebreak.

Millie (#6): F/Nickname for (Germanic) Millicent (#7), labor strength; for Camilla (#6), from (M. Latin) Camillus (#9), attendant at a religious service; for (Anglo-Saxon) Mildred (#2), of mild power, or alone.

At First Glance: Appears to dislike restraints and to be a comfortable, proud, unique-looking loner. Is active, assertive, aggressive, courageous, and decisive.

Day-to-Day: Is a talented parent and a sympathetic, home-loving, affectionate, peaceful companion to all. Thrives when integrated into all aspects of family life.

The Bottom Line: Wants to do things quickly and is often impulsive. Is curious, clever, and comfortable everywhere; adjusts to changing situations.

Quirks of Character: Likes sex and is off and running when stimulated.

Missy (#4): F/Is number 14 of ASPCA top 30 names./A contemptuous, familiar, or affectionate term of address for a young girl or a woman, in use since 1676.

At First Glance: Has a lush coat of colors that are harmonious with blue; has a rounded, sturdy, robust body. Appears to be rhythmic, understanding, and friendly.

Day-to-Day: Is routine oriented, self-disciplined, cautious, careful, and respectful. Thrives in a loving, peaceful, consistent lifestyle with a socially interactive family.

The Bottom Line: Wants serenity and quiet time for introspective day-dreaming. Is perceptive and comfortable observing rather than taking aggressive action.

Quirks of Character: Makes strangers uneasy until they get to know her ways.

Misty (#5): *unisex*/Is number 13 of ASPCA top 30 names./Indistinct; not clear, vague or blurred./Covered with mist; hazy.

At First Glance: Appears to be intense, aristocratic, aloof, and not fond of the limelight. Is calm, quiet, refined, poised, observant, and mystical.

Day-to-Day: Will find a way to freedom and adventure at every opportunity. Has a talent for keeping humans guessing and finding love in all the wrong places.

The Bottom Line: Wants to spend time alone and is an introspective, intelligent loner. Prefers silence; is withdrawn and shy; and does not make an effort to communicate.

Quirks of Character: Does not adapt into a socially interactive family.

Molly (#5): *F*/Is number 8 of ASPCA top 30 names./Nickname for (Hebrew) Mary (#3); wished for child.

At First Glance: Is different; is tinged with red hues, on a uniquely patterned coat, and is one of a kind. Appears to be independent, assertive, and aggressive.

Day-to-Day: Is a sociable, clever, talented escapist who has unconventional tastes and ideas. When bored or kept inactive, looks for new life experiences elsewhere.

The Bottom Line: Wants to be dependable; with firm training from a patient, consistent, dominant leader, is a constant, faithful, routine-oriented companion.

Quirks of Character: Stays aloof from intimate relationships; dislikes noise.

Morris (#2): *M*/(Latin) Maurus (#3)./(Roman) Mauricius (#6); a dark-skinned military leader./(English) From Maurice (#7).

At First Glance: Is spirited, mischievous, clever, challenging, and unrestrained. Appears to be an unconventional, adventurous, self-promoting politician.

Day-to-Day: Is sensitive, affectionate, nervous, and mystical. Is a caring,

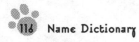

lifetime companion, who is excellent for the elderly and always willing to snuggle.

The Bottom Line: Thrives when an important member of a conventional, food-loving, harmonious family. Is comfortable indoors and stays close to home.

Quirks of Character: Makes housebreaking blunders when ignored or upset.

Muffin (#6): *unisex*/Classic./Is number 21 of ASPCA top 30 names./(Low German) *Muffen* (#2)./A light, spongy, cylindrical quick cake made with wheat flour, cornmeal, bran, or the like, used for breakfast or tea.

At First Glance: Is uplifting, happy, playful, friendly, frisky, and beautiful. Appears to be a goofy, affectionate, inquisitive tease who has a short attention span.

Day-to-Day: Has a talent for singing and loves music. Is a responsible, protective, family companion who dotes on youngsters and scavenges for food.

The Bottom Line: Wants a toy box filled with squeakies and cuddlies and brings them out to play at the drop of a hat. Is comfortable in crowds and dislikes being alone.

Quirks of Character: Has a sexual wanderlust but always comes home.

Muffy (#8): F/Nickname for Muffin (#6).

At First Glance: Appears to be guarded, introspective, finicky, aristocratic, shy, and solitary. Is startled by noise and aggressive greeters.

Day-to-Day: Is a mentally and physically determined powerhouse. Thrives with alert, athletic, energetic, robust humans who expect protection and devotion from her.

The Bottom Line: Wants to be the alpha of a group and challenges the human leader for supremacy. Is comfortable alone and requires consistent, firm behavior training.

Quirks of Character: Is best with adults who do not disturb her nap times.

Mutt (#2): *unisex*/Classic./A mongrel dog./Short for Muttonhead (#4), "a stupid person," based on the notion that sheep are stupid.

At First Glance: Appears to be a courageous, sociable, self-sufficient, agile, athletic, fearless challenge-taker and a dominant personality.

Day-to-Day: Has a talent for making friends and collecting little things.

Thrives in a peaceful home with gentle, sensitive, calm, warm-hearted, sedentary humans.

The Bottom Line: Loves to bask in the sun and wants to play. Is cute, expressive, and vocal. Gets along with children as long as the rule is "no teasing allowed."

Quirks of Character: Wants personal attention and is easily hurt if ignored.

See the Number Meanings chapter to discover the traits described by the number that accompanies each name: Macaulay (#5), Macbeth (#7), Macgraw (#3), MacGyver (#4), Macintosh (#3), Mack (#1), Macleish (#7), Macmillan (#6), Macmurray (#5), Maco (#5), Maddi (#4), Maddison (#7), Madlyn (#6), Mae (#1), Maestro (#1), Magda (#8), Magee (#4), Magnolia (#9), Magnum (#6), Maguire (#2), Mahalia (#9), Maidie (#5), Maisie (#2), Manley (#7), Manny (#4), Manuel (#3), Mara (#6), Maranda (#7), Marcel (#7), Marcela (#8), Marci (#8), Marco (#5), Mardi (#9), Mardy (#7), Margaret (#2), Marge (#8), Mari (#5), Mariah (#5), Marianne (#3), Maribelle (#5), Marie (#1), Marilyn (#2), Mario (#2), Mark (#7), Marko (#4), Marlee (#9), Marlo (#5), Marlon (#1), Marni (#1), Marshall (#3), Martha (#7), Marita (#8), Marjorie (#8), Marti (#7), Martina (#4), Marty (#5), Marvin (#5), Mary (#3), Marylou (#6), Mason (#8), Matilda (#6), Matlock (#3), Matrix (#4), Matt (#9), Matthew (#9), Matti (#9), Mattie (#5), Maud (#3), Maureen (#5), Maury (#6), Maverick (#1), Mavin (#5), Maxim (#6), Maxine (#3), Maxy (#9), Maynard (#4), Mazie (#9), Medora (#2), Meg (#7), Megan (#4), Mel (#3), Melly (#4), Mendel (#8), Mercedes (#9), Mercy (#1), Merton (#4), Mervin (#9), Meyer (#3), Michelle (#4), Mick (#9), Micky (#7), Midas (#1), Midge (#2), Mika (#7), Mikah (#6), Mikki (#8), Milady (#1), Mildred (#2), Miles (#4), Milford (#5), Millard (#6), Millicent (#7), Millie (#6), Milo (#4), Milton (#2), Mimi (#8), Mindy (#2), Minerva (#1), Ming (#7), Mitzvah (#9), Moe (#6), Mona (#7), Monday (#9), Monica (#1), Monique (#4), Monte (#4), Monty (#6), Moose (#4), Morley (#7), Mortimer (#3), Morton (#5), Moses (#8), Mueller (#5), Muffie (#6), Muggs (#4), Muldoon (#4), Mummy (#4), Muppet (#2), Murdock (#4), Murphy (#2), Murry (#5), MuShu (#1), Mutzie (#4), Mylie (#1), Myra (#3), Myrna (#8), Myron (#4).

Nabby (#8): *unisex*/Nickname for Nab (#8); to seize or catch something suddenly.

At First Glance: Is a polished, skillful, shining example of the breed. Is peaceful, easygoing, and graceful. Appears to be self-assured, tolerant, youthful, and impressive.

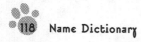

Day-to-Day: Has boundless mental and physical energy. Thrives with a strong leader who enjoys vigorous exercise and athletic play. Is a determined, shrewd protector.

The Bottom Line: Wants to be dependable and self-sufficient; is courageous and confidently takes on all challenges. Is comfortable outdoors with room to run and roam.

Quirks of Character: Is aloof, nervous, and confused when serenity is upset.

Nana (#3): F/(Japanese) Apple (#5)./Baby talk for grandmother, nurse, or nursemaid.

At First Glance: Appears to be concerned with self-preservation. Is alert, energetic, proud, different, bold, independent, and inquisitive; takes the initiative.

Day-to-Day: Is a multitalented, vocal, happy, entertaining communicator. Thrives in an interactive, fun-loving, playful, sociable family; dislike being alone.

The Bottom Line: Wants a peaceful and loving environment. Is sensitive, enjoys being helpful, and integrates into any group in a gentle, unassuming manner.

Quirks of Character: Wants to be the alpha of a group and rejects weak leadership.

Nellie (#3): F/From (Greek) Helen (#8), *helios*, "sun"; daughter of Zeus (#8) and Leda (#4)./(Irish) Helen; light or sun./(Greek) Eleanor (#7); pity./Nickname for (Greek-English) Nellwyn (#6); bright friend.

At First Glance: Is unpretentious, sweet, gentle, quiet, and receptive. Appears to be shy, hesitant, nervous, and approachable.

Day-to-Day: Thrives in a happy, unregimented, friendly environment, with humans who communicate and appreciate an amusing, frisky, youthful, family companion.

The Bottom Line: Wants to do her own thing; dislikes firm commands and routine activities. Is comfortable playing with anything and will have a good time.

Quirks of Character: Gets bored easily and has a short attention span.

Nelson (#7): M/(Irish) Son of Neil (#4)./From (Gaelic) Niall (#3), (Irish) Neil (#4); champion, cloud, or passionate.

At First Glance: Is unrestrained, inquisitive, messy, playful, daring, and friendly. Appears to be clever, funny, charming, goofy, and gregarious.

Day-to-Day: Is an intelligent, talented investigator and intuitive protector. Needs quiet time to recoup energy. Is a picky eater and does not appreciate noise at mealtimes.

The Bottom Line: Wants to be treated with tenderness, diplomacy, and affection. Is comfortable with gentle, sensitive, easygoing humans in an unregimented lifestyle.

Quirks of Character: Needs variety. Returns after leaving home for adventure.

Nibbles (#9): *unisex*/Classic./Gently taking a small or cautious bite./Eating a little of a thing.

At First Glance: Is muscular, sturdy, square, and conventional for the breed. Appears to be cautious, slow moving, quiet, dignified, and receptive to commands.

Day-to-Day: Has a unique talent for understanding human emotions and actions. Is peaceful, youthful looking, graceful, helpful, charming, and very emotional.

The Bottom Line: Wants freedom to roam outdoors and learns from experience. Is always sexually stimulated, is clever, loves new experiences, and is prone to mood swings.

Quirks of Character: Cannot sit still and is aggressive when restrained.

Nicky (#8): *unisex*/Nickname for (F, Latin) *Vera icon,* Veronica (#6); (F, Latin) Form of Bernice (#2); true image./Nickname for (M, Greek) Nicholas (#9); victory people.

At First Glance: Is a first for the breed or very different, with bold patterns and coloration. Appears to be active, alert, independent, assertive, aggressive, and bold.

Day-to-Day: Is a self-sufficient, territorial, shrewd, mental and physical powerhouse who is not trusting of other animals and is happiest as the only pet and sole protector.

The Bottom Line: Sniffs everything diligently, wants to examine every nook and cranny, and is comfortable alone. Prefers small groups to crowds and dislikes noise.

Quirks of Character: Is a finicky eater who will go hungry if necessary.

Ninja (#3): *unisex*/(Japanese) From *nin*, "persevere," and *ja*, "person."/A person trained in Japanese fourteenth-century martial arts and employed especially for espionage, sabotage, and assignations.

> *At First Glance:* Is unobtrusive, unassuming, calm, shy, quiet, soft voiced, and unimpressive. Appears to be gentle, subdued, retiring, and sweet; blends into a group.

> *Day-to-Day:* Is an attention-getting communicator who loves to play with toys and instigates games. Bristles with personality, is amusing, and has a charming, cute manner.

> *The Bottom Line:* Is the alpha of a group and wants leadership. Prefers to work alone and is not very emotional. Overt shows of affection are not necessary to his or her happiness.

> *Quirks of Character:* Is often unfriendly and disinterested in companionship.

Nipper (#6): *unisex*/Someone or something that nips./A tool such as pliers or pincers./A foretooth of a horse./(British) A young boy./(Old English) A pickpocket or petty thief.

> *At First Glance:* Is distinctive and one of a kind; an original. Is dominant, forceful, and alert. Appears to be a bold, assertive, daring personality.

> *Day-to-Day:* Is protective, loving, dignified, disciplined, and responsible. Has a talent for nurturing humans and other pets. Enjoys family interaction and loves children.

> *The Bottom Line:* Wants personal freedom and is a clever, impatient, enthusiastic traveler and a cunning, curious escape artist who bores easily and learns from experience.

> *Quirks of Character:* Is extremely unselfish, brave, and compassionate.

Nolan (#2): M/(Irish) Surname, O'nuallian (#9), descendant of Nuallan (#3); champion, or chariot fighter.

> *At First Glance:* Is sturdy, muscular, strong, stable, sure footed, and square. Appears to be cautious, respectful, disciplined, dependable, and conventional.

> *Day-to-Day:* Is sensitive, easygoing, emotional, friendly, gentle, unassuming, and wants everyone to be happy. Does not like exactitude; loves to be indulged.

> *The Bottom Line:* Wants a quiet, peaceful, serene environment. Is refined and comfortable with a small adult group of calm, sedentary humans.

Quirks of Character: Needs freedom to enjoy an occasional amorous adventure.

Norman (#3): M/(Scandinavian) Man of the north./(Old English) Northman (#4), Norseman (#9), or from Normandy.

At First Glance: Attracts attention. Is hasty, curious, and impulsive; has a striking, unusual coat and unconventional physique. Appears to be entertaining.

Day-to-Day: Has a multifaceted personality, is changeable, and is beloved by all. Is a welcome addition to any group and loves to be involved in human activities and travels.

The Bottom Line: Is a cautious, intelligent, observer in time of trouble. Pay attention if he acts stranger than usual. He is psychic and may warn of danger.

Quirks of Character: Has an overactive libido that is always turned on.

Nugget (#2): *unisex*/A solid lump or mass; especially precious metal./Anything small of great value or significance./A bite-size piece of food, usually batter fried./A Tidbit (#1), a choice or pleasing bit of food or information.

At First Glance: Is friendly, playful, entertaining, frisky, and happy. Appears to be decorative, youthful, and beautiful. Has beautiful, expressive eyes and a memorable voice.

Day-to-Day: Is high-strung, nervous, and sensitive. Prefers to be cuddled and does not like vigorous play. Needs love on a steady basis. Learns tricks and trains quickly.

The Bottom Line: Is a powerful personality and a strong influence in the family or territory. Takes challenges and is courageous, confidant, and determined when necessary.

Quirks of Character: Is hesitant, indefinite, and purposeless when left alone.

See the Number Meanings chapter to discover the traits described by the number that accompanies each name: Nadia (#2), Nadina (#7), Nan (#2), Nanette (#7), Nani (#2), Nanny (#5), Naomi (#7), Napoleon (#2), Nash (#6), Natalie (#8), Nate (#4), Nathaniel (#3), Navajo (#9), Neal (#5), Ned (#5), Neda (#6), Neddy (#7), Neelia (#1), Nehru (#3), Neil (#4), Nesbit (#6), Nessa (#4), Nestor (#1), Nevada (#2), Nevil (#8), Neville (#7), Newbury (#9), Newley (#3), Newman (#7),

Newport (#3), Newt (#8), Newton (#1), Nichole (#3), Nick (#1), Nickie (#6), Nietzsche (#1), Nigel (#2), Nikki (#9), Niko (#4), Nikolas (#9), Niles (#5), Nili (#8), Nilo (#5), Nimitz (#1), Nimoy (#4), Nina (#2), Nini (#1), Nino (#7), Nipton (#7), Nissan (#4), Nita (#8), Nitty (#7), Niven (#1), Nixon (#4), Noah (#2), Nobel (#3), Nola (#6), Nolte (#3), Nomad (#2), Nona (#8), Nora (#3), Norbert (#2), Norbie (#9), Noreen (#8), Nori (#2), Norma (#7), Norris (#3), Norton (#6), Norvell (#8), November (#4), Nowell (#9), Nubby (#1), Nunzio (#8), Nureyev (#2), Nuri (#8), Nyusha (#7).

O'Hara (#7): M/(Irish) A chief's name, descendant of Chief Eaghra (#4), bitter, sharp.

At First Glance: Is a powerful, self-reliant, alert, energetic authority. Appears to be strong, disciplined, enthusiastic, lush, expensive, and exceptional for the breed.

Day-to-Day: Is a talented observer, hunter, and investigator. Is not overly emotional; thrives with quiet, calm, refined adult humans and is happy when left alone.

The Bottom Line: Is an excellent choice for police, military, or guard duty. Is comfortable in a businesslike lifestyle, where his problem-solving abilities are appreciated.

Quirks of Character: Is not overly friendly and is detached from human interest.

Olga (#8): F/(U.S., German) Holy./(Russian) Helga (#6), from (Old Norse) *heill.* (M) Helge (#1); prosperous, happy, holy./From (Latin) (F) Olea (#6), and (M) Oliver (#9) or Olaf (#7); peace.

At First Glance: Is a first for the breed or one of a kind. Is active, alert, self-sufficient, and in control of the situation. Appears to be very independent.

Day-to-Day: Shines as a physical and mental powerhouse and is a keen judge of human behavior. Is a shrewd protector, who requires handling by athletic humans.

The Bottom Line: Wants time to be alone and a quiet, serene space in which to recoup energy and maintain emotional equilibrium. Is highly intelligent and wise.

Quirks of Character: Is humiliated when criticized publicly.

Ollie (#8): *unisex*/Nickname for (*F.* Old Latin) Olea (#6), Olena (#2); for (*F.* Old Norse, Russian, German) Olga (#8), Olive (#9); for (Latin, Italian, German) (*F*) Olivia (#5), Olivette (#9), Olva (#5), Olympia (#1), and (*M*) Oliver (#9), Olvan (#1); for (*unisex,* Hebrew) Ola (#1); for (*M.* Scandinavian) Olaf (#7); for (*M.* French, German, Danish) Olivier (#9); for (*M.* Portuguese, Spanish) Oliverio (#6).

At First Glance: Appears to be friendly, comfortable, understanding, responsible, dignified, and serious. Is sturdy and robust, with a lush coat trimmed with blue.

Day-to-Day: Is a concerned, businesslike worker and protector. Thrives with active, strong, athletic humans who love vigorous play and extensive outdoor exercise.

The Bottom Line: Wants to be obedient, learns easily, and has a kind, gentle nature. Is not happy alone and gets emotionally upset when criticized or reprimanded.

Quirks of Character: Has spurts of irresponsibility when sexually stimulated.

O'Malley (#2): *unisex*/(Irish) Melia (#4); surname, and seafaring clan from Clew Bay in west Mayo County.

At First Glance: Radiates strength and is powerful, energetic, self-confident, sociable, and masterful. Appears to be top breed, expensive, and fastidiously groomed.

Day-to-Day: Is gentle, "soft," affectionate, soft voiced, unassuming, and subdued. Has nervous energy and may appear hesitant or indecisive due to active psychic ability.

The Bottom Line: Wants to be happy, playful, and unregimented. Is not picky and is comfortable with friendly humans who enjoy humor, fun, and being entertained.

Quirks of Character: Has bouts of moodiness and melancholy when lonely.

Oprah (#4): *F*/(*F*) form of (*M,* Hebrew) Ophrah (#3); fawn.

At First Glance: Is robust, sturdy, stable, calm, quiet, and serious. Appears to be maternal, interested, understanding, sympathetic, firm, and conscientious.

Day-to-Day: Is a strong, energetic, routine-oriented, self-disciplined worker. Thrives with a down-to-earth, structured family whose life centers on home.

The Bottom Line: Wants peace, silence, and privacy. Is comfortable with

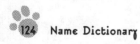

calm, introspective humans who value her intelligence, wisdom, and refinement.

Quirks of Character: Wants to dominate all situations and is an assertive alpha.

Oreo (#8):
unisex/Brand name of a chocolate cookie with white cream filling./*Disparaging:* A black person who is regarded as having adopted the characteristic mentality, values, and behavior of middle-class white society, often at the expense of his or her own heritage.

At First Glance: Is a relaxed, graceful, magnetic, classic example of the breed. Appears to be a tolerant, compassionate, sociable, emotional, sensitive communicator.

Day-to-Day: Is a strong, shrewd, impressive, convincing problem solver, who thrives with active, athletic, hardworking, disciplined humans who exorcise vigorously.

The Bottom Line: Wants to be the leader and is powerful. May be clumsy with small children and must have a dominant teacher. Is calm and quiet unless provoked.

Quirks of Character: Protection training is unnecessary; is an instinctive guardian.

Oscar (#2):
M/(Old English) God spear./(Gaelic) Deer lover; son of Oisin (#3)./Dutch, M & F/Annual award by the Academy of Motion Pictures Arts and Sciences./Represents the letter *O* in communications.

At First Glance: Looks athletic, sturdy, strong, and square. Appears to be conventional, self-disciplined, respectful, orderly, cautious, and slow moving.

Day-to-Day: Is cooperative, affectionate, sensitive, peaceful, and quiet; needs to be encouraged to play or work. Needs people around and expects unconditional love.

The Bottom Line: Wants mental stimulation and a calm, serene, private space for reflection and rest. Is comfortable in the country, away from city noise and confusion.

Quirks of Character: Understands human nature and is extremely brave.

Oswald (#2):
M/(Ancient Germanic, Old English, French) God rule./Nicknames: Ozzie (#9), Ozzy (#2), Waldo (#1).

At First Glance: Is sturdy, unassuming, and plain; does not require grooming. Appears to be cautious, respectful, dignified, reliable, and unable to be rushed into anything.

Day-to-Day: Wants to be loved by all and to do gentle, little things for family, friends, and other pets. Is peaceful, emotional, sensitive, devoted, and easygoing.

The Bottom Line: Is a thinker and needs privacy and silence. Is frightened easily, runs and hides when loud noises sound, and becomes depressed when alone too much.

Quirks of Character: Gets stuck in a rut of routines and cannot abide changes.

Otto (#7): *M/*(Ancient Germanic) Autha (#6); wealth./(Currently Dutch, English, German, Hungarian, Polish).

At First Glance: Is traditional, slow moving, cautious, dignified, and restrained. Appears to need vigorous exercise and to be strong, muscular, patient, and obedient.

Day-to-Day: Observes, investigates, and is reserved. Has determination and is unlikely to retreat or give in. Needs a calm, quiet, private space, and enjoys being alone.

The Bottom Line: Wants to be free of responsibility and needs a variety of toys. Is very vocal and has a sense of humor, a distinctive voice, and extremely expressive eyes.

Quirks of Character: When emotionally upset, wets, blinks eyes, and is bossy.

Owen (#3): *M/*(Gaelic) Eoghan (#5); youth, or yew born./(Greek) From Eugenios (#5); well-born aristocrat./(Welsh) Eugene (#3), from (Greek) Oen (#7), lamb; or (Old Celtic) Eoghunn (#3); or possibly from the Celtic god Esos (#4)./(English, French, M & F).

At First Glance: Is independent, active, alert, self-sufficient, decisive, and different from any other. Appears to be a loner who shows determination, initiative, and courage.

Day-to-Day: Wants to entertain and be entertained. Thrives in a happy, active, crowded household with humans who appreciate a fun-loving, affectionate companion.

The Bottom Line: Wants to work with others and is sensitive to household atmosphere and everyone's feelings. Is comfortable when unregimented.

Quirks of Character: Is nervous and irresponsible when the household is upset.

Oxford (#1): M/A low, sturdy shoe laced over the instep./A city and university in England./A cotton cloth of tight basket weave, used primarily for shirts./Nickname: Ox (#3).

At First Glance: Is refined, aloof, introspective, graceful, poised, and unapproachable. Appears to be intelligent, observant, investigative, and quiet.

Day-to-Day: Is an active, alert, courageous leader who aims to be a dominant force. Thrives working alone, is intelligent, and is not overtly affectionate or fun loving.

The Bottom Line: Wants little responsibility and no rules or regulations. Takes situations at face value and often misses seeing problems. Is eternally youthful.

Quirks of Character: Refuses to adhere to disciplines, is careless and lazy.

Ozzie (#9): M/Nickname for (Old English, Old German, French) Oswald (#2), Os (#7), "god," and *weald,* "rule."

At First Glance: Appears to be aristocratic, sleek, quiet, detached, and inwardly calm. Is peaceful, unresponsive, and introspective; does not want to be touched.

Day-to-Day: Wants to be involved with human activities and to be pleasant and entertaining. Is capable of being a service provider for anyone who needs assistance.

The Bottom Line: Forms intimate relationships and wants to be physically close to loved ones. Is sensitive to everyone's feelings; is thoughtful, devoted, and obedient.

Quirks of Character: Is upset by changes and finds it difficult to adapt.

See the Number Meanings chapter to discover the traits described by the number that accompanies each name: Oakie (#5), Oakley (#6), Obadiah (#4), Obelia (#8), Oberon (#6), Oboe (#1), O'Brien (#9), O'Connor (#7), Octavia (#8), October (#6), Odelia (#1), Odell (#3), Odessa (#9), Odet (#8), Odetta (#2), Oedipuss (#9), Ogden (#9), Ohio (#2), Okalani (#9), O'Keefe (#2), Oko (#5), Olay (#8), Olin (#5), Olsen (#2), Olympia (#1), Oma (#2), Omaha (#2), Ona (#3), Oona (#9), Opus (#8), Oralee (#2), Oralia (#2), Orchid (#3), Orelle (#4), Oren (#7),

Oriana (#4), Oriel (#5), Orla (#1), Orlo (#6), Ormand (#2), Orpha (#4), Orpheus (#3), Orphy (#1), Orrin (#2), Orris (#7), Orsa (#8), Orval (#5), Orvis (#2), Orwell (#4), Orzo (#2), Osbert (#7), Osgood (#3), Oshkosh (#5), Osiris (#8), Oskar (#1), Oslo (#7), Ossi (#8), Oswin (#8), Otis (#9), Ouija (#2), Outie (#7), Outlaw (#2), Ozzy (#2).

Patches (#9): *unisex*/Is number 27 of ASPCA top 30 names./Scraps of material attached to a larger piece of material; used to mend, conceal a hole, reinforce, or decorate.

At First Glance: Is happy, youthful, charming, playful, and beautiful. Appears to be kind, friendly, and amusing. Flits from one thing to another in an entertaining manner.

Day-to-Day: Is peaceful in the house, calm, loyal, brave, and loving. Thrives in a natural environment, and is a fine companion for the homebound, elderly, or infirm.

The Bottom Line: Is well behaved, sympathetic, dignified, parental, comfortable with children, and protective of the home. Loves food and may be prone to overweight.

Quirks of Character: Is aggressive when restrained with loud, angry commands.

Patsy (#9): *unisex*/Nickname for (Latin) Patricius (#8), Patricia (#5) from Patrick (#6); nobleman.

At First Glance: Is fast moving, alert, proud, independent, self-confident, and shows initiative. Appears to be unique and boldly patterned, with red tinges in the coat.

Day-to-Day: Is best suited to service training for the elderly, homebound, and people with disabilities. Thrives in a relaxed, peaceful environment.

The Bottom Line: Wants to manage activities, is shrewd, and has a businesslike approach to everything. Is comfortable with consistent mental and physical exercise.

Quirks of Character: Needs privacy for rest and is nervous when left alone.

Paws (#5): *unisex*/Classic./The feet of a quadruped having claws./Human hands, especially large or clumsy ones.

At First Glance: Is square, sturdy, muscular, solid, and conventional for the breed. Appears to be cautious, slow, respectful, dignified, unemotional, and undistinguished.

Day-to-Day: Is a frisky, sensual, sexual, unrestrained, adventurous, curious, clever risk-taker who learns from experience and lacks concentration. Is difficult to train.

The Bottom Line: Wants to do things his or her own way and prefers being alone to being restrained. Is an active instigator who is forceful and bold.

Quirks of Character: Is submissive and cowardly with a firm leader.

Peanut (#5): *unisex*/The protein-rich pod of the peanut vine, usually containing two nuts or seeds, which may be eaten raw, roasted, made into peanut butter, oil, margarine, soap, etc./A small, insignificant person or thing.

At First Glance: Is an unconventional, striking, frisky, unrestrained, youthful, venturesome politician, who promotes fun, activity, and sociability.

Day-to-Day: Wants freedom and will not be mentally or physically confined. Is comfortable with changes of location and adapts to various time schedules.

The Bottom Line: Wants to roam the countryside or seashore to befriend and be helpful to everyone. Understands human nature. Stays by the side of anyone in trouble.

Quirks of Character: Is spiteful and manipulative when disappointed.

Pearlie (#3): F/Nickname for Pearl (#7)./From the English name for the mass formed in the shells of some mollusks./Birthstone for June that supposedly imparts health and wealth.

At First Glance: Appears to be a loner who looks different, is distinctive for the breed or unique and brightly colored. Is alert, active, proud, self-sufficient, and assertive.

Day-to-Day: Is a happy-go-lucky extrovert. Is a playful, sociable, entertaining companion who loves children and has a diversified variety of personalities and tricks.

The Bottom Line: Wants love from all and a protective partner who is gentle, sensitive, and attentive. Is generally adaptable, understanding, and easygoing.

Quirks of Character: Will fight like a demon when denied freedom.

Pepper (#4): *unisex*/Is number 15 of ASPCA top 30 names./(Latin) *Piper*

(#1)./Pungently aromatic condiment; the dried berry (peppercorn), either whole or powdered.

At First Glance: Is frisky, brightly and beautifully colored, with a decorative coat, expressive eyes, and a memorable voice. Appears to be amusing, friendly, and youthful.

Day-to-Day: Enjoys the stability of routines and disciplines. Is a loyal, devoted, and cautious worker. Loves extensive exercise and wants to know what to do and does it.

The Bottom Line: Wants to be active and indicates alpha authority over other pets. Is comfortable doing things alone and is very creative with toys and responsibilities.

Quirks of Character: Is cold, aloof, and uncaring when unappreciated.

Peppy (#6): *unisex*/Full of energy: lively, bouncy, spirited, and zippy.

At First Glance: Is bright eyed, expressive, and frisky, with a lush, colorful coat and an attention-getting form and face. Appears to be sweet, kind, friendly, and playful.

Day-to-Day: Is conscientious and parental. Thrives as an important part of an interactive, sociable, conventional family. Dislikes leaving home and is possessive.

The Bottom Line: Wants to be with people and other pets; is unhappy alone. Is comfortable with easygoing humans who laugh and play and do not stick to schedules.

Quirks of Character: Has a secret hiding place during household discord.

Pet (#5): *unisex*/Classic./A special loved one./A pampered, indulged, or unusually spoiled or favored child or animal./Someone who is treated with kindness and consideration./A domestic, pleasure animal.

At First Glance: Is a polished, skillful, peaceful, classic example of the breed. Appears to be kind, friendly, relaxed, well behaved, and charismatic.

Day-to-Day: Is extremely curious, clever, outgoing, and active; demands attention due to a dislike for disciplines and confinement. Learns from experience.

The Bottom Line: Wants to do everything, see everything, and visit away from home. If confined, is comfortable looking out a window. When unrestrained, is happy.

Quirks of Character: Is a spiteful martyr when ignored or disciplined harshly.

Pluto (#3): *M*/Classic./Mythology: dark and gloomy side of the Lower World./Son of (*M*) Saturn (#3) and (*F*) Rhea (#5); brother of Jupiter (#9), Neptune (#5), Zeus (#8)./Mate: Persephone (#4). Planet farthest from the sun.

At First Glance: Is furry, flighty, and fun. Appears to be beautiful, colorful, bright, entertaining, kind, gentle, friendly, and happy to be the center of attention.

Day-to-Day: Is a multitalented, conscientious, expressive, lovable companion. Thrives with happy-go-lucky, unregimented, sociable, optimistic humans.

The Bottom Line: Wants to be of service in a peaceful environment. Is everybody's generous, sympathetic, compassionate older brother and the neighborhood guardian.

Quirks of Character: Is an overly possessive, often smothering busybody.

Pooch (#3): *unisex*/Classic./Informal: Dog (#8).

At First Glance: Is magnetic, polished, skillful, graceful, relaxed, and attractive to all. Appears to be emotional, cooperative, intuitive, self-disciplined, and receptive.

Day-to-Day: Loves to play and is not interested in structured activities. Enjoys expressive, friendly, fun-loving humans and is a charming talker, singer, and dancer.

The Bottom Line: Wants to do a variety of things each day and to be free from worries or regimentation. Is childlike and comfortable being an adored, pampered pet.

Quirks of Character: Does not control strength with smaller children or pets.

Pookie (#8): *unisex*/Classic./Nickname, origin unknown./(Irish, Dublin) Slang: malignant spirit.

At First Glance: Is a polished, skillful, graceful, relaxed, peaceful, confident subliminal communicator who appears to be wise and everyone finds attractive.

Day-to-Day: Shines as a dominant, strong, mentally and physically agile guardian. Takes challenges and is a dependable, trustworthy, hardworking, businesslike athlete.

The Bottom Line: Wants to win and requires firm handling and professional training. Is comfortable with active, disciplined, authoritative humans.

Quirks of Character: Mood and focus change rapidly. Must be kept busy.

Precious **(#7):** *unisex*/Classic./(Latin) *Pretiosus* (#7), "from great price."/Highly esteemed or cherished./Obviously contrived to charm or is overnice or overrefined.

At First Glance: Is unpretentious, sweet, gentle, shy, quiet, cooperative, and charming. Appears hesitant, unassuming, patient, and receptive to gentle handlers.

Day-to-Day: Is intelligent, investigative, introspective, and reserved. Has secret hiding places and enjoys silence, peace, calm humans, and being alone in order to rest and think.

The Bottom Line: Wants to learn about everything and is a curious hunter and an unconventional companion. Is comfortable when unrestrained and free to explore.

Quirks of Character: Due to childhood controls, is aggressive when dominated.

Prince **(#2):** *M*/(Latin) *Princeps* (#1), "the first chief."/Member of a royal family other than the sovereign, or the son of a king or emperor./One highly esteemed among his peers.

At First Glance: Appears to be mature, understanding, dignified, interested, and comfortable. Is rotund, with a durable, no-fuss coat that is tinged with blue and silver.

Day-to-Day: Is attentive and tries to accommodate in a quiet, unassuming manner. Thrives with sensitive, gentle, tolerant, humans who appreciate his mystical abilities.

The Bottom Line: Is uncomfortable with mental or physical limitations. Wants freedom to explore the unknown, cannot abide boredom, and has an active libido.

Quirks of Character: Is a seductive, sensual Don Juan who lacks self-control.

Princess **(#4):** *F*/Classic./Is number 22 of ASPCA top 30 names./(French) *Princesse* (#9)./Female member of the royal family other than the queen; the consort of a prince./A woman considered to have the qualities or characteristics of female royalty.

At First Glance: Appears to be expensive, distinctive, and top of the breed. Is mentally and physically strong, alert, and energetic. Has authority and self-reliance.

Day-to-Day: Is a serious, dignified, cautious, self-disciplined, conscientious worker who is routine oriented and who shows little emotion. Thrives in a scheduled environment.

The Bottom Line: When unobserved, is a frisky, adventurous, sexual, sensual seeker of new experiences. Wants freedom to follow her curiosity and learn from experience.

Quirks of Character: Wants autonomy and is aggressive when too controlled.

Pudgy (#1): *unisex*/From the noun Pudge (#8)./Adjective, meaning short, fat, or thickset and plump.

At First Glance: Is attractive to all and is a polished, skillful, youthful, emotional communicator. Appears to be friendly, relaxed, sympathetic, tolerant, and wise.

Day-to-Day: Is a creative, active, intelligent, investigative, alert leader. Enjoys solitary work and play, is not overly affectionate and fights controls and restraints.

The Bottom Line: Is assertive, aggressive, and independent. Is comfortable when left alone. Is courageous, inventive, and wants to be appreciated and praised lavishly.

Quirks of Character: Hides from humans when feeling moody or melancholy.

Pumpkin (#1): *unisex*/(Greek) *Pepon,* "melon."/Large yellow or orange rounded fruit, cooked as a vegetable./(West Indian) Calabasa (#4); green with yellow flesh.

At First Glance: Appears to be reserved, quiet, poised, peaceful, introspective, and regal. Is standoffish and shy with humans. Has a mystical quality and seems wise.

Day-to-Day: Is best suited to independent activities; works best alone and left to his or her own devices and interests. Dislikes restraints and should be watched with children.

The Bottom Line: Wants to be the center of attention and is a show-off. Entertains, talks nonstop, and has an amazing memory, a bundle of tricks, and amusing manners.

Quirks of Character: Is a homebody who disappears for sexual adventures.

Puppy (#4): *unisex*/(Vulgar Latin) *Puppa* (#7)./(Latin) *Pupa* (#9); girl, doll./(Middle French) *Poupee* (#6); doll or toy./A dog who is less than one year old./Reproachful: an inexperienced, impertinent, or conceited young person.

At First Glance: Is beautiful, decorative, youthful, colorfully entertaining, and attention getting. Appears to be amusing, expressive, very vocal, and charming.

Day-to-Day: Is a solid, stable, serious, self-disciplined, busy worker. Thrives in a routine-oriented household where schedules are constant and humans are patient.

The Bottom Line: Wants to be an individual, is purposeful, and tries to do things his or her own way. Is comfortable taking the initiative when leadership is indicated.

Quirks of Character: Is insecure when alone and seeks privacy when crowded.

Puss (#3): *unisex*/Nickname for Cat (#6)./A playful, coquettish girl, or a woman viewed as a sex symbol./A face or mouth./A weak or feeble person./A hare.

At First Glance: Is relaxed, graceful, polished, skillful, and a beautiful example of the breed. Appears to be tolerant, sympathetic, loving, understanding, and peaceful.

Day-to-Day: Loves to play, entertain, sing, talk, and capture everyone's attention. Is unhappy alone, good with other pets, and very affectionate, imaginative, and amusing.

The Bottom Line: Wants to be free of responsibility, is easygoing, flits from one thing to another, and charms his or her way to do a variety of carefree things.

Quirks of Character: Wants to be boss. Is assertive and angry when controlled.

See the Number Meanings chapter to discover the traits described by the number that accompanies each name: Pablo (#1), Paddington (#5), Paddy (#5), Pagan (#3), Paige (#2), Painter (#2), Paisley (#6), Pal (#2), Palmer (#2), Paloma (#4), Palomino (#5), Pam (#3), Pamela (#3), Pammy (#5), Pan (#4), Panda (#9), Pandora (#6), Panther (#1), Papa (#7), Pappy (#2), Paprika (#1), Paris (#9), Parish (#8), Parker (#6), Parnell (#6), Parry (#6), Pat (#1), Patch (#3), Pati (#1), Patience (#1), Patrice (#9), Patricia (#5), Patrick (#6), Paul (#5), Paula (#6),

Paulette (#1), Pauli (#5), Paulina (#2), Pauline (#6), Pavlova (#8), Pawlina (#4), Pawnee (#1), Paxton (#9), Peabody (#5), Peanuts (#6), Pearcy (#5), Pearl (#7), Pearla (#8), Pebbles (#7), Pedro (#4), Peepers (#3), Peggy (#6), Pele (#2), Pendleton (#6), Penelope (#7), Penrod (#9), Peony (#3), Pepi (#1), Pepita (#4), Pepito (#9), Perceval (#4), Percy (#4), Perlie (#2), Pesky (#4), Pete (#1), Peter (#1), Petey (#8), Petrice (#4), Petula (#3), Petunia (#5), Peyton (#5), Phantom (#6), Pheobe (#6), Philie (#5), Philip (#7), Phineas (#9), Phoebe (#6), Phoenix (#1), Phyllis (#2), Pia (#8), Piccolo (#1), Picket (#1), Pickles (#3), Pierpont (#5), Pierre (#8), Piggy (#1), Piglet (#6), Pilar (#2), Pilot (#9), Pinkerton (#5), Pinky (#3), Pinto (#2), Pip (#5), Piper (#1), Pirate (#6), Pisces (#8), Pistol (#1), Plato (#1), Plucky (#7), Poco (#4), Pogo (#8), Poindexter (#4), Pointer (#7), Pokey (#9), Pollack (#7), Polly (#8), Polo (#4), Poncho (#8), Popeye (#1), Porgy (#9), Porter (#2), Portnoy (#6), Potsie (#3), Prancer (#3), Presley (#1), Preston (#8), Pretty (#5), Prez (#2), Priscilla (#9), Prissy (#7), Prophet (#8), Prowler (#8), Pru (#1), Prudence (#5), Pryor (#2), Pucci (#7), Puck (#6), Puff (#4), Puffer (#9), Pugsly (#1), Punky (#6), Purrfect (#8), Purrlie (#9), Purrly (#2), Pushkin (#8), Pyewackett (#3), Pygmalion (#4).

Queenie (#4): F/Classic./Nickname for Queen (#8); a female sovereign ruler, the wife or widow of a king, a woman eminent in power or attractions./A female cat./The only fertile female in a colony of social insects (ants, bees, termites) whose function is to lay eggs./A promoted, powerful chess pawn./A picture playing card./(British) Rock music group./(French) La (#4) Reine (#6), "the queen"; nickname for Franz (#2) Joseph (#1) Hadyn (#7)'s Symphony no. 85 in B-flat Major in honor of Queen Marie (#1) Antoinette (#6).

At First Glance: Is unpretentious, conventional, and does not require grooming. Appears to be patient, sturdy, strong, dignified, stable, and self-disciplined.

Day-to-Day: Thrives in a well-organized routine and is dependable, devoted, loyal, and enduring. Has energy, wants to be of service, and works hard at everything.

The Bottom Line: Is empathetic with other pets and understands human nature. Wants to be a heroine in times of need and is comfortable in a natural environment.

Quirks of Character: Changes loyalties when bored. Is impatient when upset.

Quentin (#1): *M/*(Latin) Fifth./*(F)* Quinta (#1); five, fifth child.

At First Glance: Appears to be plain, a bit plump, shy, quiet, hesitant, and unassuming. Is receptive to friendliness; has a soft voice and gentle manner.

Day-to-Day: Is an active, alert, independent alpha who assumes leadership and requires firm authority. Thrives working alone; is forceful and assertive.

The Bottom Line: Wants to be sure that anyone entering the house or near loved ones is not a threat; if challenged, is a shrewd, powerful, courageous defender.

Quirks of Character: Has a lively libido and takes off for a romp occasionally.

Quimby (#6): *M/*(Old Norse) At the mother's house.

At First Glance: Is striking, unconventional, unrestrained, and frisky. Appears to be curious, youthful, mischievous, self-promoting, vocal, and friendly to all.

Day-to-Day: Is a parental communicator who gets involved in household and neighborhood activity. Nurtures children and assumes responsibility for their welfare.

The Bottom Line: Is a creative, courageous, assertive leader who is difficult to train. Is comfortable being the boss, wants autonomy, and vies for dominance.

Quirks of Character: Is highly intuitive. Warns of incoming storms or danger.

Quincy (#8): *M/*(Norman) Baronial surname, derived from (Latin) Quintus (#4); fifth.

At First Glance: Appears to be a loner who is groomed, controlled, and perfect for the breed. Is aristocratic, reserved, quiet, calm, poised, introspective, and aloof.

Day-to-Day: Is a mentally and physically powerful, poised, shrewd, courageous leader and guardian. Thrives with extensive exercise and strong, athletic humans.

The Bottom Line: Wants independence and to do things alone. Is comfortable taking the lead and directing his efforts. Is not friendly and is disinterested in socializing.

Quirks of Character: Is fearful and melancholy if left alone too long.

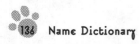

Quinley (#4): *M/*(Irish Gaelic) From Quinlin (#6), powerful one.

At First Glance: Appears to be a bold, spirited, self-promoting politician. Is striking, unconventional, messy, mischievous, restless, and looking for attention.

Day-to-Day: Has strength, energy, and self-discipline. Thrives in a conventional, routine-oriented, slow-moving environment with calm, predictable humans.

The Bottom Line: Wants vigorous exercise, work, and athletic play. Is comfortable and sociable with active adults and children. Needs consistent, confident leadership.

Quirks of Character: Is nervous and withdrawn amidst noise and confusion.

Quinn (#3): *M/*(Irish) Surname, O'Cuinn (#4); descendent of Cuinn (#7)./From (*M.* Gaelic, Celtic) Conn (#1); wise leader, or council.

At First Glance: Has a neat, impressive coat of harmonious colors and is a classic example of the breed. Appears to be relaxed, sociable, tolerant, and attractive to all.

Day-to-Day: Is a playful, happy, optimistic, friendly, vocal entertainer. Brings out the child in everyone. Thrives in a busy, crowded, fun-loving environment.

The Bottom Line: Wants to make everyone love him and is always interested and expressive. Is comfortable when unregimented and doing a variety of things.

Quirks of Character: Is very impatient and lacks concentration for training.

See the Number Meanings chapter to discover the traits described by the meanings of names that follow: Quaggy (#6), Quasi (#4), Quasimodo (#6), Quayle (#9), Queasy (#7), Quebec (#8), Queeny (#6), Quibbler (#5), Quiche (#9), Quicken (#8), Quickie (#3), Quico (#2), Quigley (#6), Quillan (#5), Quinella (#1), Quinette (#3), Quint (#9), Quintina (#6), Quipster (#8), Quirkie (#9), Quizzie (#5).

Rags (#9): *unisex/*(Scandinavian) Rough hair./Old or worn clothes; torn, frayed or woven scraps of material; tattered pieces of cloth./Derogatory: tabloid newspapers, something of low value or in poor condition./Slang: fashion industry products and nautical sails./(British) College students' boisterous practical jokes.

At First Glance: Appears to be mentally and physically powerful, dominating, businesslike, and energetic. Is impressive, expensive, and a healthy example of the breed.

Day-to-Day: Understands everybody and everything and is accepted as a peer by humans. Is an empathetic service worker for the needy, elderly, lonely, or disabled.

The Bottom Line: Wants to do things creatively and responds to commands in unique ways if at all. Is independent, self-sufficient, and able to detach from emotions.

Quirks of Character: Clings to commanding leaders and is submissive.

Rambo (#4): *M/A* fanatically militant or violently aggressive person./Fictional character: *First Blood* (1972), by David (#4) Morrell (#7), depicted on film by Sylvester (#1) Stallone (#8)./Acronym: **R**otten **A**ctor, **M**ucho **B**ox **O**ffice./Slang: heroin (#6).

At First Glance: Is full bodied, robust, strong, conventional for the breed, and walks with a rhythmic gait. Appears to be interested, sympathetic, tolerant, and patient.

Day-to-Day: Is systematized, thorough, loyal, routine oriented, practical, cautious, and dependable. Enjoys energetic digging and work that produces tangible results.

The Bottom Line: Wants private time and a quiet space for rest and reflection. Is intelligent, calm, intuitive, guarded, and works well alone or with small adult groups.

Quirks of Character: Is overly protective and bossy when emotionally upset.

Rascal (#9): *unisex*/A deceitful, unreliable, unscrupulous person or a trickster; a playful, mischievous person or animal.

At First Glance: Is a self-examining, quiet, reflective, and introspective observer. Appears to be patient, tolerant, and aristocratic while examining nature, not people.

Day-to-Day: Is friendly, understanding, and unselfish. Thrives when trained to serve disabled, lonely humans in need of assistance. Attracts friends and recognition.

The Bottom Line: Wants to stay out of the limelight and is sensitive, unassuming, shy, and helpful. Is comfortable with one partner and is an affectionate friend.

Quirks of Character: Has an unusual voice and is too chatty when nervous.

Red (#9): *unisex/*(Latin) *Ruber* (#3), *rufus* (#4)./Various hues resembling
the color of tomatoes, blood, strawberries, rust, etc.

At First Glance: Appears to be a self-disciplined, serious, sturdy worker. Is muscular, square, and quietly dignified. Has an unemotional, cautious approach.

Day-to-Day: Is loved and appreciated for showing unselfish, compassionate service to all. Cares very little for routines and disciplines. Follows his or her heart.

The Bottom Line: Is a friendly charmer who wants to meet new people and experiences. Travels with ease, learns from experience, and makes changes comfortably.

Quirks of Character: Has unexpressed hostility and fights when restricted.

Rex (#2): M/Classic./(Latin) King (#5).

At First Glance: Is a robust, rhythmic, average-for-the-breed, happy communicator who appears to be concerned with children, friendly to adults, and helpful to all.

Day-to-Day: Bonds with one special female and is an affectionate, peaceful, sensitive partner for life. Thrives with gentle handling and is a good student.

The Bottom Line: Loves to be outdoors and enjoys unrestricted freedom to follow his curiosity. Is sensual, sexual, and prone to occasional travels and surprising escapades.

Quirks of Character: When upset, is stubborn, overprotective, and possessive.

Ringo (#9): M/Beatles (#1) drummer and actor, Ringo Starr (#4), born
Richard (#7) Starkey (#9) (July 7, 1940).

At First Glance: Is fun loving, frisky, cute, youthful, self-expressive, and unrestrained. Appears to be colorful, brightly embellished, and attention getting.

Day-to-Day: Is an understanding, thoughtful, sympathetic "big brother" and friend to all. Understands human nature, is generous with affection, and rarely meets a stranger.

The Bottom Line: Wants a stable, harmonious, socially interactive home and to be involved in community activities. Is comfortable with groups and dislikes being alone.

Quirks of Character: Blinks eyes, is self-insistent, and suspicious when upset.

Rin Tin Tin (#1): M/Classic./Radio, TV, movie character (c. 1920s through 1990s): German (#4) Shepherd (#2), heroic dog of the Old West./Small boy companion, Rusty (#4)./Nickname: Rinty (#5).

At First Glance: Is different, one of a kind, or a first. Appears to be alert, active, independent, intelligent, self-confident, strong willed, assertive, and forceful.

Day-to-Day: Is a quick-acting, self-motivated individual who won't follow anyone around the house or allow strangers into his territory without a challenge or his approval.

The Bottom Line: Understands human frailty and wants to be of service to anyone in need. Is comfortable as a companion or aid to an elderly, handicapped, or lonely human.

Quirks of Character: Forgets responsibilities to follow his lust or curiosity.

Rizzo (#4): unisex/(Italian) Surname, from Ricco (#3); curly, a curly haired person.

At First Glance: Is a guarded, introspective, quiet, calm, reserved loner. Appears to be intelligent, poised, wise, observant, cautious, and finicky.

Day-to-Day: Is a down-to-earth, strong, hard-working, routine-oriented, and dignified schedule-watcher, who keeps busy detailing the home and guarding the territory.

The Bottom Line: Wants stability and a harmonious, understanding, conscientious, sociable, homebound, musical family to love, protect, and comfort.

Quirks of Character: Assumes too much responsibility and is overly possessive.

Rocket (#9): unisex/(Italian) Rocchetta (#3)./(Germanic origin) Rocca (#4); a distaff, rock (#2)./Artificial firework used as a projectile for various purposes./Any vehicle propelled by a rocket engine./To rise straight up./Blunt lance head used in a joust./A plant remarkable for its evening fragrance.

At First Glance: Is indifferent to humans and observes the environment.

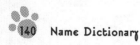

Appears to be a sleek, quiet, calm, introspective, cautious, shy, aristocratic loner.

Day-to-Day: Has an understanding of human emotions, activities, and weaknesses. Is brave, loving, and compassionate. May be trained to serve handicapped humans.

The Bottom Line: Is sensitive, affectionate, and gentle. Wants one-to-one companionship; is friendly, charming, and adaptable; and dislikes being alone.

Quirks of Character: When ignored or slighted, is sulky, apathetic, and sly.

Rocky (#9): M/Is number 26 of ASPCA top 30 names./Nickname for tough individualists or bodybuilders./A physical, unemotional, hard person./Abounding in rocks./Shaky./Having a trying time.

At First Glance: Is unconventional and striking, with unusual patterns and a colorful coat. Appears to be curious, clever, charming, friendly, adaptable, quick, and changeable.

Day-to-Day: Thrives when able to roam and befriend neighbors. Is a sociable, sympathetic, generous, compassionate, sentimental do-gooder and a brave defender.

The Bottom Line: Is routine oriented, patient, devoted, dignified, trustworthy, and enduring. Is comfortable being told what to do and working to do the right thing.

Quirks of Character: Makes himself scarce and hides until loud noises or crude handlers disappear.

Rover (#6): M/Classic./(Middle English from Middle Dutch) *Roven,* "to rob."/A pirate./Someone who is inconsistent, leads a changeable life, or alters positions in a game or sport.

At First Glance: Approaches with caution and is a sturdy, muscular, square, conventional example of the breed. Is unemotional, serious, disciplined, and respectful.

Day-to-Day: Responds to affectionate, sympathetic, responsible humans and is a homebody who shares an interest in all activities. Dislikes being left alone.

The Bottom Line: Wants to be helpful, is unpretentious, and has a strong desire for peace and harmony. Is a comfortable follower who expects to be kept clean and neat.

Quirks of Character: Responds to neediness with compassion or disdain.

Ruff (#6): *unisex*/Classic./A unique collar on the neck of an animal, bird, or fish; an old-fashioned tight collar./Game, similar to whist (#7)./Synonym: trump (#7), as in cards./Low, vibrating beat of a drum./To exhibit pride or haughtiness./Slang: a good, excellent person.

At First Glance: Is eager to play and make friends. Approaches happily, confident that he or she is welcome. Appears to be decorative, fluffy, frivolous, and beautiful.

Day-to-Day: Is a serious, protective homebody and guardian. Enjoys being part of a close-knit, harmonious, sociable family. Thrives on caring for children and other pets.

The Bottom Line: Wants to be free of repetitious patterns and rigid disciplines. Is easygoing, comfortable, and entertaining when talking, creating games, and being happy-go-lucky.

Quirks of Character: Acts like an anxious martyr when following commands.

Rusty (#4): *unisex*/Classic./Is number 29 of ASPCA top 30 names./Nickname for (*M,* Old French) Rousel (#9), little red; or (English) Russell (#7); or a person with red hair or a ruddy complexion./The surface condition of iron or steel when a reddish brown, reddish yellow, yellowish red rust-fungus results from oxidation after iron or steel is exposed to air and moisture./Dulled in color by age or use./A person whose skills decline due to neglect or misuse and is stiff, inept, or slow.

At First Glance: Is brightly colored, cute, friendly, decorative, and fluffy. Attracts admirers due to his or her attention-getting, vocally and physically expressive manner.

Day-to-Day: Likes to keep busy and is routine and schedule oriented. Is devoted, serious, patient, cautious, trustworthy, and initially slow to learn or follow commands.

The Bottom Line: Wants to dominate. Is motivated to do things his or her own way and needs constant control. Responds to praise and is unemotional about food.

Quirks of Character: Goes to a secret space to avoid noise and confusion.

See the Number Meanings chapter to discover the traits described by the number that accompanies each name: Rabbi (#5), Rabbit (#7), Racer (#9), Rachel (#2), Radcliffe (#1), Rae (#6), Rafferty (#9), Raffi (#4), Raider (#1),

Rake (#8), Raleigh (#6), Rally (#5), Ralph (#1), Rambler (#6), Ramon (#7), Ramona (#8), Ramsey (#9), Randall (#8), Randy (#8), Rani (#6), Raphael (#7), Rapunzel (#5), Raquel (#2), Rasputin (#1), Raven (#6), Ray (#8), Raymond (#9), Reba (#8), Rebecca (#1), Redd (#4), Redford (#7), Reeves (#2), Regan (#9), Regent (#6), Reggie (#6), Regina (#9), Reginald (#7), Regis (#4), Reigner (#4), Reilly (#9), Remus (#4), Rennie (#2), Reno (#7), Reuben (#2), Rhea (#5), Rhett (#8), Ribbons (#7), Ricardo (#5), Richard (#7), Rick (#5), Ricky (#3), Riddler (#7), Rigby (#7), Rikki (#4), Riler (#8), Riley (#6), Rio (#6), River (#9), Roamer (#7), Robbie (#6), Roberta (#7), Robin (#4), Robyn (#2), Rocco (#9), Roddy (#3), Rodney (#9), Roger (#9), Rogue (#3), Rojo (#4), Roland (#1), Rolf (#6), Rollie (#8), Rollo (#9), Romulus (#2), Ronald (#1), Ronda (#7), Ronnie (#3), Rosco (#7), Roscoe (#3), Rose (#3), Rosey (#1), Rosie (#3), Rosita (#1), Ross (#8), Rowdy (#4), Roxi (#3), Roy (#4), Rubin (#1), Ruby (#3), Rudolf (#4), Rudolph (#4), Rudy (#5), Rufus (#4), Ruggles (#8), Runner (#9), Runyon (#8), Rupert (#8), Russ (#5), Russell (#7), Ruthie (#9), Ryan (#4).

Sam (#6): *unisex*/Is number 2 of ASPCA top 30 names./Nickname for (M. Hebrew) Shimshon (#6), Samson (#9); sun (mate: Delilah [#6]; the delicate)./(M. Hebrew) Shemuel (#2), Samael (#6), and Samuel (#8); name of God, or God has heard./(F. Hebrew) Samala (#2), Samuela (#9); his name is El (God)./(F. Hebrew) Samara (#8); a guardian or caretaker./(F. Aramaic) Samantha (#5); the listener./(F. Arabic) Sama (#7), generosity; Samira (#7), lively conversationalist; Samiya (#5), elevated./(M. Arabic) Sami (#6), lofty; Samir (#6), partner; Samy (#4), sublime or hears./(M. Arabic) Sami (#6); listener./(M. Greek) Samouel (#5)./(M. Italian) Samuele (#4).

> **At First Glance:** Appears to be seductive, self-promoting, and striking. Is a friendly, enthusiastic, curious, noisy, quick, changeable, affectionate, attention-getting tease.
> **Day-to-Day:** Likes to be held, hugged, and stroked, and to be involved in all household and community activities. Is keeper of the kitchen and parent to all.
> **The Bottom Line:** Is independent, assertive, and bossy; does not want to be restrained. Is motivated to fight when challenged but cuddles soon after.
> **Quirks of Character:** Is routine oriented and confused when schedules change.

Samantha (#5): F/Is number 19 of ASPCA top 30 names./(Aramaic) The listener./Variations: Samanthe (#9), Samanthi (#4), Samanthia (#5), Samanthy

(#2), Samatha (#9), Samella (#9), Sammantha (#9), Symantha (#2)./Nicknames: Sam (#6), Sammi (#1), Sammie (#6), Sammy (#8).

At First Glance: Is unassuming, unpretentious, hesitant, shy, and content to wait to be noticed. Appears to be sensitive, docile, sweet, undemanding, cuddly, and receptive.

Day-to-Day: Loves being outdoors. Does not know the meaning of caution and tempts fate with her curiosity. Is unpredictable and full of life, boundless energy, and charm.

The Bottom Line: Wants to play, flirt, tease, and avoid work or responsibility. Is motivated to talk incessantly and attract attention; entertains at the drop of a hat.

Quirks of Character: Is extremely independent and refuses to be controlled.

Sandy (#9): *unisex*/Color of sand./Nickname for (F) Alexandra (#8), originated from Greek goddess Hera (#5) and *alexein* (#7), "to defend"; for (M) Alexander (#3), Alexandros (#5); defender of men./(F, Spanish) Cassandra (#8), from (Greek) Kassandra (#7)./Sandra (#3); nickname for Alessandra (#4) (F, Italian), Alexander (#3)./(M, Scottish) Alexander./(British) Sanborn (#2), Sanborne (#7), from the sandy brook; Sanford (#5), from the sandy ford; Santon (#2), from the sandy farm./Variations: Sandee (#3), Sandi (#2), Sandie (#7), Sandya (#1), Sandye (#5)./(F, Irish) Tawney (#7); warm, sandy color of a lion's coat.

At First Glance: Is brightly colored, alert, active, forceful, one of a kind, a first for the breed, or just different. Appears to be a bold, assertive, self-sufficient loner.

Day-to-Day: Seems to be an understanding, compassionate, unselfish peer to humans. Is depended upon to oversee the family welfare and the neighborhood activity.

The Bottom Line: Wants to take charge and is a dynamic personality. Needs consistent exercise and dislikes taking a backseat while someone else leads the way.

Quirks of Character: Cannot cope with loud, rude humans or disorganization.

Scamp (#7): *unisex*/Classic./(Old French) *escamper*, "to run away."/A rascal; a mischievous person./One who does things superficially or is neglectful.

At First Glance: Appears to be serious, responsible, and conscientious.

Has a lush coat trimmed with blue, and is comfortable and interested in humans and other pets.

Day-to-Day: Prefers a quiet, reflective lifestyle. Is not inclined to vigorous activity. Is a dignified, refined, intelligent, questioning, peaceful, and investigative aristocrat.

The Bottom Line: Wants autonomy and dislikes regimentation. Is motivated to do things creatively and is assertive when too restricted. Does not take commands well.

Quirks of Character: Seems aloof and is terrified when left alone too long.

Scooter (#5): *unisex*/Classic./Nickname for someone who walks fast, makes swift, darting or high speed movements./A child's foot-operated, two-wheeled vehicle.

At First Glance: Is robust, with a conventional, harmoniously colored lush coat tinged with blue. Appears to be quiet, mature, interested, and responsive to children.

Day-to-Day: Is a free spirit. Is a rebel who ignores routines and schedules. Enjoys new activities, is clever and mischievous, and loves a good chase inside the house or out.

The Bottom Line: Is a powerful, shrewd personality and has little fear of other animals or strangers. Wants dominance, is self-reliant, and is motivated to win.

Quirks of Character: Is vengeful if feeling harmed by a perceived injustice.

Scottie (#1): *unisex*/Classic./(Scottish) Old breed of usually black, long-haired terrier; has an erect tail and ears./(Late Latin) Scott (#5); Scotchman./(M. Old English) Nickname for Scott (#5); for a person from Scotland, possibly from Scot (#3); for tattoo (#1) or a Scotsman who has tattoos./(Italian) Scotti (#5)./(Irish) Scuit (#9).

At First Glance: Is muscular, energetic, powerful, fastidiously groomed, and tops for the breed. Appears to be confident and self-disciplined; has an air of authority.

Day-to-Day: Wants to do things his or her own way and is not about to be controlled without a battle of wits and courage. Is an independent, proud, alert, active loner.

The Bottom Line: Wants a peaceful, harmonious, cooperative, easygoing lifestyle. Is motivated to bond with one human, who will be treated with love, respect, and affection.

Quirks of Character: Has temper tantrums and is destructive when confined.

Scout (#6): *unisex*/Classic./(Latin) *Auscultare* (#4); to hear with attention./One who seeks information; follows for the purpose of observation.

At First Glance: Appears to be well fed, comfortable, concerned, and conventional for the breed. Is dignified with adults and very understanding and loving with children.

Day-to-Day: Is a homebody. Thrives with socially interactive, agreeable, loving, responsible humans who understand a need for affection, companionship, and treats.

The Bottom Line: Wants to be helpful and needs to be needed. Is compassionate, intuitive, and motivated to watch over, defend, and serve anyone needy or in trouble.

Quirks of Character: Never forgets an injustice or neglect and will get even.

Scrappy (#8): *unisex*/Classic./Full of fighting spirit; feisty; aggressive and determined.

At First Glance: Is a beautiful, graceful, relaxed, classic example of the breed. Appears to be peaceful, intelligent, intuitive, skillful, disciplined, and approachable.

Day-to-Day: Is a dominant, shrewd, courageous fighter and defender. Has a sociable, discriminating personality and is an efficient, businesslike, trustworthy, dependable worker.

The Bottom Line: Wants to win at everything. Is motivated to be competitive and needs the companionship of athletic, able-bodied, active humans for play and exercise.

Quirks of Character: Runs from confusion, sudden noises, and turbulence.

Shadow (#7): *unisex*/Classic./Is number 6 of ASPCA top 30 names./Someone who follows another, especially secretly./An inseparable companion./The absence of light in a form; partial darkness; a reflected image; shaded or darker portion of a picture.

At First Glance: Is a magnetic and charismatic polished, skillful, youthful beauty. Appears to be peaceful, easygoing, confident, sociable, and aware of the environment.

Day-to-Day: Is intelligent, observant, self-examining, refined, and calm. Enjoys a serene atmosphere and is not fond of noisy, vigorous activity or young, careless children.

The Bottom Line: Wants privacy and has a quiet, secret space for daily rest and reflection. Is motivated to look and make guarded decisions before taking action.

Quirks of Character: Is often disloyal, self-indulgent, and purposeless.

Shamu (#8): F/Classic./(M) Namu (#4), name of the first orca (whale) in captivity. Second whale captured was female, and to differentiate between the sexes, she was named Shamu; stage name for whales that perform at California's Sea World.

At First Glance: Has a dark, easily groomed, thick coat. Is conventional for the breed. Is muscular, sturdy, and strong. Appears to be plain, dignified, and patient.

Day-to-Day: Is a sociable powerhouse of strength, self-discipline, and efficiency. Thrives with space to run, play, and work. Needs firm leadership and training.

The Bottom Line: Wants stability, is routine oriented, and adheres to schedules. Is respectful, cautious, and motivated to try to understand what is expected and to do it.

Quirks of Character: Cannot stop talking when nervous or emotionally upset.

Sheba (#8): F/Classic./Is number 25 of ASPCA top 30 names./(Latin, Arabic, Biblical) Saba (#5)./Nickname for (Hebrew) Bathsheba (#3), from Batsheva (#6), daughter of the oath, or seventh daughter (mate: David [#4]; son: Solomon [#4])./Variation: Sheva (#1)./Kingdom in Arabia.

At First Glance: Is unpretentious, peaceful, docile, and friendly to gentle, calm, and quiet humans. Appears to be "soft," easygoing, and content to stay in the background.

Day-to-Day: Has tremendous mental and physical energy. Requires extensive exercise and firm leadership. Is a shrewd, courageous guardian of the home and family.

The Bottom Line: Wants to be involved in all relationships and activities. Is comfortable in a full household and maintains emotional stability when feeling secure.

Quirks of Character: Is indecisive and submissive when challenged.

Siggy (#4): *unisex*/Nickname for (*M*, Old German) Siegmund (#2), Sigmund (#6), victorious protector; for Siegfried (#1), Seigrred (#4), Sigfrid (#9), conquering peace; for Siegbert (#4), Sigebert (#4), bright victory; for Sighard (#3), conquering firmness; for Sighelm (#2), conquering helmet; for Sigmar (#4), conquering fame; for Sigrad (#4), conquering council./Sigurd (#6); (Icelandic) hero and (Teutonic) conquering guard./(Scandinavian-Teutonic) Sigvor (#9); conquering prudence./(Teutonic) Sigwald (#3); conquering power./(*F*, German) Siegfreda (#2), Sigfreda (#6)./Sigrada (#5); victory./(German-Italian) Sigismonda (#2)./(French) Sigolene (#5), Sigolaine (#1), Sigrade (#9)./(Scandinavian) Sigrid (#3), Sigritt (#3), Sigrin (#4).

> **At First Glance:** Steps right in to be friendly and helpful. Is understanding, vocal, and unpretentious. Appears to be comfortable, robust, rhythmic, and conventional.
>
> **Day-to-Day:** Puts effort and energy into everything and works well with other pets and humans. Is cautious, conscientious, respectful, self-disciplined, loyal, and dependable.
>
> **The Bottom Line:** Is refined and dislikes loud, sudden noise and rowdy or careless children. Wants a peaceful, quiet, private place for daily rest, relaxation, and observation.
>
> **Quirks of Character:** Is questioning, nervous, and slow to act in time of trouble.

Silver (#4): *unisex*/Classic./Whitish gray or a soft, lustrous white color; a precious metal.

> **At First Glance:** Is a powerful personality with a strong, agile body; is top of the breed, with fastidious grooming. Appears to be competitive, self-confident, and commanding.
>
> **Day-to-Day:** Is slow to learn, but once trained, is obedient, routine oriented, and loyal. Needs to be busy, to work, and to exercise daily. Loves to dig and do physically taxing things.
>
> **The Bottom Line:** Wants to be outdoors, free to enjoy new sensations, people, and experiences. Is motivated to avoid boredom and pulls a variety of surprising stunts.
>
> **Quirks of Character:** Is compassionate when humans feel badly or are sick.

Simba (#8): *M*/Classic./(East Africa, Kenya, Tanzania) in Swahili (#9), a people and language name, or Kiswahili (#2), language of literature and commerce; lion.

At First Glance: Is reserved, quiet, calm, refined, observant, and introspective. Appears to be proud, aloof, intelligent, cautious, poised, dignified, and mystical.

Day-to-Day: Is dominant, powerful, and inclined to take over and do things well. Thrives when active and is a shrewd, self-disciplined, businesslike, controlling defender.

The Bottom Line: Wants to be boss and is a leader for less assertive pets and weak trainers. Is motivated to master any situation, strives for independence, and is a loner.

Quirks of Character: Is submissive when challenged by loud, aggressive humans.

Skipper (#4): *unisex*/Classic./Master or captain of any vessel or a team./One that skips./Nicknames: Skip (#1), Skipp (#8), Skippie (#4), Skippy (#6).

At First Glance: Appears to be expensive, fastidiously groomed, vigorous, athletic, and a winner for the breed. Is a powerful, dominant, self-disciplined personality.

Day-to-Day: Works to perform duties responsibly and is detail conscious, routine oriented, and devoted. Is slow moving, cautious, serious; requires rigorous exercise.

The Bottom Line: Wants personal freedom to explore outdoors. Is motivated to find escape routes and is a clever adventurer when sensually and sexually stimulated.

Quirks of Character: Is surprisingly gentle, wise, and comforting in a crisis.

Skippy (#6): M/Classic./Nickname for Skipper (#4).

At First Glance: Is groomed, well formed, agile, strong, and dominant. Appears to be expensive, self-confident, disciplined, sociable, dependable, and mentally balanced.

Day-to-Day: Is a parental homebody who centers his interests around loved ones. Loves to eat and may be prone to scavenging and begging. Thrives with loving humans.

The Bottom Line: Spends mental and physical energy. Requires calm, quiet, private time for rest and introspection. Is motivated to observe and think before taking action.

Quirks of Character: When disturbed by confusion, is impulsive and hasty.

Smoky (#2): _unisex_/Classic./Is number 5 of ASPCA top 30 names./Appearing as a cloud of grayish blue to bluish or dark gray fine or solid liquid particles in a gaseous medium, resulting mainly from the burning of organic material./Variations: Smokey (#7), Smokie (#9).

At First Glance: Appears to be lost in thought, quiet, peaceful, and aloof. Is dignified, poised, well mannered, and standing back to look things over thoroughly.

Day-to-Day: Is sedentary, easygoing, cooperative, and affectionate. Enjoys collecting things, sharing gentle activities, and relaxing on someone's lap.

The Bottom Line: Wants to know what is expected and will do it. Is comfortable with routines and schedules and slowly plods along in a cautious, systematic manner.

Quirks of Character: Has a way of disappearing in the midst of hectic activity.

Snoopy (#5): _unisex_/Classic./Nosey, curious, inquisitive./Variations: Snoopee (#8), Snoopie (#3). Popular comic strip and cartoon character.

At First Glance: Is unpretentious, sturdy, square, strong, and muscular, with a dark, thick, durable coat that does not require grooming. Appears to be cautious and respectful.

Day-to-Day: Keeps everyone guessing, is unpredictable, lacks concentration. Is unrestrained, enthusiastic, energetic, cleverly manipulative, mischievous, and demanding.

The Bottom Line: Is motivated to be assertive and cannot be forced into a mold. Aims to take over the household and wants to do things alone; is aggressive when regimented.

Quirks of Character: Wants privacy, hides when crowded, and hates being alone.

Snowball (#8): _unisex_/Classic./Snow, rounded and tightly pressed into a ball./Increase and accelerate rapidly./Ball of crushed ice with fruit syrup, or a ball of ice cream trimmed with coconut and chocolate syrup./Plant with white, trumpet-shaped flowers.

At First Glance: Is out of the ordinary, alert, active, forceful, and not intimidated easily. Appears to be intelligent, intense, proud, self-sufficient, and short on social skills.

Day-to-Day: Is a dependable, shrewd, commanding guardian and a zealous athlete. Needs to be busy, trained to disciplines, and exercised extensively. Is a powerhouse.

The Bottom Line: Wants time to think things through and process thoughts before taking action. Is motivated to ignore the obvious, remain quiet, and react to intuition.

Quirks of Character: Cannot keep quiet and is a pest when emotionally upset.

Snowflake (#7): *unisex*/Classic./A watery, uniquely shaped crystal congealed into a white, transparent ice particle that falls from the clouds.

At First Glance: Appears to be cautious, slow moving, respectful, and disciplined. Is precise, dignified, solid, stable, down-to-earth, and conventional for the breed.

Day-to-Day: Is quiet, calm, aristocratic, and unemotional. Needs privacy and dislikes noise, confusion, and to be handled roughly. Is a finicky eater and likes to be clean.

The Bottom Line: Is motivated to be free of responsibility and is too easy-going to bother with disciplines. Wants a variety of toys and is always interested and entertained.

Quirks of Character: Is unpredictable, curious, impulsive, and accident prone.

Snuffy (#1): *unisex*/Classic./Sulky, annoyed, angry./(Scottish, Gaelic) Old-fashioned face./Like snuff (tobacco blended with other ingredients that is sniffed, not smoked) in color or substance.

At First Glance: Appears to be relaxed, youthful, virile, graceful, skillfully disciplined, and groomed to a polish. Is beautiful, magnetic, and appealing to all.

Day-to-Day: Is an independent, inventive, unemotional, controlling, assertive, intense loner who is impatient inside or out. Needs training and firm handling.

The Bottom Line: Is very active, controlling, and motivated to refer everything to his own likes or dislikes. Wants praise, but is rarely accommodating or satisfied.

Quirks of Character: Is noisy and impulsive when sensing impending danger.

Socks (#4): *unisex*/Classic./(Greek) *Sukkhos* (#5), "slipper."/Cover for feet and lower leg.

At First Glance: Appears to be intelligent, observant, peaceful, poised, and reserved. Is sleek, graceful, cautious, and not about to perform tricks or vie for attention.

Day-to-Day: Learns by repetition, works diligently once trained, and is routine oriented, respectful, and dependable. Is content to dig, play, and work with others.

The Bottom Line: Is motivated to protect and serve loved ones. Requires care, is not independent, dislikes being alone, and wants to be involved in all group activities.

Quirks of Character: Is panicked by harsh-sounding, loud, angry commands.

Sparkey (#5): *unisex*/Classic./Nickname for a beau or a lover; bright, animated person; a brisk; showy gay man./Variations: Sparkee (#3), Sparkie (#7).

At First Glance: Is a dominant, fastidiously groomed, businesslike powerhouse. Appears to be expensive, sociable, energetic, agile, and capable of concentrated effort.

Day-to-Day: Is a seductive, sexy, clever, curious, and resilient sensualist with a love of mental and physical freedom. Tries anything that is new and exciting; is lucky.

The Bottom Line: Is motivated to protect loved ones and is possessive and jealous. Wants harmonious interaction at home and strives to avoid stress and unpleasantness.

Quirks of Character: Has secret hiding places and disappears when upset.

Spike (#6): *unisex*/Classic./To add vitality or zest./A pointy nail or implement./An ear of corn./A surge of intermittent electrical current./A sharp increase and fall of prices or rates./To add liquor to a nonalcoholic beverage.

At First Glance: Is active, alert, unregimented, and different. Appears to be a first for the breed or to have a unique ancestry. Stands alone and is confident and proud.

Day-to-Day: Is a protective homebody who loves music and gets involved in all community activity. Thrives with loving families and is influential in relationships.

The Bottom Line: Wants freedom, gets caught in the moment, and is always sexually stimulated. Learns from experience, is spontaneous, and is difficult to housebreak.

Quirks of Character: Is impulsive; sires or produces unwanted litters.

Spot (#7): *unisex*/Classic./A small, usually round mark or eruption on the skin; a stain on fabric or a mark on a playing card./A place or locality./(British) Small quantity of anything.

At First Glance: Is a dominant original. Appears to be a distinctive, alert, proud, assertive, bold individual who is in perpetual motion and is self-controlled with humans.

Day-to-Day: When secure, is quiet, refined, sedentary, and introspective. Prefers privacy and dislikes noise and the confusion of a socially active, family lifestyle.

The Bottom Line: Wants all the comforts of home and feels protective. Is motivated to protect the territory, is possessive of food, and responds to music.

Quirks of Character: Plays the martyr when rejected, hurt, or ignored.

Stormy (#2): *unisex*/Classic./Nickname for Storm (#4); tempestuous weather or emotions.

At First Glance: Appears to be sleek, aristocratic, quiet, calm, and listening for comments. Is introspective and thoughtful as he or she observes the environment.

Day-to-Day: Prefers to depend upon one sensitive, trustworthy human; does not feel secure with changes or pressures. Enjoys gentle handling and is receptive to disciplines.

The Bottom Line: Wants structure and the stability that a planned, routine-oriented, scheduled lifestyle implies. Is motivated to be respectful, cautious, and to exercise regularly.

Quirks of Character: When fearful, goes to a secret hiding place and mopes.

Sugar (#3): *unisex*/Classic./Nickname for someone who has a sweet personality or as flattery to cover something unpleasant./A sweet, white or less-refined, brownish yellow crystalline substance generally obtained from the evaporated juice of sugarcane or beets.

At First Glance: Appears to be physically and mentally powerful, with possibilities of being constructive or destructive. Demonstrates authority, self-control, and sociability.

Day-to-Day: Is playful, trusting, conscientious, charming, and amusing. Enjoys toys, games, and being the center of attraction. Loves children and hates being alone.

The Bottom Line: Wants a stable, secure, routine-oriented, scheduled lifestyle. Is comfortable when exercised regularly and is motivated to be dependable and trustworthy.

Quirks of Character: Is mean, jealous, and spiteful if confined outdoors alone.

Sunny (#3): *unisex*/Classic./Nickname for Sunshine (#1); a cheerful, warm and bright personality and appearance.

At First Glance: Is receptive to the friendliness of gentle, calm humans. Appears to be clean, neat, sensitive, quiet, unpretentious, gentle, and self-conscious.

Day-to-Day: Thrives on affection, play, and fun-loving relationships; creates imaginative games. Is extremely vocal, has a fine memory, and enjoys socializing.

The Bottom Line: Wants to do things creatively and forgoes disciplines for a variety of interests. Is motivated to take the initiative, is daring, and resents controls.

Quirks of Character: Needs quiet and solitude when eating.

Sunshine (#1): *unisex*/Classic./The rays of the sun.

At First Glance: Is quiet, unpretentious, and appears to communicate through feelings. Is sensitive to the surrounding atmosphere and environment.

Day-to-Day: Enjoys doing things alone and is not content following disciplines and routines. Resents taking orders and prefers to be daring and to take the initiative.

The Bottom Line: Wants dominance and is a mentally and physically powerful personality. Is motivated to be shrewd and instigates athletic, vigorous exercise and play.

Quirks of Character: Is curious and cleverly finds escapes from confinement.

See the Number Meanings chapter to discover the traits described by the number that accompanies each name: Sabina (#1), Sable (#3), Sabrina (#1), Sabu (#7), Sacha (#5), Saffron (#7), Sage (#5), Saint (#9), Sake (#9), Sal (#5), Salem (#5), Sally (#6), Salty (#5), Samauri (#1), Samba (#9), Sanders (#8), Sandford (#9), Sandie (#7), Sandman (#3), Sandor (#8), Sapphire (#2), Sasha (#3), Satin (#9), Saucy (#6), Sausage (#1), Savage (#1), Savannah (#8), Sawyer (#1), Scarlett (#8), Schnappsie (#2), Schnieder

(#4), Schnookie (#9), Schultz (#1), Scully (#2), Scupper (#8), Sebastian (#9), Sedrick (#6), Selby (#9), Selma (#5), Selwyn (#8), Senator (#2), Señor (#8), Señora (#9), Sergei (#9), Seth (#7), Seymour (#8), Shamrock (#7), Shane (#2), Shannon (#4), Sharkie (#8), Sharon (#3), Sharpie (#4), Shawnee (#3), Sheena (#7), Sheik (#7), Shelby (#8), Sheldon (#5), Shelley (#5), Shep (#3), Sheri (#5), Sheridan (#6), Sheriff (#8), Sherlock (#1), Sherman (#6), Sherwood (#8), Sheryl (#6), Shiksa (#4), Shirley (#6), Sid (#5), Siddy (#7), Sidney (#4), Sidwell (#3), Siegfried (#1), Siggi (#6), Sigmund (#6), Simon (#7), Simone (#3), Simpson (#6), Sinbad (#4), Sinclair (#4), Siren (#2), Skeeter (#2), Skylar (#5), Sleepy (#1), Slick (#9), Slinky (#9), Slugger (#8), Sluggo (#9), Smoochie (#6), Smoochy (#8), Snappy (#1), Sneaky (#3), Sneezy (#4), Sniffer (#5), Snoogie (#3), Snookums (#1), Snuggles (#5), Snyder (#4), Solomon (#4), Sox (#4), Spacey (#6), Spanky (#5), Sparkie (#7), Spats (#3), Specs (#8), Speedy (#2), Spencer (#8), Sphinx (#9), Spicy (#9), Spock (#1), Spooky (#2), Sporty (#5), Spunky (#7), Squeaky (#9), Stanley (#6), Star (#4), Stella (#6), Stevie (#8), Stewart (#7), Stoli (#3), Stoney (#8), Strega (#7), Stretch (#3), Stuart (#9), Stubby (#8), Studley (#7), Sturges (#1), Suki (#6), Sullivan (#2), Susan (#2), Susie (#1), Suzette (#8), Sven (#6), Swayze (#9), Sweetness (#3), Sweets (#1), Swiftie (#1), Swifty (#3), Swinton (#6), Swoozie (#4), Sybil (#4), Sydney (#2), Sylvester (#1), Sylvia (#7).

Tabbie (#3): F/Classic./Nickname for (Aramaic) Tabitha (#7); gazelle or doe./Tabby (#5).

At First Glance: Appears to be well fed, comfortable, self-controlled, serious, understanding, and trustworthy. Has a rhythmic step and soft coat with a bluish tint.

Day-to-Day: Loves to have fun and is charming, amusing, vocal, playful, and inventive. Is fond of children, ignores disciplines, does tricks, and craves attention.

The Bottom Line: Wants friends, good food and a home-loving family to latch onto and help. Is motivated to be protective and lend a hand; gets involved in everything.

Quirks of Character: Is curious and unintentionally gets into odd situations.

Tabitha (#7): F/Classic./(Aramaic) Gazelle or doe./(Hebrew) Roebuck./(Greek) Dorcas (#6)./Variations: Tabatha (#8), Tabbatha (#1), Tabbetha (#5), Tabbitha (#9), Tabea (#2), Tabetha (#3), Tabithe (#2), Tabytha (#5).

At First Glance: Is unconventional, undisciplined, lively, curious, and quick. Appears to improvise and is restless when handled. Has charm and is very seductive.

Day-to-Day: Is an aloof, refined, aristocratic, quiet, introspective well of secrecy. Enjoys resting in the sun, observing the scene, and sleeping. Goes hunting alone.

The Bottom Line: Is "soft," cuddly when approached, and wants to select handlers. Is motivated to be cautious, exacting, and to cling to one special friend.

Quirks of Character: Is very independent, but lacks initiative.

Taffy (#4): *unisex*/Classic./(Welsh) (*M*) David (#4), darling or beloved; (*F*) Davida (#5), Tafline (#4), Vida (#9), beloved./Sweet, chewy candy made by boiling down molasses or brown sugar until thick, pulling by hand or machine until glossy and holds a shape./Form of flattery.

At First Glance: Is striking, unconventional, colorful, and self-promoting. Appears to be curious, enthusiastic, amusing, quick, frisky, charming, and undisciplined.

Day-to-Day: Is slow to learn, but once trained, thrives on work, exercise, routines, and schedules. Is a dignified, respectful, trustworthy family assistant and companion.

The Bottom Line: Is a powerful personality and a shrewd, courageous, self-disciplined problem solver and guardian. Collects and protects personal property.

Quirks of Character: Disappears when rattled by sudden noise and confusion.

Teddy (#4): *unisex*/Nickname for (*M*, Old English) Edward (#1), rich guard; for (Greek) Theodoros (#2), Theodore (#9), gift of God; for (*F*) Theodorus (#8), God's gift; for (*F*) Theodora (#5), Dorothea (#5).

At First Glance: Is unusually patterned, has striking colors, and is unique. Appears to be assertive, alert, active, proud, self-confident, and independently ready to take a risk.

Day-to-Day: Enjoys a regimented, stable lifestyle in which expectations are clearly defined and there is little spontaneity. Is serious, always keeps busy, and is reliable.

The Bottom Line: Wants to have a best friend for play and easygoing activities. Is very trusting, loves company, and enjoys being entertained and amusing others.

Quirks of Character: Is extremely suspicious and aloof when emotionally upset.

Thumper (#2):
unisex/Classic./Someone who rhythmically pounds hard with a hand, a blunt object, or something thick or heavy, and repeatedly makes a thudlike sound.

At First Glance: Is friendly, furry, funny, flighty, and frolicsome. Appears to be attractive, charming, bristling with personality, talkative, and extremely expressive.

Day-to-Day: Is obedient, affectionate, sweet, unassuming, and dependent on humans for security and stability. Is easygoing, sensitive, "soft," and has no regard for rigidity.

The Bottom Line: Is motivated to use physical and mental energy and needs constant athletic activities to maintain emotional balance and dependability.

Quirks of Character: Is exceptionally intuitive and brave or in the other extreme, unaware and selfishly cowardly.

Thunder (#9):
unisex/Classic./(Latin) Tonitrus (#1)./(Old English) Thunor (#6)./Crackling, booming sound produced by rapidly expanding air along the path of the electrical discharge of lightning./Use words or move noisily, fast, heavily, forcefully.

At First Glance: Is one of a kind and stands alone. Appears to be alert, proud, confident, courageous, self-involved, unemotional, and forceful. Takes the initiative.

Day-to-Day: Is attractive, charming, peaceful, and loving to all. Never meets a stranger; feels compassion and empathy for anyone needy, lonely, or disabled.

The Bottom Line: Is mentally, emotionally, and physically powerful. Wants to protect the home, serve loved ones, and win at whatever he or she does.

Quirks of Character: Is selfish, cruel, and cold when treated unfairly.

Tiffany (#9):
F/(Greek) Theophania (#7); manifestation of God, or revelation of God./Nicknames: Tifa (#9), Tiff (#5), Tiffa (#6), Tiffee (#6), Tiffie (#1), Tiffy (#3).

At First Glance: Is first of the breed or one of a kind. Appears to be alert, active, impatient, proud, daring, assertive, and content doing things alone.

Day-to-Day: Is a caring, dependable, peaceful, intelligent, wise service provider. Loves to roam in natural surroundings, understands human nature, and is youthful.

The Bottom Line: Wants authority and is a capable of autonomy. Is motivated to solve problems in a businesslike, efficient manner and is a shrewd judge of character.

Quirks of Character: Shuts humans out and is inactive when emotionally upset.

Tiger (#5): M/Classic./Is number 18 of ASPCA top 30 names./(Latin) *Tigris* (#1)./Undomesticated, carnivorous, large, tawny colored and black-striped cat, with a black-ringed tail, nearly white throat and belly; is native to Asia and the East Indies./A furious, bloodthirsty person.

At First Glance: Is magnetic, graceful, polished to a shine, and classic for the breed. Appears to be peaceful, well disciplined, and interested in searching the horizon.

Day-to-Day: Is unpredictable. Loves to be free outdoors to meet new people and experiences, dislikes being restrained by routines and schedules, and hates repetition.

The Bottom Line: Is motivated to be free of responsibility. Wants to be around humans, adapts to changes, is flexible, and follows his curiosity to learn from experience.

Quirks of Character: Has passionate likes and dislikes; is loving or selfish.

Tigger (#3): M/Is number 28 of ASPCA top 30 names./Variation: Tiger (#5)./Fictional character: bouncy, happy, tigerlike friend of Winnie (#2) the Pooh (#9), Kanga (#7), and Roo (#3).

At First Glance: Is sleek, quiet, calm, aristocratic, poised, and introspective. Appears to be intelligent and observant; stays aloof from noises and confusion.

Day-to-Day: Is an easygoing, frisky, multitalented attention getter. Talks and sings, is an inventive game-player, loves children's toys, and has an extraordinary memory.

The Bottom Line: Wants to be free, unrestrained, and outdoors as much as possible. Is motivated to look for escape routes, ignore disciplines, and get into mischief.

Quirks of Character: Understands human emotions and is empathetic and wise.

Tiny (#5): *unisex*/Someone or something that is very small.

At First Glance: Purebred or mix, is perfect for whatever it is. Appears to be calm, aristocratic, poised, intelligent, quiet, observant, thoughtful, and unapproachable.

Day-to-Day: Is always energetic and on the go. Is frisky, amusing, charming, playful, and unrestrained. Follows his or her curiosity and cleverly gets in and out of trouble.

The Bottom Line: Is a puzzle and a loner. Wants the perfection of his or her expectations; when disappointed, hides and stays away from household activities.

Quirks of Character: Is fearful of being hurt and avoids emotional ties.

Tippy (#5): *unisex*/Applied to boats that heel over easily under sail, or anything unsteady.

At First Glance: Appears to be an uncaring, aloof, unemotional, quiet, reserved, dignified loner. Is observant, introspective, and nervous. Relaxes if made to feel safe.

Day-to-Day: Is a self-promoting, frisky, clever politician who loves to tease and charms his or her way out of trouble. Overindulges in food, sex, and travel adventures.

The Bottom Line: Wants to be loved but is not overtly affectionate or inclined to get close to anyone. Is motivated to live in a quiet, peaceful atmosphere. Seeks privacy.

Quirks of Character: Watches TV and stares intently when humans speak.

Tommy (#5): *M*/Nickname from (Aramaic) Tomea (#9), Thomas (#4); twin./Variations: Thompson (#3), Toma (#4), Tomas (#5), (Italian) Tomaso (#2), (German) Thoma (#3), (Polish) Tomasz (#4).

At First Glance: Is different and colorful. Appears to be active, alert, self-confident, assertive, aggressive, intelligent, and determined to get what he wants.

Day-to-Day: Thrives with happy-go-lucky, easygoing, unconventional humans. Is a tease who loves new activities, is sociable and charming, and keeps everyone on their toes.

The Bottom Line: Wants to have stability and is serious about disciplines and schedules. Is motivated to do what is expected and, once trained, follows the rules.

Quirks of Character: Is not flexible and is nervous with young children.

Tootsie (#4): *F/A* sweetheart; a darling, or a prostitute./Variations: Tootsee (#9), Tootsy (#6), Tootsy-Wootsy (#9).

At First Glance: Appears to be unafraid, frisky, self-promoting, enthusiastic, and charming. Is striking, colorful, and unconventional. Makes friends quickly and easily.

Day-to-Day: Is slow to learn, cautious, loyal, and enduring. Needs routines and schedules to maintain emotional balance. Loves to dig and hunt; is a passionate worker.

The Bottom Line: Wants authority and is a trustworthy, shrewd, discerning guardian. Is motivated to be sociable but may be too athletic to play with small children.

Quirks of Character: Is willful and destructive if restrained indoors.

Toto (#7): *unisex*/(Latin) *In toto,* "completely"; *toto caelo,* "by the entire extent of the heavens, diametrically."/Computer reference: default scratch file for French-speaking programmers./Acronym: **T**ongue **O**f **T**he **O**cean./(Asian) Sports lottery./Fictional character: Dorothy's dog, *The Wizard of Oz,* by L. Frank Baum.

At First Glance: Is sturdy, square, neat, muscular, and conventional for the breed. Appears to be respectful, cautious, conscientious, serious, trustworthy, and unemotional.

Day-to-Day: Enjoys solitude and quiet; needs time each day for rest and introspection. Is observant and thinks before taking action. Prefers adults to children.

The Bottom Line: Is very vocal and friendly when strangers arrive. Is motivated to be an entertaining extrovert but lacks the physical stamina for play or socializing.

Quirks of Character: Is protective. Prefers to be indoors, interacting with family.

Tramp (#5): *unisex*/Classic./Vagabond, hobo, bum, or disreputable wanderer./Sexually promiscuous woman./Walk with a firm and resounding step.

At First Glance: Appears to be strong, muscular, and neat, with dark conventional coloring and a square formation. Is slow, cautious, quiet, earthy, and respectful.

Day-to-Day: Prefers to be outdoors, free to explore and make friends. Is frisky, curious, and clever; lacks concentration. Learns from observation and experience.

The Bottom Line: Wants independence and dislikes restraints, routines, or schedules. Is motivated to be selfish and bossy, and to do things his or her way.

Quirks of Character: Is secretive and finds hiding places when nervous.

Trigger (#3): *unisex*/Classic./A small, projecting lever that when squeezed releases the cock and activates a firearm./Initiate events or reactions.

At First Glance: Is sleek, regal, self-confident, calm, and quiet, remains aloof from human contact or activities. Appears to be self-contained, introspective, and intelligent.

Day-to-Day: Is animated, charming, self-expressive, talkative, friendly, playful, and happy. Thrives with easygoing, youthful humans who have a good sense of humor.

The Bottom Line: Wants freedom to meet new people and unknown experiences. Is always on the go and into mischief. Is motivated to be outdoors and is easily bored.

See the Number Meanings chapter to discover the traits described by the number that accompanies each name: Taboo (#8), Taddy (#9), Tailor (#3), Talbot (#7), Tallulah (#6), Tally (#7), Tamara (#9), Tammy (#9), Tandy (#1), Tang (#6), Tango (#3), Tank (#1), Tanner (#9), Tante (#6), Tanya (#7), Tapper (#4), Tarry (#1), Tarzan (#8), Tasha (#4), Tate (#1), Tati (#5), Tatters (#4), Tattoo (#1), Tatum (#3), Taurus (#1), Taylor (#1), Ted (#2), Teena (#9), Telly (#2), Tempest (#8), Templeton (#3), Terence (#7), Terry (#5), Tessa (#1), Tessie (#5), Testy (#8), Thackery (#1), Thatcher (#2), Thea (#7), Thelma (#5), Theo (#3), Theta (#9), Thing (#4), Thor (#7), Thoreau (#7), Thorndyke (#3), Thorney (#6), Throckmorton (#8), Thud (#8), Thurber (#2), Thurgood (#9), Thurman (#5), Thursday (#8), Thurston (#9), Tia (#3), Tierney (#6), Tilda (#1), Tildy (#7), Tilly (#6), Tim (#6), Tina (#8), Tipper (#3), Tippie (#3), Tisa (#4), Tish (#2), Tisha (#3), Titan (#1), Tito (#1), Titus (#8), Toady (#2), Tobias (#3), Toby (#8), Toddy (#5), Toffee (#3), Tolstoy (#9), Tom (#3), Tommie (#3), Toni (#4), Tonic (#7), Tony (#2), Tonya (#3), Toodles (#9), Topaz (#6), Topper (#9), Topsie (#3), Toro (#5), Tory (#6), Tosha (#9), Toshi (#8), Totsie (#7), Tottie (#8), Touche (#9), Touchy (#2), Toulouse (#2), Tovah (#3), Toy (#6), Tracer (#2), Tracy (#4), Trader (#3), Trapper (#4), Traveler (#2), Travis (#8),

Travolta (#1), Treacher (#6), Treasure (#8), Treat (#1), Tremain (#8), Trent (#5), Trenton (#7), Trevor (#8), Trina (#8), Trinket (#7), Trish (#2), Triton (#6), Trojan (#6), Trooper (#8), Trotsky (#2), Troy (#6), Trudie (#5), Truman (#6), Trumbull (#2), Trumpet (#5), Trusty (#6), Tsar (#4), Tucker (#6), Tucks (#2), Tucson (#2), Tuesday (#5), Tuffy (#6), Tugs (#4), Tulip (#6), Tunney (#9), Turner (#6), Turnip (#8), Tutu (#1), Twister (#6), Twitty (#9), Twyla (#9), Ty (#9), Tyler (#8), Tyrone (#7), Tyson (#3).

Ulysses (#3): M/(Latin) Odysseus (#1), "I hate," from (Greek) odyssesthai, "to hate."

At First Glance: Is muscular, strong, surefooted, dark, and earthy. Appears to be cautious, self-disciplined, patient, conscientious, respectful, and conventional.

Day-to-Day: Is a perky, happy, cute, charming, and trusting playmate for youngsters and fun-loving adults. Develops a large vocabulary, is talkative, and needs attention.

The Bottom Line: Is motivated to keep busy and has a powerful presence in the home and territory. Wants vigorous exercise and needs businesslike, athletic handlers.

Quirks of Character: Trembles and is submissive when confined or controlled.

Uma (#8): F/(Sanskrit) Flax (blue-flowered herb)./Hindu goddess, Parvati (#6)./Variation: Umeeka (#2).

At First Glance: Appears to be dignified, calm, unemotional, self-disciplined, cautious, and respectful. Is conventional, with a dark natural coat and a square frame.

Day-to-Day: Is an energetic, intelligent, discerning, self-reliant worker and guardian. Has mental and physical strength; requires firm leadership and strong handlers.

The Bottom Line: Wants to know what to do and does it. Is motivated to follow routines, maintains a stable daily schedule and is a loyal, calm, practical companion.

Quirks of Character: Is lazy and overly dependent when emotionally upset.

Una (#9): F/(Latin) One./(Old Irish) Oona (#9)./(Native American, Hopi) Remember.

At First Glance: Is unconventional, striking, and attention getting. Appears to be willful, easily distracted, frisky, friendly, and quick. Is a rambunctious, silly clown.

Day-to-Day: Is unselfish, compassionate, empathetic, peaceful, and helpful. Stays at the side of anyone who is needy, lonely, sick, emotionally disturbed, or handicapped.

The Bottom Line: Wants stability and needs a patient, consistent, calm trainer. Learns slowly; once into a daily routine and secure, is dependable and loyal.

Quirks of Character: Is fearful and weak minded when controlled rigidly.

Uncle (#1): M/(Latin) Avunculus (#8); A maternal uncle./The brother of one's father or mother, or the husband of an aunt./Kindly or familiar address for an elderly man./Someone who is a source of encouragement and advice./A pawnbroker.

At First Glance: Is quiet, docile, unassuming, shy, and unpretentious. Is undisciplined, but appears to be kind, gentle, sensitive, hesitant, and respectful.

Day-to-Day: Enjoys working, hunting, and playing alone. Is independent and inventive. Is alert, active, intelligent, and forceful; asserts his leadership aggressively.

The Bottom Line: Wants dominance and is a powerful personality with tremendous energy and stamina. Is emotionally balanced when exercised vigorously every day.

Quirks of Character: Has a lust for the ladies and is a seductive adventurer.

Upton (#5): M/(Anglo-Saxon) From the high town./(English) Upper place or farm.

At First Glance: Is frisky, enthusiastic, unrestrained, and rambunctious. Appears to be self-promoting, amusing, and restless. Has a colorful, striking appearance.

Day-to-Day: Is a sociable, active, clever mimic, who learns from observation and experience. Is curious, accident-prone, self-indulgent, and a keen judge of character.

The Bottom Line: Wants to be useful and volunteers to stay by the side of anyone who is lonely or needs a helping hand. Thinks of others before himself.

Quirks of Character: Runs away and never fails to return home.

Uranus (#4): M/(Late Latin from Greek) Ouranos (#4)./Mythology: person-ification of the sky; son and lover of Gaea (#5), earth; father of the Cyclopes (#8), Chronos (#2) (time), and the Titan (#1) giants, heavyweights./Giant planet, seventh from the sun.

At First Glance: Approaches with a rhythmic step and a paternal attitude. Is robust, comfortable, and conventional. Appears to be dignified and approachable.

Day-to-Day: Is a hard worker who depends upon disciplines and routines, and maintains schedules. Thrives in a practical, stable environment with patient, dependable humans.

The Bottom Line: Wants and requires time for rest and reflection. Looks for secret hiding places and a serene, quiet space for privacy. Is an unso-ciable, refined loner.

Quirks of Character: Due to childhood restraints, is unfriendly when con-trolled.

Ursa (#5): *unisex*/(Latin) Bear (#8)./(F, Danish, Dutch, German, Italian, Norwegian, Spanish) Ursula (#2).

At First Glance: Is different, one of a kind, or first for the breed. Appears to be active, intelligent, alert, courageous, bold, assertive, aggressive, and independent.

Day-to-Day: Is mischievous, unregimented, adventurous, curious, and clever; prefers to be irresponsible. Gets bored easily and needs to be out-doors to roam and make friends.

The Bottom Line: Is slow to learn. Needs patient, detailed training; but once into a routine, is steadfast and responsible. Is motivated to use energy working quietly.

Quirks of Character: When disciplined loudly or aggressively, is submis-sive.

Ursula (#2): F/(Latin) Little bear.

At First Glance: Is muscular, strong, steady, and neat; not groomed to be decorative. Appears to be natural, earthy, and conventional for the breed.

Day-to-Day: Is shy, quiet, gentle, and sensitive. Loves to collect toys and food; begs to be cuddled. Enjoys group activities but prefers to bond with one human.

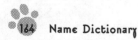

The Bottom Line: Is an intelligent, observant, sedentary aristocrat who needs privacy and a serene atmosphere. Is motivated to analyze. Hesitates before taking action.

Quirks of Character: Is very assertive when restrained mentally or physically.

See the Number Meanings chapter to discover the traits described by the number that accompanies each name: Udall (#5), Uggams (#5), Ugly (#2), Ula (#7), Ulani (#3), Ullman (#1), Ultra (#9), Umar (#8), Umber (#5), Umberto (#4), Ump (#5), Umpire (#1), Unger (#2), Unicorn (#4), Urchin (#1), Uri (#3), Ursella (#7), Ursi (#4), Usher (#8), Ushi (#3), Ustinov (#3), Utah (#5), Utoo (#8), Utopia (#1), Uzi (#2).

Vanna (#7): *F*/(Hebrew) God's gift./Nickname for (English) Savannah (#8), large, grassy plain; for (Greek) Vanessa (#9), butterflies./From (*M*) Evan (#6), (Welsh) youth, (Celtic) young fighter, (Scottish), right-handed./Nickname: Van (#1); from the family of . . ., or a covered wagon./(Cambodian) Khmer (#1); from expression meaning "golden."

At First Glance: Appears to be seductive, unrestrained, charming, frisky, clever, quick, and curious. Is colorful, unusually patterned, striking, and attention getting.

Day-to-Day: Is thoughtful, quiet, calm, reserved, and intelligent. Thrives with gracious, sensitive, faithful, trusting humans who are not athletic, very sociable, or active.

The Bottom Line: Companionship is essential: Wants to adapt to everyone's needs and is comfortable with intimate, loving relationships and a peaceful atmosphere.

Quirks of Character: When emotionally upset, is stubborn, weak, and selfish.

Velvet (#5): *unisex*/(Latin) *Villus* (#5); shaggy hair or fleece./Soft and smooth to sight, hearing, touch, or taste./Originally silk fabric having short, close pile of erect threads; inferior qualities made from silky pile on cotton, rayon, polyester, or linen back./Gambling winnings, profit, or gain beyond expectation.

At First Glance: Has a dark, thick, natural coat and is muscular, sturdy, and square. Appears to be cautious, respectful, self-disciplined, quiet, dignified, and unemotional.

Day-to-Day: Is a curious, playful, adaptable, sensual, charming politician who is spontaneous and unregimented. Has frequent mood swings and does not live by the rules.

The Bottom Line: Wants to be left alone to initiate activities. Is confident, enterprising, and courageous. Accepts challenges with determination and daring.

Quirks of Character: Is self-absorbed and edgy; creates a crisis to gain attention.

Venus (#9): F/(Latin) Love./Mythology: goddess of beauty and love./Second planet from the sun.

At First Glance: Is different, first of a breed, or of unique ancestry. Appears to be alert, active, proud, assertive, aggressive, self-confident, quick acting, and independent.

Day-to-Day: Absorbs surrounding vibrations and understands human emotions and activity. Is compassionate, loving, responsible, peaceful, self-disciplined, and helpful.

The Bottom Line: Is a powerful mental and physical presence and loves to take on challenges. Is comfortable with strong, firm, athletic, dependable, controlled humans.

Quirks of Character: Due to childhood restraints, is inappropriately independent.

Veronica (#6): F/(Latin) From *vera icon* (#6), "true image."/Form of pagan Greek goddess of victory, Nike (#3), Berenike (#6)./(English) Berenice (#7), Bernice (#2); bringing victory./Nicknames: Ranna (#3), Ronna (#8), Ronni (#7), Ronnie (#3), Ronny (#5), Vera (#1), Vero (#6), Vonnie (#7).

At First Glance: Is beautiful and decorative, with an abundant, golden coat and an expectant, enthusiastic, childlike expression. Appears to be happy and is very vocal.

Day-to-Day: Is a homebody who thrives on social interaction, responsibility, and love. Is a musical, patient, industrious, teachable student who learns—or tries—to sing.

The Bottom Line: Is happy-go-lucky; wants attention and is miserable when left alone. Delights in amusing and entertaining, stays youthful, and is trusting and playful.

Quirks of Character: When upset, is a petulant, poor listener who fights controls.

Vicky (#7): F/Nickname for (Latin) Victoria (#7); victory.

At First Glance: Is an impressive, magnetic personality. Is groomed to a polish, skillfully trained, strong, youthful, and beautiful. Appears to be courteous and kindly.

Day-to-Day: Prefers a calm, secluded spot for rest and reflection and is not extremely active. Is quiet, refined, questioning, investigative, and best with adults.

The Bottom Line: Is withdrawn; wants silence and peace and to escape from noise and confusion. Enjoys natural surroundings and is shy and highly intuitive.

Quirks of Character: Wants privacy and is nervous and fearful when left alone.

Victor (#6): M/(Latin) Victor, conqueror.

At First Glance: Is groomed to a polish, skillfully trained, strong, youthful, and beautiful. Appears to be courteous and kindly. Is an impressive, magnetic personality.

Day-to-Day: Is paternal, understanding, sociable, and involved in all household activity. Makes the kitchen his headquarters and focuses on home, family, and friends.

The Bottom Line: Wants to be with people all the time. Loves music and social interaction. Is inclined to be possessive and is comfortable with children and other pets.

Quirks of Character: Is easily bluffed and avoids a fight when threatened.

Victoria (#7): F/(Latin) Victory./Nicknames: Vicki (#9), Vickie (#5), Vicky (#7).

At First Glance: Appears to be relaxed, interested, and peaceful. Has natural beauty. Is a youthful, sociable, skillfully trained, polished example of the breed.

Day-to-Day: Is aristocratic, aloof, introspective, and sedentary. Prefers solitude and quiet; tends to observe rather than become involved in athletic exercise or games.

The Bottom Line: Wants to be sure of commands before acting and is slow to follow instructions. Is dignified and comfortable with poised, refined, careful adults.

Quirks of Character: Is very noisy and trembles when frustrated by supervisors.

Vinnie (#1): M/Nickname for (Latin) Vincent (#6), conqueror./Variation: Vinny (#3).

At First Glance: Has a striking attitude and appearance; attracts attention. Is frisky, curious, enthusiastic, and fast moving. Appears to be a clever, amusing charmer.

Day-to-Day: Is independent and wants to do things his own way. Tries to lead the leader and is assertive, aggressive, forceful, and self-sufficient. Needs patient training.

The Bottom Line: Wants freedom; fights physical restrictions and mental controls. Is comfortable in a nonroutine environment with easygoing humans.

Quirks of Character: Is sexually self-indulgent and sires litters indiscriminately.

Virgil (#5): M/(Latin) From Vergilius (#5) (from an expression whose meaning is lost). The virginal or unbloomed./Variation: Vergil (#1).

At First Glance: Is striking, seductive, sensual, and unrestrained. Appears to be a charming, youthful, curious, clever, impulsive, changeable, enthusiastic adventurer.

Day-to-Day: Enjoys freedom from mental and physical restraints. Learns from experience. Is happy outdoors, bores easily, and creates a variety of surprising activities.

The Bottom Line: Is comfortable when needed. Understands human emotions and behavior. Wants to be helpful and is drawn to anyone in physical or emotional pain.

Quirks of Character: Is very talkative and noisy when ignored or upset.

Virginia (#8): F/Originally, (Latin) Verginia (#4), from family name, (M) Verginius (#7); later association from Latin, Virgo (#8), maiden, virgin, chaste.

At First Glance: Is quiet, investigative, and confident; avoids human contact. Appears to be aristocratic, poised, introspective, wise, intelligent, and guarded.

Day-to-Day: Is a self-disciplined, discerning, powerful personality who requires consistent, vigorous exercise and play. Enjoys social interaction with athletic humans.

The Bottom Line: Needs to work independently. Is an alert, fast-moving, creative playmate who prefers to initiate activity. Is comfortable with submissive companions.

Quirks of Character: When emotionally upset or frustrated, is dull and lazy.

Vladimir (#7): M/From (Slavic) *volod* (#5), "rule," and *meri* (#9), "great."/(Russian, Czech) To rule with greatness, and world prince./(Germanic) Walter (#7); ruler of the army.

At First Glance: Is mature, serious, stocky, and conventional for the breed. Appears to be well fed, comfortable, sympathetic, and interested in making friends.

Day-to-Day: Is an observer and stays aloof from rough play and small children. Thrives with adults. Enjoys the countryside and prefers to be alone in a crowd.

The Bottom Line: Wants to be boss and is an independent loner. Is comfortable in a one-pet family with patient, firm leadership and room to do things creatively.

Quirks of Character: When sympathy and compassion are needed, he is there.

Vyacheslav (#1): M/Classic./(Russian, from German) Wenceslaus (#5), (Slavic) Wencelsas (#2); possesses glory.

At First Glance: Appears to be cute, playful, happy, and decorative. Is a shiny, golden, handsome blond who attracts attention for his expressive eyes and loud voice.

Day-to-Day: Insists on being left to his own devices and impatiently avoids training, routines, and schedules. Enjoys hunting alone and is first in line for food and attention.

The Bottom Line: Is uncomfortable in crowds and with crude handlers, noise, and confusion. Wants private time and a secluded space for observation, rest, and reflection.

Quirks of Character: Gets into a rut; forms habits that are impossible to break.

See the Number Meanings chapter to discover the traits described by the number that accompanies each name: Vadim (#4), Val (#8), Valaria (#1), Valdemar (#4), Valdez (#7), Valentina (#8), Valerie (#9), Valli (#2), Vamp (#7), Vandal (#9), Vanderbilt (#8), Vandyke (#1), Vanni (#6), Vaughn (#1), Veda (#5), Velasquez (#1), Venetta (#6), Venice (#4), Verdi (#4), Verdon (#6), Vergie (#3), Vermont (#8), Verna (#6), Verne (#1), Vernon (#7), Vesta (#4), Viceroy (#7), Vichy

(#4), Vicki (#9), Vickie (#5), Victory (#4), Vidal (#3), Vidor (#5), Viking (#9), Vinton (#4), Viper (#7), Virginny (#1), Vixen (#2), Voodoo (#5).

Wags (#5): *unisex*/Originally (Swedish) *vagga* (#2); to rock the cradle./(Middle English) *Waggen* (#3); moves repeatedly from side to side, up and down, or forward and backward./Talks indiscreetly./Witty people.

At First Glance: Has a natural, thick, dark coat; has a square frame and is conventional for the breed. Is strong, muscular, and stable. Appears to be self-disciplined and cautious.

Day-to-Day: Is an active, curious, enthusiastic investigator who loves travel and games, and seeing new people and meeting new experiences. Is clever, charming, and only learns things that are interesting or serve his or her purposes.

The Bottom Line: Wants to be the leader and prefers to work alone. Confronts authoritative handling with aggressive behavior. Is self-centered and unfriendly.

Quirks of Character: Pretends to be docile and submissive when angry.

Walker (#7): *unisex*/Classic./(Old English) *Wealcare* (#5); clothes washer./(Anglo-Saxon) A fuller of cloth; (M) one who trod the cloth, and (F) thickener of cloth.

At First Glance: Is striking, brightly colored, and uniquely patterned. Appears to be proud, alert, active, unemotional, and intelligent. Stands alone.

Day-to-Day: Is a secretive, investigative loner who avoids young children and noisy adults. Is slow to react to disciplines and is quick to escape when approached by strangers.

The Bottom Line: Is a homebody who enjoys a comfortable environment and abundant meals and snacks. Is comfortable protecting loved ones and wants appreciation.

Quirks of Character: Stays by the side of humans or pets who are sick or needy.

Wally (#1): *unisex*/Nickname for (Germanic) *wil helm* (#1), (F) Wilhelmina (#7), Wilhelmine (#2); determined protector./Nickname for (M, Old French) Wallace (#3); Welshman./(Ancient Germanic) *Wald heri* (#8), (M & F) Walter (#7); commander of the army.

At First Glance: Appears to be sweet, subdued, unpretentious, and plain. Is shy, quiet, gentle, hesitant, sensitive, insecure, and content to remain in the background.

Day-to-Day: Will not follow the leader. Is active, alert, courageous, proud, and independent. Creates his or her rules, demands attention, and prefers to go it alone.

The Bottom Line: Is a powerful, dependable, dominant, shrewd protector who is comfortable and calm when exercised vigorously and trained to work.

Quirks of Character: Is nervous and impulsive when left alone too long.

Watson (#2): M/(Old High German) Surname, from son of Walter (#7).

At First Glance: Is dark, with a thick, natural coat; is solid, muscular, strong, and square. Appears to be slow moving, cautious, respectful, disciplined, and dignified.

Day-to-Day: Is gentle, quiet, unassuming, and sensitive. Enjoys giving and receiving affection and is content with one-to-one companionship and an easygoing lifestyle.

The Bottom Line: Is upset by noise and confusion. Wants peace, quiet, and uninterrupted time to observe and meditate. Is shy and is comfortable alone in a crowd.

Quirks of Character: Is curious and incautious. Gets into surprising situations.

Whiskers (#4): unisex/Classic./(Middle English) *Wisker* (#4), from *wisken* (#9) (to whisk); anything that whisks./Hairs of the beard growth on the sides of the face or on the chin./Long, stiff projecting hairs or bristles (*vibrissa* #9) growing near the mouth or on the head of certain animals./Whisky (#5).

At First Glance: Is a powerful, handsome, energetic, expensive winner. Is controlled, self-confident, and sociable. Appears responsible and behaves appropriately.

Day-to-Day: Enjoys being cautious and thorough; relies upon routines, schedules, and systematic humans. Is happy knowing what to do and living up to expectations.

The Bottom Line: Wants to be free, is vital and experimental outdoors, and enjoys discovering new people and experiences. Is a bodily alert, clever, adventurous hunter.

Quirks of Character: Is aggressive when boxed in or threatened by restraints.

Whitey (#9): *unisex*/Offensive or condescending term for a white person or white people collectively./(Caribbean, British) Pinkie (#1).

> *At First Glance:* Approaches slowly and cautiously. Is sturdy, stable, muscular, strong, dark, square, and conventional for the breed. Appears to be respectful and natural.
>
> *Day-to-Day:* Is unselfish, peaceful, kind, emotional, and brave. Thrives when trained to serve anyone who is sick or handicapped. Understands human nature and is perceptive.
>
> *The Bottom Line:* Wants to be with people and make friends. Is adaptable, flexible, clever, enthusiastic, sociable, and comfortable in any circumstance or condition.
>
> *Quirks of Character:* Has secret hiding places when upset by noise or confusion.

Whizzer (#7): *unisex*/A centrifugal machine for drying things like grain, sugar, nitrated cotton./Something that whizzes./Whiz (#3), Whizz (#2); a whirring or hissing sound, or a person that moves swiftly./Nickname: Wiz (#4), from Wizard (#9), a person who does something very well./Vulgar idiom: "to take a whiz," to urinate.

> *At First Glance:* Is unpretentious, plain, and shy. Has a soft voice and appears to be sweet, subdued, gentle, hesitant, insecure, unassuming, and tentatively receptive.
>
> *Day-to-Day:* Is an intelligent, observant, refined, quiet, sedentary, and peaceful loner. Prefers the company of considerate adults to the noise and activity of young children.
>
> *The Bottom Line:* Is always sexually stimulated and is impulsive when bored. Is comfortable when free to explore outdoors and unconcerned about handlers expectations.
>
> *Quirks of Character:* Stays at the side of anyone who is lonely, in pain, or is needy.

Whoopie (#1): *unisex*/(Middle English) *Whopen*./Whoopee (#6); noisy, boisterous revelry and merrymaking./A shout of joy./Slang: "to make whoopie," to make love.

> *At First Glance:* Appears to be "soft," peaceful, unassuming, and easygoing. Is not impressive or aggressive. Has a gentle, kind, and diplomatic manner and is receptive.
>
> *Day-to-Day:* Is an unemotional, independent loner who prefers to be dif-

ferent and never follows the pack. Takes challenges and never backs down from a confrontation.

The Bottom Line: Wants vigorous exercise and athletic play. Is a mentally and physically powerful personality; is a comfortable leader and a dependable defender.

Quirks of Character: Is impatient and mischievous when restricted indoors.

Will (#2): *unisex*/From (German) (M) William (#7), (F) Willa (#3); will helmet, resolute guardian./Short or nickname for (M) Wilbert (#8), Wilbur (#4), Wilford (#6), Wilfred (#5), Wilfrid (#9), Wilhelm (#1), Willard (#7), Willem (#2), William (#7), Willis (#3), Wilmer (#8), Wilson (#2), Wilton (#3)./Nicknames: (M) Wille (#7), Willee (#3), Willie (#7), Wills (#3), Willy (#9), and (F) Willow (#4).

At First Glance: Is quiet, unobtrusive, unassuming, and content to remain in the background while absorbing the environment. Appears to be receptive and approachable.

Day-to-Day: Is content with calm, clear, gentle commands and prefers peaceful, easygoing, thoughtful handlers who make comfort, affection, and friendliness important.

The Bottom Line: Is unselfish, understands human emotions and activities, and is eager to be of service. Is comfortable in a natural environment, free to explore outdoors.

Quirks of Character: Is detached and uncommunicative when emotionally upset.

Willa (#3): *F*/(German) Will helmet, resolute guardian./Nickname for Willabella (#8), Willamina (#4), Willamine (#8).

At First Glance: Appears to be sweet, gentle, unassuming, and content to remain in the background. Is hesitant. Is friendly and receptive to calm, quiet, considerate handlers.

Day-to-Day: Loves to play, has a fine memory, and is very funny and talkative. Enjoys children and other pets and is trusting, kind, conscientious, optimistic, and happy.

The Bottom Line: Wants to do things her own way and is an independent leader when possible. Is comfortable when left alone to be an alert, courageous protector.

Quirks of Character: Intimidated by brash, detached, authoritative leaders.

Windy (#3): *unisex*/Windblown, breezy weather./Wordy, prolonged talk lacking in substance./(Scottish) Boastful./Variations: Windee (#6), Windie (#1).

At First Glance: Is undisciplined, frisky, friendly, restless, curious, and charming. Appears to be unconventional for the breed or a striking example of mixed ancestry.

Day-to-Day: Loves to play and is a happy, trusting, sociable friend to humans and other pets. Is unregimented, talks incessantly, and makes a game out of behavior training.

The Bottom Line: Is an extroverted introvert. Insists upon private time and a serene place to rest and recoup energy. Is comfortable with calm handlers or alone in a crowd.

Quirks of Character: Is emotionally unresponsive. Fears bonding with anyone.

Winnie (#2): *unisex*/(F) Nickname for Edwina (#2) and for all names that begin with *Win* or *Wynn*./Variations: Winnee (#7), Winney (#9), Wynnee (#5), Wynney (#7), Wynnie (#9).

At First Glance: Is a robust, serious, conventional example of the breed. Has a lush blue and silver coat and appears to be well fed, kind, friendly, and comfortable.

Day-to-Day: Is "soft," sweet, gentle, parental, cooperative, and mystically intuitive. Bonds with one special female human, showers her with affection, and influences her life.

The Bottom Line: Enjoys exercising outdoors; wants constant change and adventure. Is often headstrong and hasty when restricted by commands or fences.

Quirks of Character: Hesitates and is fearful when walking through doorways.

Winston (#6): M/(Old English) Wynnstan (#4); joyful stone./Nicknames: Win (#1), Winnee (#7), Winnie (#2), Winney (#9), Winst (#4).

At First Glance: Is a skillful, polished, magnetic, multicolored, shining example of the breed. Appears to be peaceful, relaxed, and tolerant; is energized when approached.

Day-to-Day: Gives and attracts love. Is a musical, teachable, serious, attentive, helpful, sympathetic homebody who enjoys nurturing, comforting, protecting loved ones.

The Bottom Line: Wants to be involved in all social and work activities.

Feels responsible for everything and is comfortable supervising and teaching children and pets.

Quirks of Character: Disappears occasionally to enjoy a sexual adventure.

Wizard (#9): M/A person who has magical powers, or one wise in the ways of magic and sorcery; uses his skill to help or harm others./One who is skillful and gives an outstanding, unexpected and/or excellent job./Nicknames: Wiz (#4), Wizzee (#4), Wizzey (#6), Wizzie (#8), Wizzy (#1).

At First Glance: Is a dominating, powerful presence and personality. Has strength, energy, and depth. Appears to be a self-confident, sociable winner for the breed.

Day-to-Day: Is intuitive, clear sighted, imaginative, and unselfish. Understands human nature and helps anyone who is sick, lonely, disabled, or emotionally needy.

The Bottom Line: Is independent, innovative, self-sufficient, courageous, and alert. Dislikes following routines, challenges leaders, and prefers to do things his own way.

Quirks of Character: When nervous or upset, bites his paws relentlessly.

Wolf (#2): M/Classic./(Latin) *Lupus* (#5)./(Greek) *Lykos* (#1)./(Old English) *Wulf* (#8)./Wild, predatory animal of the dog family that lives and hunts in a pack./A man who tries to have sex with many women./Nicknames: Wolfee (#3), Wolfie (#7), Wolfey (#5)./Variations: Wolfe (#7), Wolve (#5).

At First Glance: Attracts attention. Is unusual with an unconventional, faulty physique and a changeable, energetic, charming, unrestrained, and impatient personality.

Day-to-Day: Prefers an easygoing, peaceful, unregimented lifestyle and is quiet, calm, refined, and unassuming. Is sensitive, friendly, and content with small things.

The Bottom Line: Wants roots and thinks food is symbolic of love. Is a homebody who is wary of strangers. Protects, nurtures, teaches, and shows affection to loved ones.

Quirks of Character: When emotionally upset, is anxious, indecisive, and bossy.

Woofy #3: *unisex*/Nickname for Woof (#5); pet talk.

At First Glance: Is unpretentious, simple, unassuming, and shy. Has a soft, neutral coat and a gentle, sweet face. Appears to be hesitant, insecure, modest, and receptive.

Day-to-Day: Is a happy-go-lucky, unregimented, and unscheduled game player. Loves children, plays with other pets, and continuously tries to be the center of attention.

The Bottom Line: Has an independent personality and is creative and content being alone. Is comfortable when allowed to display leadership, usefulness, and courage.

Quirks of Character: Is frightened by noise; hides from crowds or confusion.

See the Number Meanings chapter to discover the traits described by the number that accompanies each name: Waddle (#4), Wade (#6), Wadsworth (#5), Wafer (#8), Waffle (#8), Wagner (#5), Walden (#5), Waldo (#1), Wallaby (#4), Wallace (#3), Waller (#8), Wallie (#8), Wallis (#4), Walt (#2), Walton (#4), Wanda (#7), Wanton (#6), Warden (#2), Waring (#9), Warlock (#2), Warner (#7), Warrior (#3), Warwick (#7), Watcher (#6), Weasel (#2), Webb (#5), Wednesday (#1), Weezer (#1), Weezie (#1), Welby (#4), Wellington (#5), Wembley (#4), Wesley (#8), Westie (#9), Weston (#6), Whale (#4), Wharton (#9), Wheatley (#9), Wheaton (#5), Wheedle (#8), Wheelie (#4), Wheezie (#9), Whiffer (#3), Whistler (#6), Whitman (#7), Whitney (#5), Whittaker (#7), Wiggles (#1), Wilcox (#5), Wilder (#8), Wiley (#2), Wilfred (#5), Wilhelm (#1), Wilhelmina (#7), Wilkie (#6), Willard (#7), Willis (#3), Willoughby (#8), Willow (#4), Wilma (#4), Wilson (#2), Wilt (#1), Wilton (#3), Winchell (#5), Winchester (#7), Windsor (#3), Winona (#4), Winters (#9), Winthrop (#6), Wolfgang (#4), Wong (#5), Woodbury (#6), Woodrow (#5), Woodson (#6), Woodstock (#8), Woodward (#4), Wordsworth (#1), Wrigley (#9), Wyatt (#8), Wyler (#2), Wynn (#4), Wyoming (#7).

Xavier (#7): M/(Arabic) Bright./From (Basque) Etxaberri (#3) or Etcheberria (#4); new house./Nickname: Xavi (#2)./Variation: Zavier (#9).

At First Glance: Is different. Has a red-tinged, brightly colored coat and is one of a kind or a first for the breed. Appears to be alert, active, confident, and independent.

Day-to-Day: Prefers to observe and does not take action until sure of the result. Is quiet, contemplative, reserved, and thrives with considerate adults in a calm environment.

The Bottom Line: Is parental and responsible. Enjoys loving and being loved. Wants a stable, dignified home; centers interests on helping and protecting loved ones.

Quirks of Character: Will not leave the side of anyone in pain or trouble.

Xena (#8): *F/(Greek) From (M) Xenos (#5); strange guest./Variations: Xenia (#8), Xina (#3), Xinia (#3), Zena (#1), Zenia (#1), Zina (#5).*

At First Glance: Is content to wait to be noticed before encouraging affection. Appears to be plump and has an unpretentious, neat, soft, neutral, orange-tipped coat.

Day-to-Day: Is creative, productive, disciplined, sociable, and dominant whenever possible. Works at protecting and defending loved ones and the territory.

The Bottom Line: Is a foodaholic who interprets food as love. Wants a socially interactive, harmonious, stable home with responsible humans who enjoy music.

Quirks of Character: Is disrespectful and arrogant when forced to be inactive.

See the Number Meanings chapter to discover the traits described by the number that accompanies each name: X-Man (#7), X-Ray (#5), Xanthe (#9), Xanthine (#5), Xantippe (#6), Xaverie (#3), Xenia (#8), Xenon (#9), Xenophon (#3), Xia (#7), Xylia (#8), Xylon (#9).

Yak (#1): *unisex/Large, stocky, shaggy-haired wild ox./To talk or chatter uninterruptedly.*

At First Glance: Is an outstanding, classic example of the breed and is charismatic, skillfully trained, and polished to perfection. Appears to be relaxed, wise, and friendly.

Day-to-Day: Is active, alert, aggressive, assertive, proud, and independent. Is content to work and play alone and is unemotional, competitive, and courageous.

The Bottom Line: Is impatient and difficult to train. Wants to be free to follow his or her routines. Finds it difficult to adhere to schedules or follow commands.

Quirks of Character: Is extremely sensitive and vulnerable when upset.

Yale (#7): M/(Teutonic) One who pays or yields./(Welsh) Ial (#4); fertile plateau or upland.

At First Glance: Appears to be free and independent thinking. Is definitely different and stands alone. Seems to be capable, proud, inquisitive, and healthy.

Day-to-Day: Prefers quiet, calm, private time and space to the noise and confusion of a bustling household. Is an observer and dislikes rough play or careless children.

The Bottom Line: Wants a stable, harmonious environment. Is loyal and protective to immediate household members. Is helpful and devoted when comfortable.

Quirks of Character: Is impulsive and surprising when sexually stimulated.

Yancy (#5): M/(Native American) An Englishman./(Early U.S.) A Yankee.

At First Glance: Has a rich coat of harmonious tones of blue. Is mature, serious, sympathetic, loving, and paternal. Appears to be agreeable, vocal, and conscientious.

Day-to-Day: Is active, quick, clever, adaptable, and mentally curious. Learns from experience, enjoys social events and being outdoors, and loves food and sex.

The Bottom Line: Is a diplomatic problem solver and a discerning, shrewd home guardian and personal protector. Is comfortable working alone or with others as leader.

Quirks of Character: Has secret hiding places. Avoids noise and upheaval.

Yankee (#7): unisex/Considered an adaptation by Native Americans of English or the French Anglais./A nickname given to the English colonists by the Dutch settlers of Connecticut and used today to describe a northerner by southerners, an American by Europeans, or an established New Englander by other Americans.

At First Glance: Runs from place to place, is curious and unrestrained. Is a charming, frisky, outgoing personality. Has a striking, unconventional appearance.

Day-to-Day: Is active on command and enjoys being an introspective observer. Prefers peaceful, quiet, private hiding places to a crowded, noisy environment.

The Bottom Line: Wants unconditional love and enjoys one-to-one com-

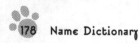

panionship. Is comfortable in a neat, serene, sensitive environment with gentle, patient humans.

Quirks of Character: Goes home with anyone who offers food or excitement.

Yaya (#7): *unisex*/Child's pronunciation of an unpronounceable name.

At First Glance: Is intriguing, enthusiastic, self-expressive, impulsive, seductive, frisky, and unrestrained. Has a striking, boldly colorful, unconventional appearance.

Day-to-Day: Is a quiet, refined, reserved, calm observer who remains alone in a crowd. Needs peaceful surroundings and is irritable if the environment is noisy.

The Bottom Line: Is vulnerable, shy, insecure, and sensitive. Tries to be helpful in little ways and is subordinate to humans and other pets. Needs gentle, patient handling.

Quirks of Character: Is arrogant and aggressive when too controlled.

Yenta (#2): F/Slang from (Latin) *gentiles* (#1), "of the same clan," through (Old Italian) *gentile* (#9), "highborn, amiable," to (Yiddish alteration) Yentl (#4), Yente (#6); generally a woman busybody or gossip./Variation: Yenti (#1).

At First Glance: Is spontaneous, unpredictable, changeable, seductive, intriguing, and curious. Tries to touch and tease everyone at one time. Makes a unique impression.

Day-to-Day: Is emotionally and physically sensitive and attentive to neatness and detail. Prefers one-to-one intimate relationships and is highstrung, finicky, and selective.

The Bottom Line: Wants to gain friends by being a friend. Is comfortable in a socially interactive, dignified, loving, comfortable, harmonious, people-filled household.

Quirks of Character: Is bossy, arrogant, and intolerant when challenged.

Yentl (#4): *unisex*/(Yiddish from the French) *Gentille,* "kind."

At First Glance: Is a distinguishable, dominant, strong, energetic, enthusiastic, powerful personality who is expensive, fastidiously groomed, and top of the breed.

Day-to-Day: Enjoys a framework and methods. Is respectful and routine oriented; thrives on work. Needs consistent exercise and regular habits to maintain stability.

The Bottom Line: Wants to have freedom to explore outdoors and seek sexual adventures. Is comfortable with a variety of people and adapts to new experiences.

Quirks of Character: Cannot keep quiet and talks incessantly when ignored.

Yogi (#2): *M*/(Sanskrit) Yogin (#7)./Reflective or mystical person who practices the Yoga (#3) philosophy, who has achieved a high level of insight and may be considered a teacher./(*F*) Yogini (#7).

At First Glance: Is an unconventional, striking figure, with a coat of unusual color combinations. Appears to be enthusiastic, friendly, frisky, curious, and uncontrolled.

Day-to-Day: Is unassuming, quiet, sweet, gentle, helpful, considerate, and cooperative. Prefers an easygoing lifestyle. Disregards rigid schedules and disciplines.

The Bottom Line: Wants love, stability, protection, and a harmonious environment. Is comfortable with socially interactive, responsible, understanding adults and children.

Quirks of Character: Stays at the side of anyone needy, lonely, or disabled.

Yoko (#3): *F*/(Japanese) Sun child, positive female child.

At First Glance: Is a magnetic, charming, strong, classic example of the breed. Appears to be peaceful, graceful, understanding, and tolerant; is absorbed by the scenery.

Day-to-Day: Is a lighthearted, entertaining, talkative, multitalented entertainer. Prefers to do a variety of things and rarely concentrates on schedules or disciplines.

The Bottom Line: Is generally happy, playful, and affectionate. Wants friends, popularity, and attention. Is comfortable in a crowded, fun-loving, unstructured home.

Quirks of Character: Is overly possessive and maternally smothers intimates.

Yorkie (#2): *unisex*/Classic./Nickname for Yorkshire (#2) Terrier (#3) and (*M*) York (#6); (Celtic) yew tree, and (English) from the bear estate or pig farm./(*F*) York, (Anglo-Saxon) Brigantia (#9); Yorkshire goddess.

At First Glance: Is an artistic, romantic, beautiful, polished, skillful, impressive personality. Appears to be youthful, strong, energetic, peaceful, relaxed, and emotional.

Day-to-Day: Is vulnerable, cautious, sweet, and sensitive to changes. Prefers one-to-one affection. Bonds with one human and is friendly to gentle, attentive handlers.

The Bottom Line: Wants unconditional love and to be babied; tends to be petty and spiteful when ignored. Is an attentive listener; is comfortable curled in a loved one's lap.

Quirks of Character: Gets bored easily; is an impulsive, curious risk-taker.

Yuri (#1): *unisex*/(M, Hindi, Polish, Russian) George (#3), farmer; from (Greek) Georgos (#5), earth worker./(F, Japanese from Sanskrit) Lily./Variation: Joeri (#3).

At First Glance: Is reserved, calm, poised, cautious, and introspective; remains an observer. Has a sleek coat of harmonious colors and is groomed to perfection.

Day-to-Day: Is an independent loner who dislikes repetitious commands or following another's way of doing things. Is demanding, strong willed, and forceful.

The Bottom Line: Takes the initiative with confidence. Wants control and is bold and enterprising. Is an alert, active, proud, quick-acting, daring, determined know-it-all.

Quirks of Character: Stays at the side of anyone emotionally upset or in pain.

See the Number Meanings chapter to discover the traits described by the number that accompanies each name: Yaakov (#3), Yacker (#9), Yahoo (#1), Yammer (#3), Yarborough (#4), Yardley (#9), Yarnie (#9), Yarrow (#1), Yasmin (#9), Yasu (#3), Yates (#7), Yeager (#7), Yeasty (#5), Yelena (#8), Yeller (#5), Yellow (#2), Yesterday (#5), Yichi (#9), Yodel (#8), Yoga (#3), Yokel (#5), Yolande (#4), Yona (#1), Yorgy (#9), York (#6), Yorke (#2), Yorty (#4), Yoshinobu (#2), Yoshinori (#6), Yoshio (#1), Yoshiro (#1), Yoshitomo (#4), Youtoo (#3), Yuki (#3), Yule (#9), Yulka (#7), Yuma (#6), Yummy (#7), Yutu (#6), Yvon (#4), Yvonne (#5).

Zach (#2): M/Nickname for Zachary (#1), form of Zacharais (#5); from (Greek) Zechariah (#7), Jehovah remembers, from (Hebrew) Zecharyah (#5)./Variations: Zack (#5), Zackie (#1), Zak (#2), Zeke (#2).

At First Glance: Is a different, boldly colored and patterned one-of-a-kind or a first for the breed. Appears to be active, alert, proud, intelligent, and investigative.

Day-to-Day: Enjoys being with people, wants to be babied, and is unassuming, sweet, gentle, and affectionate. Prefers soft toys and is not into roughhousing.

The Bottom Line: Wants to eat, play, and love when he wants. Does things his own way and has a strong will. Makes his own schedule, is demanding and territorial.

Quirks of Character: Needs consistent, vigorous exercise to release energy.

Zachary (#1): M/(Hebrew) Zcharya (#1); remembered by God, the Lord recalled./Variations: Xackery (#6), Zacary (#2), Zachery (#5), Zachory (#6), Zackary (#4)./(F) Zacharina (#9)./Nickname: Zachey (#5).

At First Glance: Is brightly colored, unusually patterned, and different. Stands alone and is bold, alert, active, intelligent, investigative, dominant, and proud.

Day-to-Day: Does things his own way and is difficult to train or submit to the controls of handlers. Is unemotional, self-reliant, creative, impatient, and very active.

The Bottom Line: Wants to be needed. Understands human nature, is empathetic, compassionate, and brave. Thrives with needy, lonely, elderly, or disabled humans.

Quirks of Character: Has secret hiding places to escape noise and confusion.

ZaSu (#4): F/Created by parents of actress ZaSu Pitts (1898–1963) from the names Eliza (#8) and Susan (#2), two aunts who wanted the baby named after them./Variation: Zazou (#8).

At First Glance: Appears to be magnetic and a classic, polished, skillful example of the breed. Is peaceful, tolerant, charming, warm, friendly, emotional, and youthful.

Day-to-Day: Is routine oriented and depends upon rules and schedules. Enjoys rolling and digging in dirt and is a tireless, strong, conscientious, self-disciplined worker.

The Bottom Line: Wants to know what is expected and does it. Is committed to home, earth, nature, and responsible humans. Needs patient handlers; is slow to learn.

Quirks of Character: Is a noisy chatterer when emotionally upset or ignored.

Zaza (#9): F/(Arabic) Flowery./(Hebrew) Movement.

At First Glance: Is quiet, proud, reserved, cautious, investigative, introspective, shy, unemotional, and aristocratic. Appears to be sleek and groomed to perfection.

Day-to-Day: Is intuitive, peaceful, talkative, kind, wise, and compassionate. Loves to roam in a natural environment, is helpful, and makes friends wherever she goes.

The Bottom Line: Wants peace, harmony, unconditional love, and constant companionship. Is a sensitive, vulnerable, adaptable, indecisive follower.

Quirks of Character: Independently refuses to follow routines or schedules.

Zeke (#2): M/Nickname for (Hebrew) Yechezkel (#1), Ezekiel (#1); God strengthens.

At First Glance: Appears to be different; has a coat of bright colors and striking patterns and is one of a kind. Is proud, alert, active, bold, assertive, and investigative.

Day-to-Day: Is gentle, sweet, adaptable, affectionate, cooperative, helpful, and sensitive. Dislikes being alone. Thrives when babied, spoiled, and cuddled consistently.

The Bottom Line: Wants to make his own rules, is impatient when restrained, and does things his own way. Is comfortable playing alone and is creative with handlers.

Quirks of Character: Is sexual and sensual and cannot be fenced in.

Zelda (#3): F/Nickname for (German) Griselda (#3); woman warrior or gray battle./(Yiddish), Luck./Nickname: Zelly (#8).

At First Glance: Appears to be maternal, tolerant, protective, understanding, sociable, comfortable, and dignified. Is a full-bodied, robust example of the breed.

Day-to-Day: Is a talkative, fun-loving, frisky, playful attention-getter with a good memory and charming, cute personality. Thrives with easygoing adults and children.

The Bottom Line: Wants to center interests on home and immediate family; distrusts strangers. Needs harmonious relationships and runs away if there is discord.

Quirks of Character: Is aggressive when taking a secondary position to leader.

Zena (#1): *F*/(Ethiopian) News./(Persian) A woman./(Greek) From Xenos (#5), stranger; Xenia (#8), hospitable./Nickname for Italian Rosina (#4); for (Latin) Rosa (#8), rose; and for (Greek) Zenobia (#9), Zeus life.

At First Glance: Is muscular, strong, and dark; does not require grooming. Has a thick, naturally dense coat and a disciplined, determined, work-oriented attitude.

Day-to-Day: Is alert, intelligent, and independent; does things her way. Enjoys investigating, hunting, and being active. Is impatient and selfish, and is best with firm adults.

The Bottom Line: Wants the stability of home and an immediate family. Is responsible and naturally maternal, and does not need to be taught to protect the territory.

Quirks of Character: When too controlled, forgets rules of housebreaking.

Zeus (#8): *M*/(Greek) Religion, mythology: bright or sky, amorous god, supreme deity./Father: Chronos (#9); mother: Rhea (#5). Brother of: Demeter (#7), Hades (#1), Hera (#5), Hestia (#8), Poseidon (#7). First love: Dione (#2). /Consort (and sister): Hera (#5)./ Children: Amphitryon (#4), Ares (#7), Athena (#4), Dardanus (#1), Hebe (#2), Hercules (#1), and more.

At First Glance: Is mystical, magnetic, emotional, relaxed, cooperative, independent, and disciplined. Appears to be a polished, skillful example of the breed.

Day-to-Day: Has a dominant, distinctive, businesslike personality; is agile, athletic, and energetic. Is polite, dependable, shrewd, discriminating, and trustworthy.

The Bottom Line: Wants consistent, challenging work, play, and exercise. Is comfortable in an orderly household with strong, authoritative, responsible leaders.

Quirks of Character: Due to childhood restraints, is aggressive when confined.

Ziggy (#2): M/Nickname for (Hungarian, German) Sigmund (#6), triumphant defender; and for (Latvian, Russian) Siegfried (#1), calm or triumphant.

> *At First Glance:* Is plain and has quiet dignity. Appears to be cautious, respectful, unemotional, and disciplined. Is muscular and sturdy; has a natural, dark coat.
>
> *Day-to-Day:* Is sweet, gentle, sensitive, affectionate, teachable, quiet, easygoing, and agreeable. Is not aggressive, needs company, aims to please, and wants approval.
>
> *The Bottom Line:* Wants a quiet, peaceful, private time each day for uninterrupted observation, meditation, and rest. Finds secret hiding places when environment is noisy.
>
> *Quirks of Character:* Best with older humans. Cannot tolerate rough handlers.

Zipper (#9): Unisex/Slide fastener; two toothed edges with a sliding tab, used for fastening clothing or objects./Someone who has energy and vitality, and who moves quickly./Nickname: Zippy (#2).

> *At First Glance:* Is plain, earthy, dark haired, and conventional for the breed. Appears to be respectful, slow moving, cautious, unemotional, quiet, and disciplined.
>
> *Day-to-Day:* Understands human emotions and activities. Is a compassionate service provider. Has a loving nature and responds sympathetically to the hurts others suffer.
>
> *The Bottom Line:* Wants freedom outdoors and is adaptable, clever, and flexible. Relates to humans and is sensual, sexual, curious, impulsive, and learns from experience.
>
> *Quirks of Character:* Is indecisive and uncontrolled when emotionally upset.

Zsazsa (#2): F/Nickname for (Hungarian) Erzsebet (#1); for (English) Elizabeth (#7), God's promise; for Zsuzsanna (#6); for (English) Susanna (#8), from (Hebrew) Shoshannah (#7), shoshan (#3), "lili."/Nickname for Susan (#2).

> *At First Glance:* Appears to be magnetic, loving, wise, and attractive to all. Is a polished, skillful, fastidiously groomed, graceful, poised, classic example of the breed.

Day-to-Day: Enjoys one-to-one, intimate relationships. Is sweet, affectionate, cooperative, charming, tactful, neat, "soft," and loves to be babied and spoiled.

The Bottom Line: Wants an easygoing, cooperative, comfortable lifestyle and unconditional love. Is content with small things when she bonds with one partner.

Quirks of Character: Is bossy, argumentative, and aggressive when restrained.

Zummo (#7): *unisex*/Nickname for someone who zooms; who moves very quickly, sometimes making a loud, low-pitched buzzing sound, or climbs very quickly./Zum (#6) acronym: **Z**imbabwe **U**nity **M**ovement.

At First Glance: Is aristocratic, sleek, and groomed to perfection. Appears to be refined, unruffled, poised, intelligent, introspective, polite, and unapproachable.

Day-to-Day: Enjoys observing and is a sedentary, investigative, questioning watcher, not a doer. Prefers careful adult handlers and dislikes noise and confusion.

The Bottom Line: Wants to be unselfish and useful. Is comfortable when trained to serve lonely or disabled humans and stays at the side of anyone who needs understanding.

Quirks of Character: Assumes responsibility for everyone and is possessive.

See the Number Meanings chapter to discover the traits described by the number that accompanies each name: Zabar (#3), Zada (#5), Zadie (#9), Zadora (#2), Zaftig (#6), Zanna (#2), Zany (#3), Zap (#7), Zapata (#2), Zappa (#6), Zenith (#1), Zenos (#7), Zero (#1), Zesta (#8), Zesty (#5), Zeze (#8), Zia (#9), Ziegfield (#2), Ziffi (#2), Zimmi (#7), Zing (#2), Zita (#2), Ziv (#3), Zombie (#7), Zoom (#6), Zora (#6), Zori (#5), Zowie (#6), Zubin (#9), Zulu (#8).

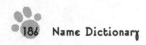

Bibliography

Books

Campbell, Florence. *Your Days Are Numbered*. Ferndale, PA: The Gateway, 1931.

The Concise Columbia Encyclopedia. New York: Columbia University Press, 1983.

Fields, Maxine. *Baby Names from Around the World*. New York: Pocket Books, 1985.

Fogle, Bruce, D.V.M. *The Complete Illustrated Guide to Cat Care & Behavior*. San Diego: Thunder Bay Press, 1999.

———. *The Complete Illustrated Guide to Dog Care & Behavior*. San Diego: Thunder Bay Press, 1999.

Hitchcock, Helyn. *Helping Yourself with Numerology*. West Nyack, NY: Parker Publishing Co., 1972.

Javane, Faith, and Dusty Bunker. *Numerology and the Divine Triangle*. Rockport, MA: Para Research, 1972.

Jung, Carl G. *Man and His Symbols*. London: Aldus Books Ltd., 1964.

Lingerman, Hal A. *Living Your Destiny*. York Beach, ME: Samuel Weiser, Inc., 1992.

Norman, Teresa. *Names Through the Ages*. New York: Berkley Publishing Group, 1999.

Rodale, Jerome I. *The Synonym Finder*. Emmaus, PA: Rodale Press, 1978.

Roquemore, Kathleen. *It's All in Your Numbers: The Secrets of Numerology*. New York: Harper & Row, 1963.

Webster's Unabridged Dictionary of the English Language. New York: Random House, Inc., 1966.

Wells, Evelyn. *What to Name the Baby*. Garden City, NY: Doubleday & Co., Inc., 1946.

Zullo, Michael. *Cat Astrology: The Complete Guide to Feline Horoscopes*. New York: Andrews McMeel, 1993.

Online Sources

www.allwords.com.

American Heritage Dictionary of the English Language, 3rd ed.; accessed on *www.bartleby.com.*

Baby Name Finder, *www.parentsoup.com/babynames/dictionary.*

www.babynamer.com.

www.babynames.com.

Baby Names, *www.parenthood.com.*

The Baby Names Searcher, *www.enlightenedsoftware.com/babynames.*

www.behindthename.com.

Cambridge Dictionary of American English; accessed on *www.uk.cambridge.org.*

www.dictionary.com.

www.dogbreedinfo.com.

www.foreignword.com.

www.hyperdictionary.com.

www.infoplease.com.

The Internet Public Library, *www.ipl.org.*

Kraemer, Elizabeth Wallis. "An Etymological Dictionary of Classical Mythology," "Influences on Personal Names," 1998; *www.kl.oakland.edu/kraemer/edcm.*

www.makewayforbaby.com/babynames.

Moms Online, *www.oxygen.com.*

Online Dictionary Database Query, *www.dict.org.*

www.xrefer.com.

www.yourbabysname.com.

www.yourDictionary.com.

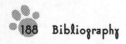

Scratch Pad

Scratch Pad

Scratch Pad

Scratch Pad

Scratch Pad

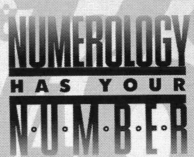